IMAGES
of America

IBERIA PARISH

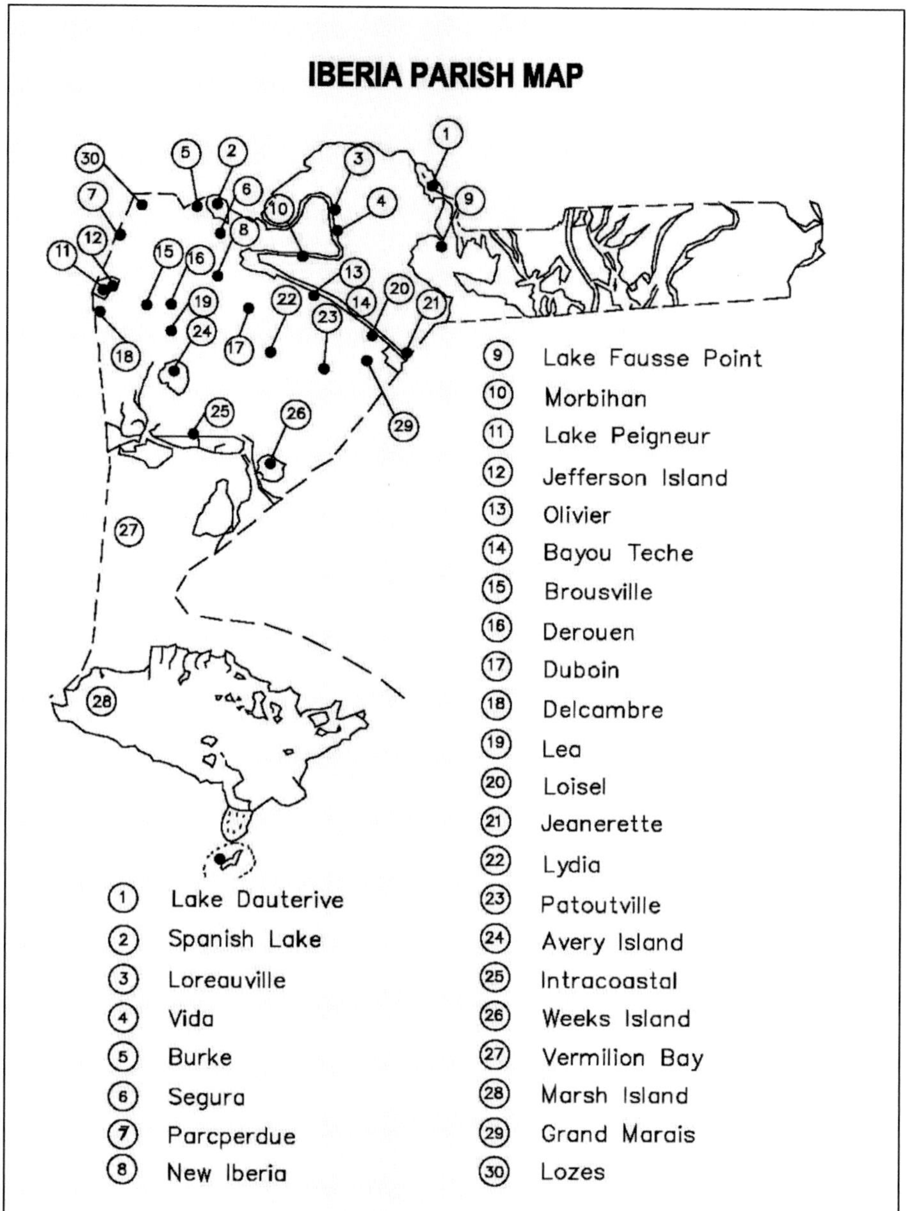

Over the past 250 years, waves of immigrants have arrived in what is now Iberia Parish, including French, Spanish, Lebanese, Italians, Afro-Caribbeans, Germans, and Acadian exiles from Nova Scotia. As seen in this map, created by architect and map designer Andrew Perrin, MA, early Iberia settlers named their communities for people, geography, or terrain. (Courtesy of Jim Bradshaw, the *Daily Advertiser.*)

On The Cover: St. Peter's College Senior Band allowed adults to perform with the students. At age 40, Hermann Hauser was an Episcopalian who enjoyed playing music with the Catholic students. He is pictured in 1936 playing his tuba with the band. Today, the Iberia Community Concert Band continues this tradition with high school students playing alongside adults at musical performances. (Courtesy of Rex Hauser.)

IMAGES
of America

IBERIA PARISH

Nelwyn Hebert and Warren A. Perrin

ARCADIA
PUBLISHING

ISBN 978-0-7385-9175-9

Published by Arcadia Publishing
Charleston, South Carolina

Printed in the United States of America

Library of Congress Control Number: 2011943841

For all general information, please contact Arcadia Publishing:
Telephone 843-853-2070
Fax 843-853-0044
E-mail sales@arcadiapublishing.com
For customer service and orders:
Toll-Free 1-888-313-2665

Visit us on the Internet at www.arcadiapublishing.com

We dedicate this book to the people who shared their stories and photographs of Iberia Parish with us, and to the next generation, to whom we bequeath this book as a part of their heritage.

To my two nieces Jennifer Bodden Chauvin and Katie Delaune, my great-niece Reagan Chauvin, and my great-nephew Carter Chauvin.
—Nelwyn Hebert

To my beloved grandchildren, Nicolas Ouellet, Lily Ouellet, Henry Perrin, Nicoline Perrin, and Louis Perrin.
—Warren A. Perrin

Contents

Acknowledgments

I want to thank Warren A. Perrin, who invited me to coauthor this book. I want to thank my parents, Howard Andre and Frances Laperouse Hebert, for instilling in me a love of family. I also thank my sisters Mary Lou Hebert Bodden and Andrea Hebert Delaune, who for years have listened to the stories and have helped plan many family reunions.

—Nelwyn Hebert

The authors would like to thank the individuals who have made contributions to this book—please forgive us if we have overlooked anyone. Shane K. Bernard has been a reliable source of historical documentation. Former sheriff Sidney Hebert was able to obtain documents for us from the New Orleans archives. Mary Perrin, Laura Gaspard, and Sam Broussard edited the manuscript. Photographs and information have come from the following: Mickey Delcambre; the Eldridge P. Theriot family; Shannon LaSalle; Edward Pratt; Janie Bayard; Jason Theriot; George and Wendy Rodrigue; Tai and Elaine Sun; Dr. Donald Voorhies; Cathy Voorhies Indest; Tracy and Sarah Migues; Ken and Mary Broussard; Rex Hauser; Ruth Broussard; Paul Schexnayder; Lewis Bernard; Lynn Breaux; Mike and Sandy Davis (Konriko Store); Perry Segura; Patricia Kahle and Cathy Schramm of Shadows on the Teche; Nancy Mixon; J.R. Bill Bailey; Pauline Gerami; Porteus Burke; Steve Davis; Darnelle Delcambre; Dr. Catherine H. Segura; Ted Viator; Dr. Andy Reaux; Sheriff Mike Neustrom; former governor Kathleen B. Blanco; Johanna Villarreal; Paul Muffoletto; Mayor Hilda Curry; Kathy Thibodaux; E. Gerald "T-Boy" Hebert; the *Daily Advertiser*; the *Daily Iberian*; Richard C. Sealy Jr.; Theresa, Marie, and Michael Musemeche; Phebe Hayes; Pat Broussard; Iberia Parish Convention and Visitors Bureau; the McIlhenny Company and Avery Island, Inc. archives; the E.A. McIlhenny Collection at Avery Island; University of Louisiana professor Michael Martin and the Center for Louisiana Studies; Greg Lamboussy and the Louisiana State Museum; Dr. Florent Hardy and the Louisiana State Archives; and Gail Garcia. Two special people who helped to gather information and photographs are Claire Mire and Rogers Romero. A manuscript by William R. Burke provided valuable information about New Iberia prior to 1899.

The authors are also indebted to Jose Manuel de Molina Bautista of Alhaurin de la Torre, Spain, who wrote *Historia de Alhaurin de la Torre en la Edad Moderna, 1489–1812*, which has a chapter in English dedicated to the founding of Nueva Iberia (New Iberia). Jose Manuel was also the contact person for the "twinning," which took place between the cities of New Iberia and Alhaurin de la Torre, Spain, in 2009 (in New Iberia) and 2011 (in Alhaurin de la Torre).

Unless otherwise noted, images appear courtesy of the Bayou Teche Museum, the Acadian Museum in Erath, and the Jeanerette Museum.

INTRODUCTION

Although France established its first Louisiana settlement in 1699, it made little effort over the following decades to explore the Attakapas region, the area that would eventually include Iberia Parish. Fear of the local Attakapas tribe warded off potential explorers, since many claimed this tribe practiced cannibalism. Whether or not the claim was true, and there are reasons for doubt, settlers nonetheless believed it, and that belief sufficed to discourage exploration. It took the courage of explorer-traders such as André Massé and Joseph Blanpain to penetrate the region—much to the annoyance of the Spanish in Mexico City, who regarded their province of Texas as stretching all the way to the Mississippi River. The viceroy of New Spain, however, declined to press the matter with French authorities in New Orleans. After all, the Catholic kings of Spain and France, both Bourbons, were traditional allies against the detested British, who increasingly encroached on both French and Spanish territories in North America. By the early 1760s, the British had garrisoned Baton Rouge.

Whether the west bank of the Mississippi belonged to France or Spain ceased to be a matter of contention when, in 1762, France, in an effort to cut their economic losses, ceded Louisiana to Spain in compensation for Spain's own losses during the French and Indian War.

Spain took a greater interest than France had in developing the Louisiana interior, doing so for several reasons. Spain wanted to populate the colony to discourage British, and later Anglo-American, incursions into its territory. Spain also wanted to increase the colony's agricultural output, which in turn would raise revenues for the poverty-stricken colony, provide a source of food (especially beef) for New Orleans, and help to integrate the colony into the economy of the larger Spanish empire.

Louisiana's most distinguished Spanish governor, Bernardo de Gálvez, vetoed the initial plan of his lieutenant, Francisco Bouligny, to settle a village on the Ouachita River in present-day northeastern Louisiana. The area was too far from New Orleans, Gálvez thought, and too close to hostile Indians. Bouligny, therefore, chose a second site on Bayou Teche, which wound its way from its mother stream, Bayou Courtableau, down through the Attakapas region for 130 miles. The alluvial lands along the Teche were extremely fertile, and the Indians who lived along its lower reaches, the Chitimacha, were known to be friendly, having agreed to a peace treaty earlier in the century.

Along the Teche, Bouligny settled a group of colonists from the Mediterranean port of Málaga, Spain; these Malagueños, however, were hardly alone. Besides the Chitimacha, Acadian exiles from Nova Scotia and their offspring already lived along the meandering bayou. These French-speaking pioneers had arrived about a decade and a half earlier. They came looking for a new homeland after world events—namely, the incessant warring of England and France—had resulted in the capture of their former homeland by the British and, nearly a half-century later, in their brutal expulsion by the British. Yale historian John Mack Faragher has called the latter event "the first episode of state-sponsored ethnic cleansing in North American history."

Even before the Acadians arrived, much of the banks of the Teche had been claimed by retired French military officers, some of them absentee landowners who had accepted their government's offer of land concessions in lieu of free passage back to the Continent. Besides a smattering of other settlers, including a few Germans and Anglos, the region boasted an increasingly large number of African slaves as well as mixed-race free persons of color (*gens de couleur libre*), both of whom exerted a profound influence on the region's history and culture.

In 1800, Napoleon coaxed Louisiana from Spain, and shortly thereafter sold it to the fledgling United States of America. The United States sent a military officer, Lt. Henry Hopkins, up the Teche to raise the American flag over the predominantly French-speaking region. The land along the bayou was now American—at least politically and legally, if not culturally.

Only a few years earlier, an entrepreneur named Étienne de Boré had invented a profitable method of making sugar from Louisiana sugarcane. As a result, many planters in the Teche region put aside cattle ranching and indigo farming and instead began to grow sugarcane. With the rise of the sugar plantation system came the steamboat, perfected by Robert Fulton not too many years earlier; the sugar refinery, with its complex, state-of-the-art rollers, evaporators, and vacuum pans; and an even greater dependence on slave labor.

The slave economy of the deep South was thoroughly entrenched in South Louisiana's sugar-growing region by the time the Civil War broke out. Armies, cavalries, and navies from both sides of the conflict soon ravaged the Teche country. Military forces moved up and down the bayou, back and forth, in a futile attempt to firmly occupy and hold the region.

When President Lincoln issued the Emancipation Proclamation in 1863, he expressly excluded the Teche Country. Intending to free slaves only in regions as yet unconquered by the North, the president, somewhat overly optimistically, regarded the lands along the Teche as conquered. Thus, slaves in the Teche country technically remained enslaved until the passage of the 13th amendment to the US Constitution in 1865.

Only after the Civil War, amid the violence and tumult of Reconstruction-era Louisiana, did the state legislature create Iberia Parish. In large part, the parish was formed because residents of New Iberia and its vicinity resented the alleged misuse of tax revenues by politicians on the St. Martin Parish police jury, headquartered farther up the Teche at St. Martinville. Moreover, these residents disliked the drudgery of having to travel to the parish courthouses at St. Martinville or Franklin, located downstream in St. Mary Parish, to conduct legal business.

Thus, Iberia Parish came into being in 1868, forged from parts of St. Martin and St. Mary Parishes, with New Iberia as its parish seat. While the parish itself was new, the peoples who comprised it had already lived there for generations, including Native Americans, French Creoles, Spanish Creoles, Acadians (or Cajuns, as they increasingly came to be called), Germans, Anglo-Americans, African Americans, and Creoles of color, among others. They would, in the coming centuries, be joined by new peoples, more recently Southeast Asians and, in a curious twist that brings the story full circle, more Spanish-speaking immigrants—not from Málaga, Spain, this time, but from Mexico and Central America.

These are the large-scale forces that created Iberia Parish, a place that in the globalization of the early 21st century continues to regard with evident pride its own rich history and culture.

—Shane K. Bernard
Historian
New Iberia

Shane K. Bernard is the author of several books, including *Cajuns and Their Acadian Ancestors: A Young Reader's History* (2008), *Tabasco: An Illustrated History* (2007), *The Cajuns: Americanization of a People* (2003), and *Swamp Pop: Cajun and Creole Rhythm and Blues* (1996).

One

The Early Years

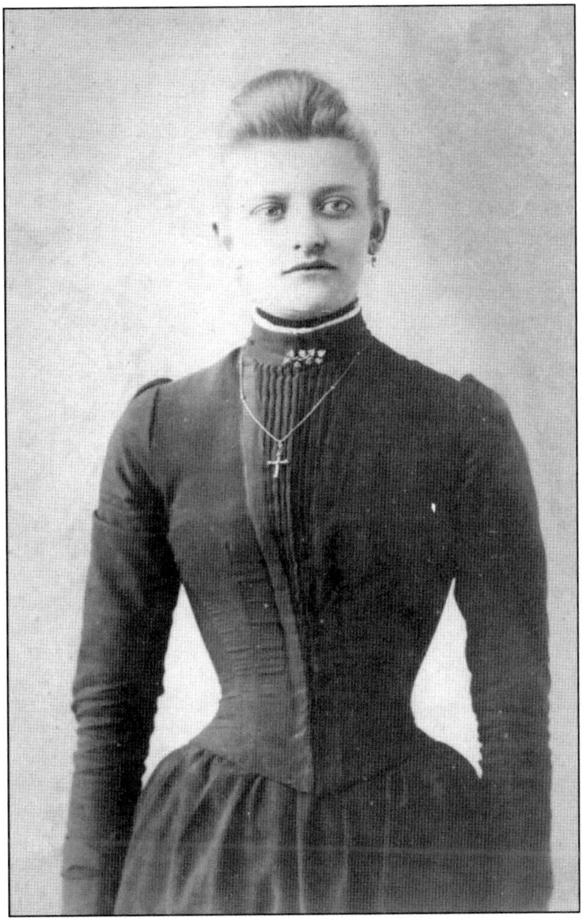

In the 1500s, Spanish explorers landed on Louisiana's coast. In the 1700s, French explorers Iberville and Bienville met the Attakapas. In 1733, Joseph Blanpain formed a partnership with them to trade pelts, horses, bear grease, and tallow. On April 10, 1805, the Louisiana Territory was divided into 12 counties, including the area known as the Attakapas, from which Iberia Parish was eventually carved. Cecile Landry Chastant (pictured), daughter of Terville Landry Jr. and Aurelia Theriot, was born near Lake Tasse (Spanish Lake) in Iberia Parish. She married Evalture Chastant and had four sons: Charles, Paul, Pierre, and Henry. In 1900, she died giving birth to Henry.

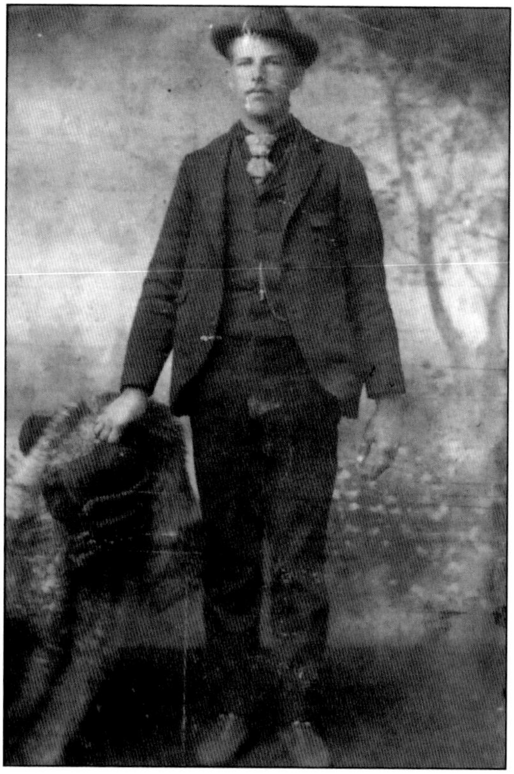

Between 1699 and 1860, several groups of French immigrants came to Louisiana. In the mid-1700s, Andre Fabry de la Bruyere signed a contract to purchase deer skins from André Massé. In 1760, Gabriel Fuselier de la Claire, the first commandant of the area, purchased land between the Teche and the Vermilion River from the chief of the Attakapas. Antoine Bernard Dauterive signed a cattle contract with eight Acadians in 1765. In 1799, Pierre Delcambre sailed from France to Louisiana. Shown in the late 1800s is his descendant Amadee Delcambre.

In 1763, the Treaty of Paris gave Spain lands west of the Mississippi River where forts were built. In 1776, Bernardo de Gálvez was named governor and brought colonists from the Canary Islands (such as the Dominguez family) and his home area of Málaga, Spain. On February 12, 1779, Lt. Col. Francisco Bouligny established a settlement on Bayou Teche. April floods forced the group to move to higher ground, and Bouligny named the new town Nueva Iberia. In 1779, the Miguez, Romero, Lagos, Riveros, Postigo, Garrido (Gary), Aguilar, Moreno, Prados, Ibanez, Segura, Artacho, Villatoro, Gomez, Ortiz, Solano, and de Puentes families came from the area around Málaga. Paul Miguez is pictured in 1917 during World War I at the age of 17.

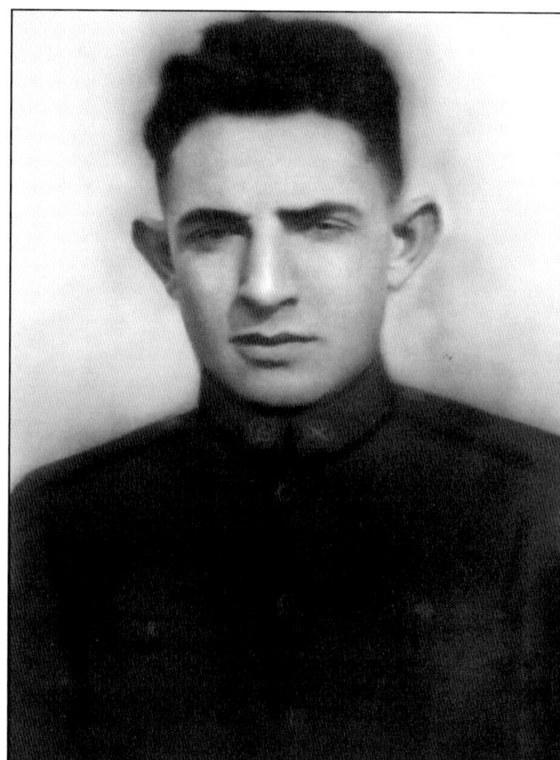

African slaves influenced the culture, language, and cuisine of Iberia Parish. In 1724, Louisiana institutionalized segregation when it adopted the *Code Noir*, a decree originally set forth by France's King Louis XIV. Following the Civil War, blacks were subjugated by Jim Crow laws. Pictured is Cornelius Manuel, father of Clara Manuel Moore. Manuel was born in eastern Iberia Parish in an area originally known as Isles Cannes, later Isle Piquant, and today as Neco Town. He and his wife farmed their land and owned a store where customers included both blacks and whites. His father, Alphonse Manuel, was a former slave and a Union veteran of the Civil War.

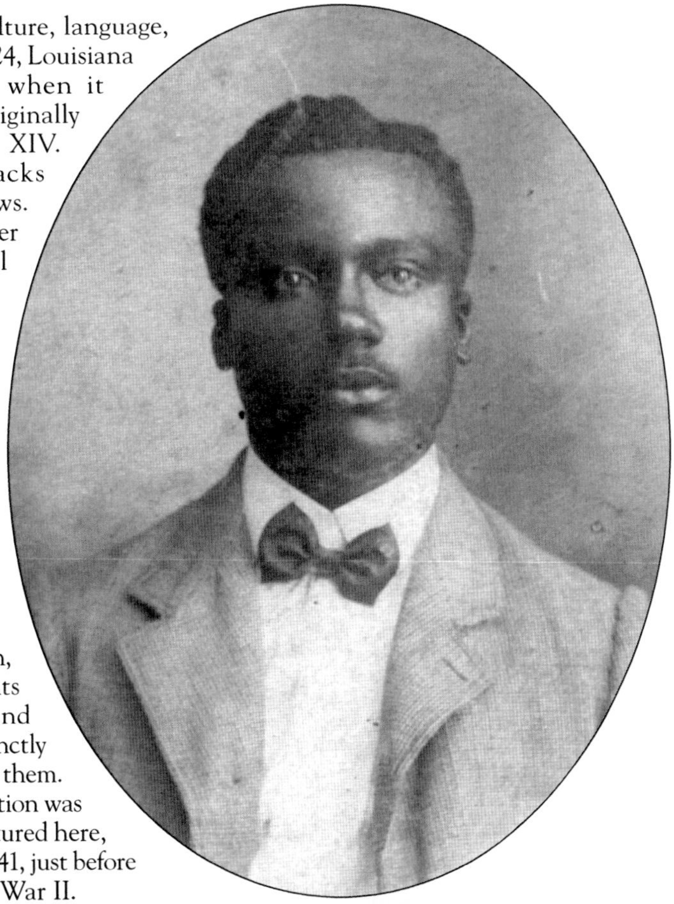

Iberia Parish was populated by Irish, Spanish, and German immigrants as well as Haitians, Italians, and Sicilians, all of whom brought distinctly different customs and cuisines with them. A previous New Iberia Pan-Am station was replaced by the service station pictured here, which opened on November 12, 1941, just before the United States entered World War II.

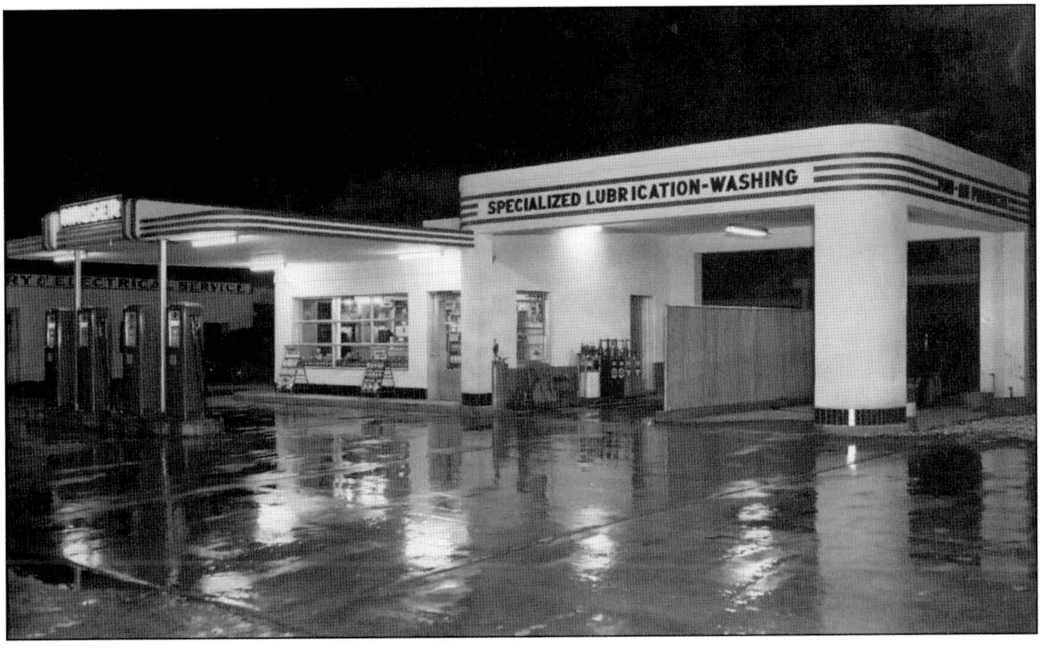

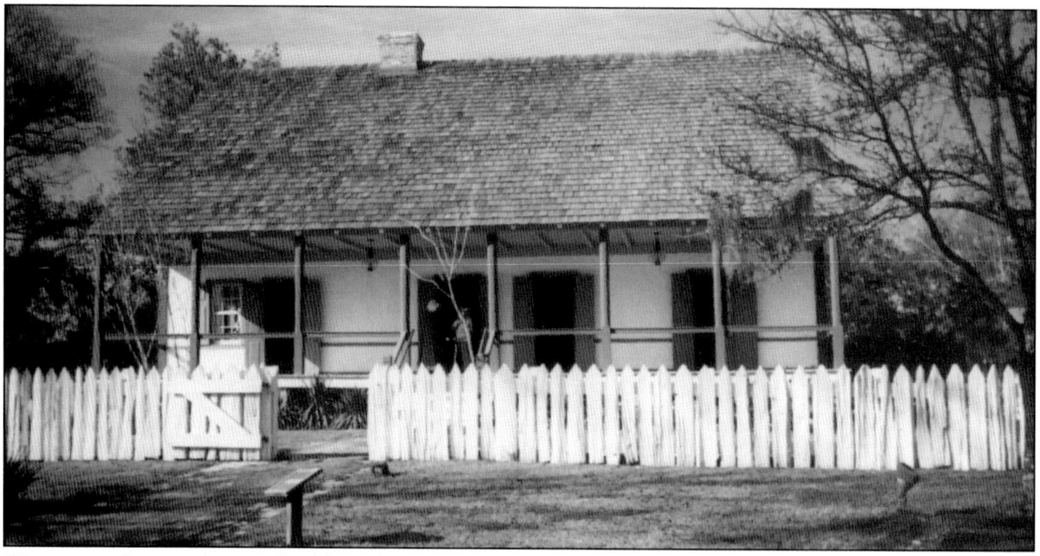

Climate influenced every building decision. The first houses were built on cypress stumps to keep them off the ground. Settlers made use of *bousillage*, an excellent insulating mixture of Spanish moss and mud. The outside walls were covered with horizontal cypress planks for protection from abundant rainfall. To combat the heat, high ceilings were the norm for Acadian houses, and windows and doors were arranged for cross ventilation. Usually, wide galleries ran the full length of the front, and a steeply pitched roof provided room for storage or sleeping and cooled the house. The historic house of Amant Broussard, son of Acadian leader Joseph "Beausoleil" Broussard, was built in 1790 near present-day Loreauville. The home is pictured at its original site (above) and today (below) at Vermilionville, a Cajun and Creole living history museum and folklife park in Lafayette. The park's director, Dr. David Cheramie, is the former director of the Council for the Development of French in Louisiana (CODOFIL). (Courtesy of Vermilionville.)

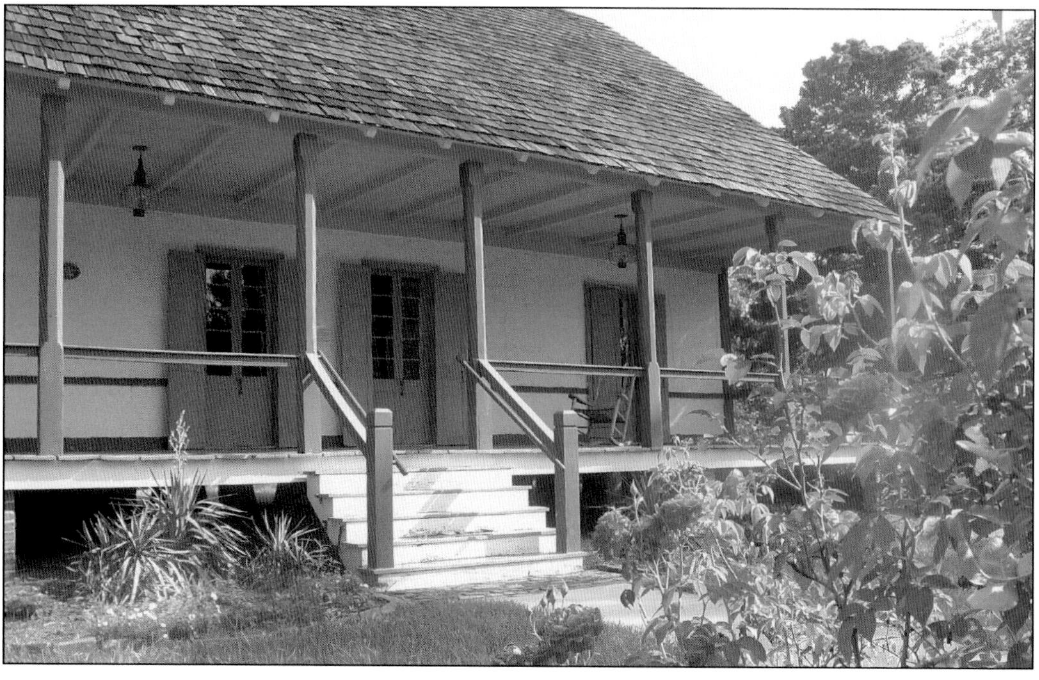

People of English descent, like the Marshes, Edwards, and Weeks, often built homes influenced by the Victorian style, which was popular in the northeast. One of the most useful elements of this style in Iberia's warm climate was the full-length front porch. In 2011, a celebration was held of the 50th anniversary of the Shadows on the Teche's designation as a National Trust Historic Site. This photograph, taken on August 17, 1947, shows the site's unique gallery featuring its classic columns. (Courtesy of the Louisiana State Archives.)

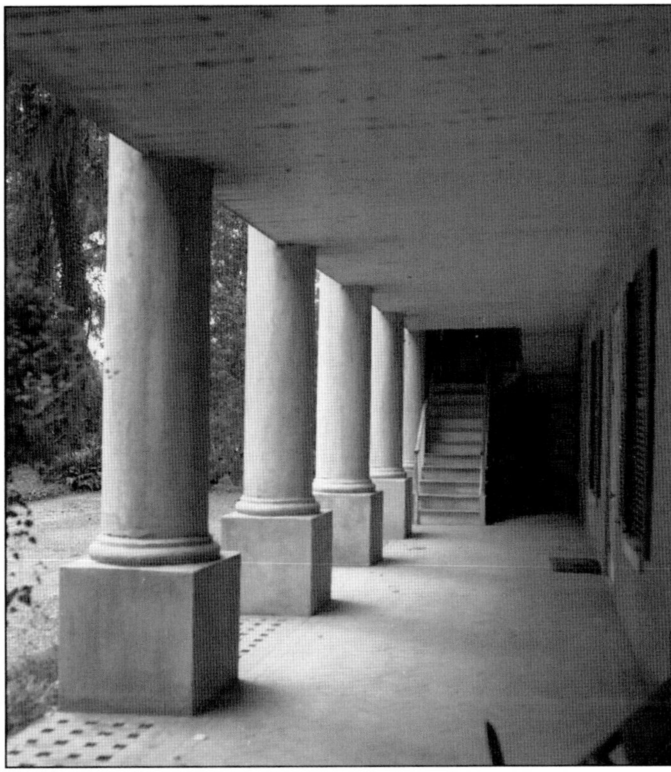

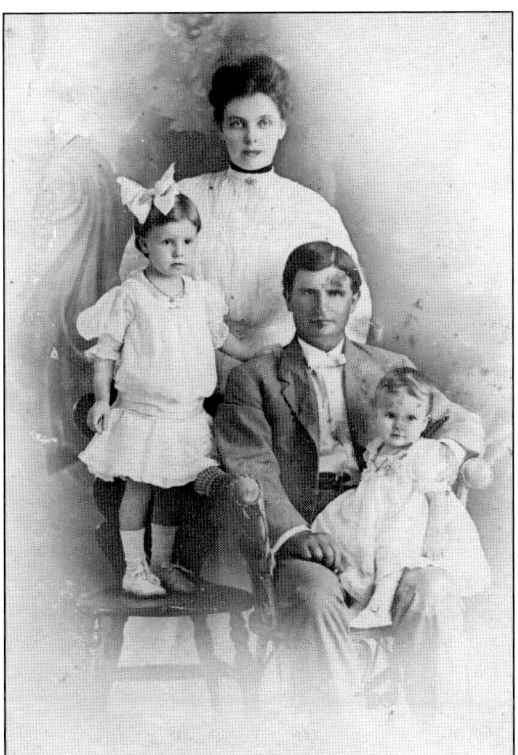

The devastating flood of 1927 displaced 100,000 people from the edge of the Atchafalaya Basin. To shelter the displaced, a Red Cross camp was set up in New Iberia, where many evacuees were first exposed to electricity and movies. A family affected by the flood is pictured in 1905. From left to right are Marie DeBlanc Landry (standing), Clara Landry Roy (standing on stool), Gabriel Landry (sitting), and Mabel Landry Lourd (sitting on Gabriel).

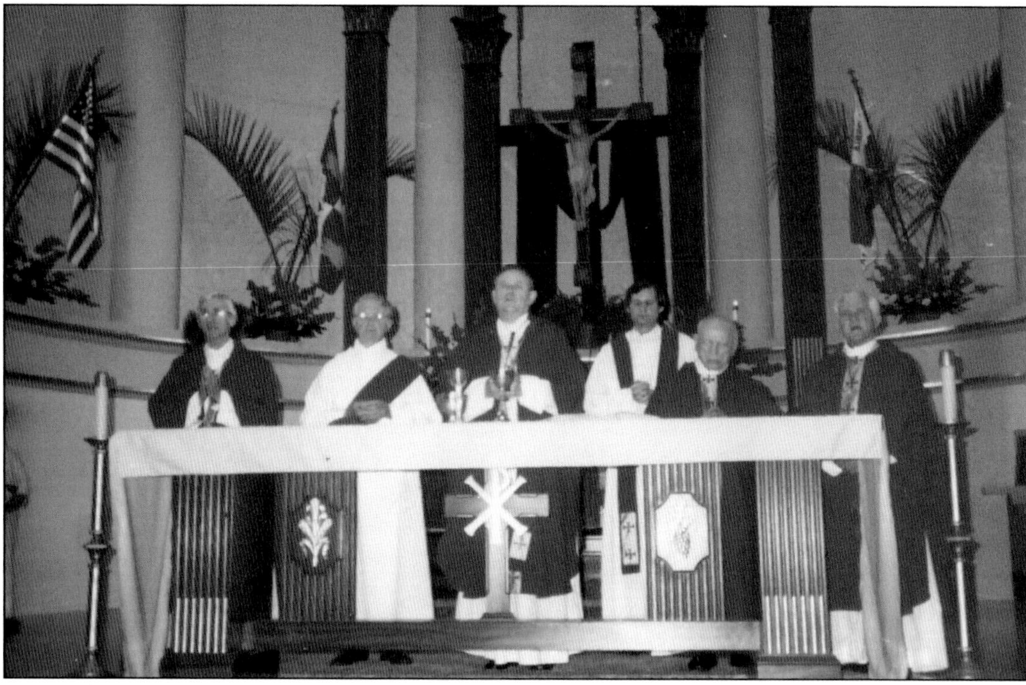

Pictured on April 8, 1979, from left to right are Msgr. Warren Boudreaux, Deacon Carl Conrad, Bishop Gerald Frey, Fr. Robie Robichaux, Bishop Maurice Schexnayder, and Bishop d'Antonio celebrating the New Iberia Bicentennial Mass in St. Peter's Catholic Church, which was established in 1838. On January 7, 1823, the First United Methodist Church held a service in New Town (New Iberia) on a New England brig on the Bayou Teche. The present sanctuary was built in 1907 and was placed in the National Register of Historic Places in 1991. Baptisms were recorded at the Episcopal Church in 1848, and the church was placed in the National Register of Historic Places in 1977. The Presbyterian Church began services in 1895, and the Jewish Temple was organized on April 26, 1897.

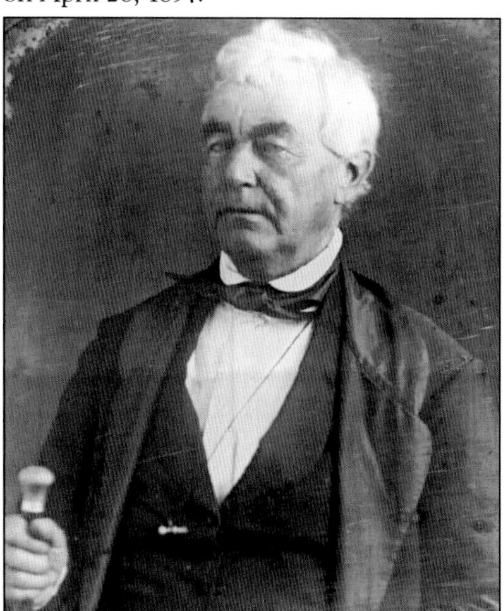

Out of the largesse of nature's bounty, Iberia Parish has given to the world the prized products of its beautiful waters, salt mines, oil sands, and lush panoramic fields of sugarcane, rice, cotton, and sweet potatoes. For passionate environmentalists like Nara Crowley of Jefferson Island, Iberia is a rich tapestry of delicate ecologies that must be preserved for future generations. In 1818, New Jersey native John Craig Marsh, pictured around 1850, settled on Petite Anse Island, now Avery Island, to grow sugarcane. The Avery and McIlhenny families of Avery Island are his descendants. (Courtesy of the Avery Island, Inc. Archives.)

The surname Romero, the largest in the parish, was introduced into Louisiana in the late 18th century when Spain was attempting to bolster the population of its newly acquired colony. In 1779, six Romero families arrived in New Orleans: five from the Canary Islands and one from Málaga, in southern Spain. Miguel Romero, his wife, Maria de Grano, and their three sons were sent to the Attakapas to help found a town on Bayou Teche, which would be called New Iberia, and to raise flax for the Spanish. Pictured are Winnie Romero (left) and Odette Delcambre Voorhies.

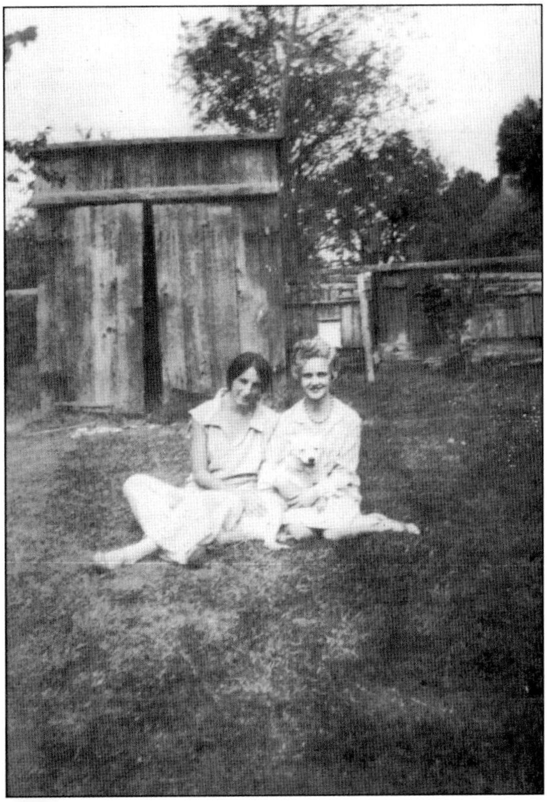

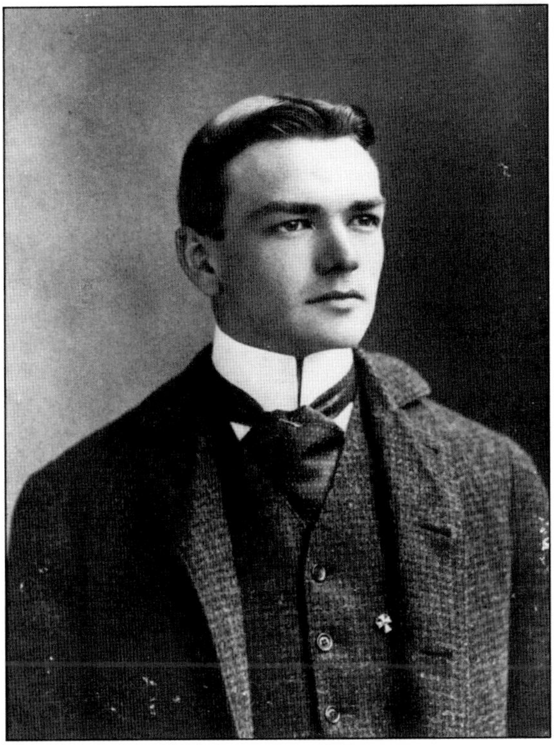

Rufus McIlhenny, son of Tabasco sauce inventor Edmund McIlhenny, served on the Iberia Parish Police Jury and as treasurer of McIlhenny Company. Iberians were hardworking and creative. Combining work with a love of good food made work more pleasant, so farmers harvesting their crops served the most delicious meal possible for their workers. Iberia's highly productive lands, totaling 426,880 acres, consist of prairie, coastal marsh, alluvial, and swamp lands. (Courtesy of the McIlhenny Company Archives.)

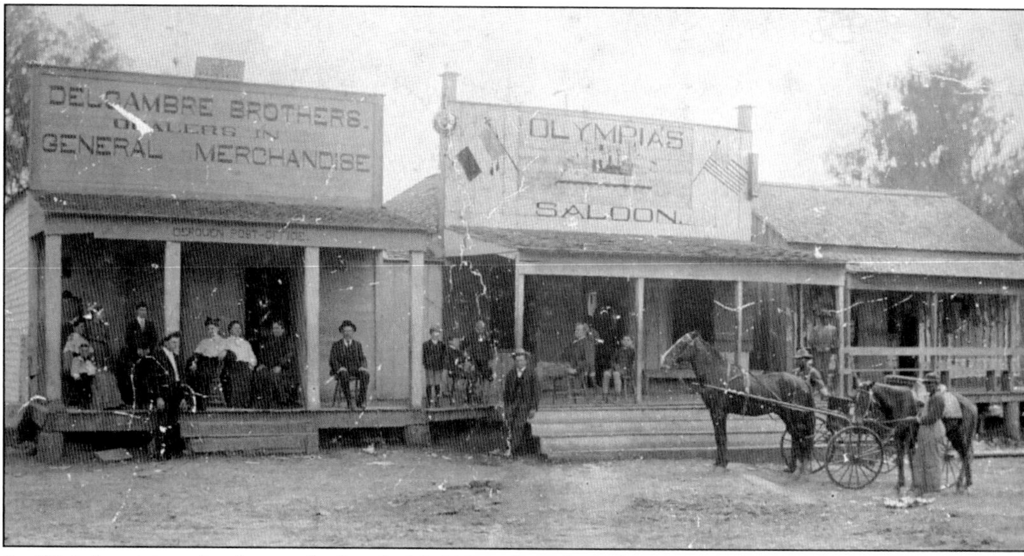

In 1911, Louisiana had a total of only 25,000 miles of roadways, mostly dirt. By 1920, 1,700 miles of roads had been upgraded with gravel or shell surfaces, 100 miles of which were located in Iberia Parish. The Bayou Teche was the hub of economic activity, and dirt or gravel roads connected smaller towns with New Iberia, making it the commercial center. Pictured in the 1920s is the general store in Derouen.

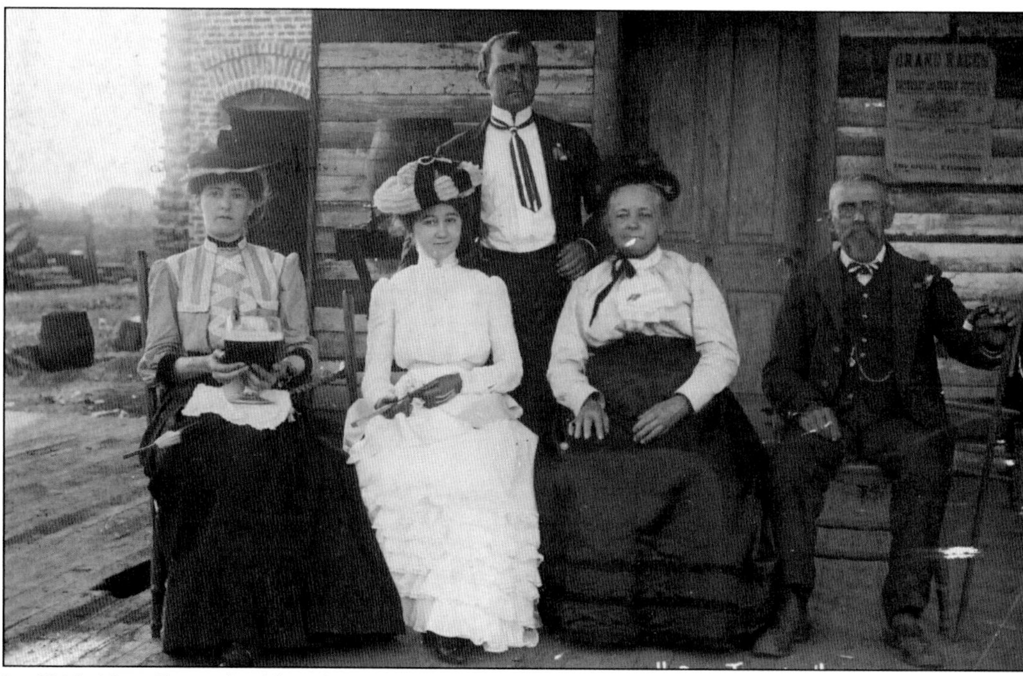

In 1920, New Iberia had hotels, sanitariums, foundries, machine shops, canning factories, rice mills, lumberyards, convents, two Catholic schools, and two banks. Antoine Moresi (far right) and his wife, Philomene Kobleur Moresi (seated next to him), are pictured in 1890 with their family members at the A. Moresi Foundry in Jeanerette. In 1891, according to historian William Henry Perrin, other industries included sawmills, brickyards, a cistern factory, a soap factory, and a cottonseed mill, which was the largest mill in the city.

Two

ATTAKAPAS DISTRICT

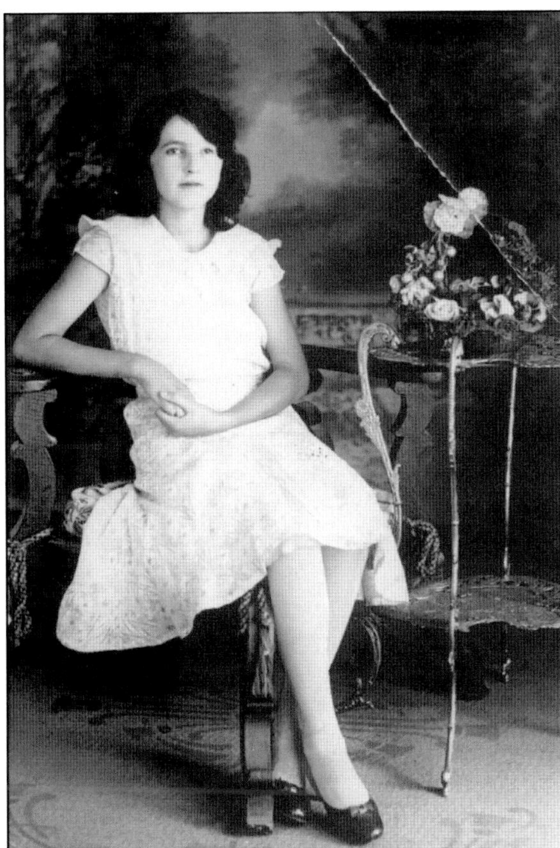

Before deportation from Nova Scotia in 1755, Acadians isolated themselves from other groups and remained politically neutral. This helped them develop a new ethnicity. In 1765, Joseph "Beausoleil" Broussard led the first large group of about 200 Acadians to Louisiana. Their new ethnicity made them different from other French-speaking peoples in North America. Pictured in 1928 is Adella Landry Broussard in New Iberia, a descendant of the first Acadians to settle in the area.

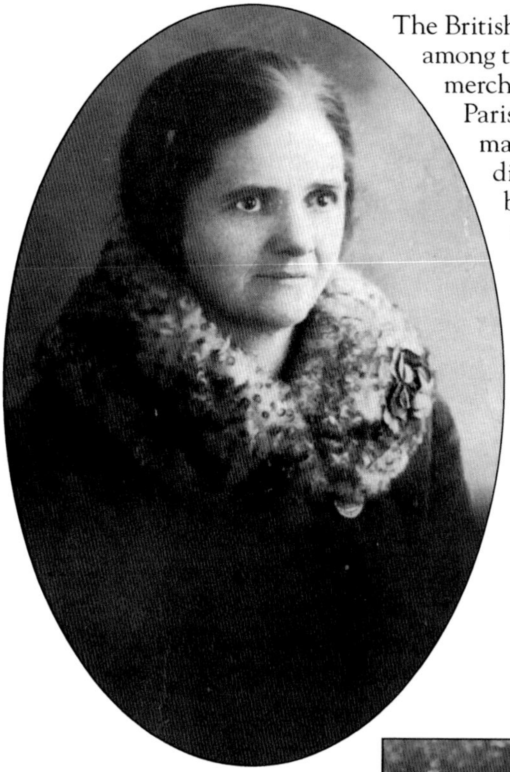

The British exiled Acadians from Acadia for many reasons, among them economic paranoia induced by pressure from merchants in the British colonies. Since the Treaty of Paris prevented them from returning to their lands, many Acadians came to Louisiana; most, however, did not arrive until 1785, when seven vessels brought 1,660 of them. Pictured is Linda Landry, a descendant of Acadian settlers, who was born in 1881 in Loreauville. Prior to moving to Biloxi, Mississippi, she and her husband, Elie Romero, farmed his father's land.

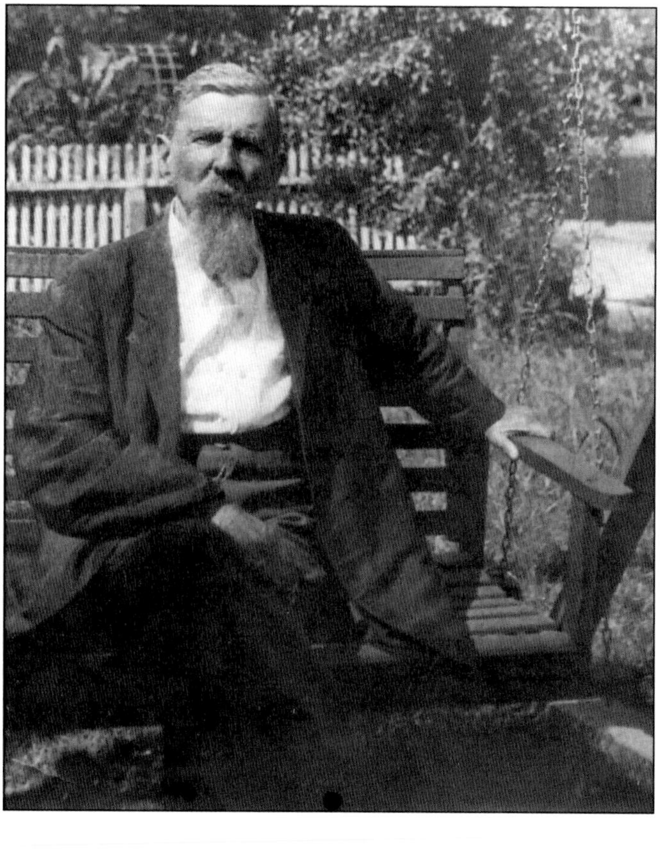

Pictured is Felix Voorhies (1839–1919), an Acadian district judge in New Iberia and an accomplished author. He wrote short stories and plays both in standard French and the local dialect for comic effect. Staged in St. Martinville, these plays contributed to the town's reputation as "le Petit Paris." In 1903, Voorhies published *Acadian Reminiscences*, a family memoir that included a chapter entitled "The True Story of Evangeline," which sparked a literary debate that continues to this day.

Today, the Broussards comprise the second largest clan in the parish with more than half in the state living in Teche country. Most Broussards trace their ancestry to two Acadian brothers, Joseph "Beausoleil" and Alexandre. The second decade of the 19th century saw the Broussards concentrated in areas near the site of their initial settlement around present-day St. Martinville, including Fausse Point on the Teche, along Bayou Petite Anse near Avery Island, Lake Peigneur, and Prairie Sorrel. This 1900 photograph shows Damas Broussard and Helen Dronet.

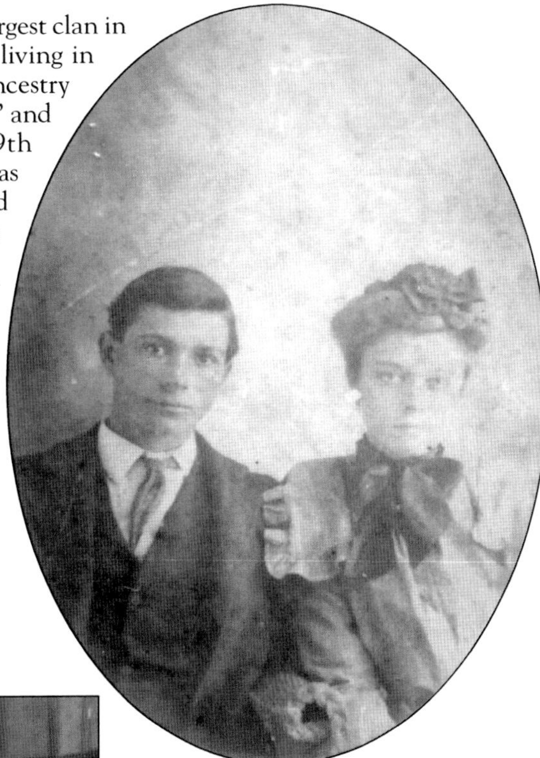

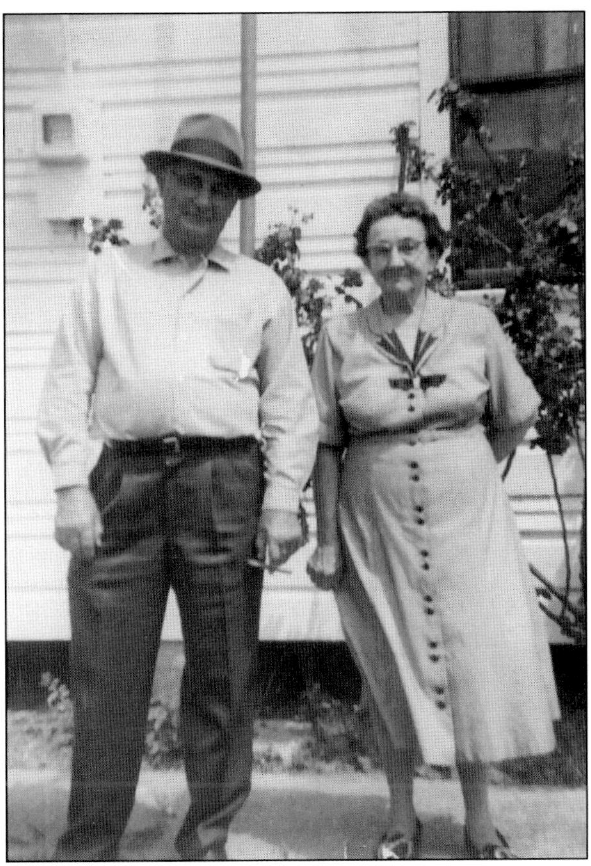

After Quebec fell in 1759, the Acadians, who had avoided deportation and started an insurgency against the British, found their struggle hopeless and surrendered. They were imprisoned for four years on Georges Island in Halifax, Nova Scotia, and were eventually allowed to depart for Louisiana in 1764. Later, in Iberia, it was common for an Acadian woman to marry a Spanish descendant, like Abara and Mae Blanchard Viator, shown in this late-1950s photograph.

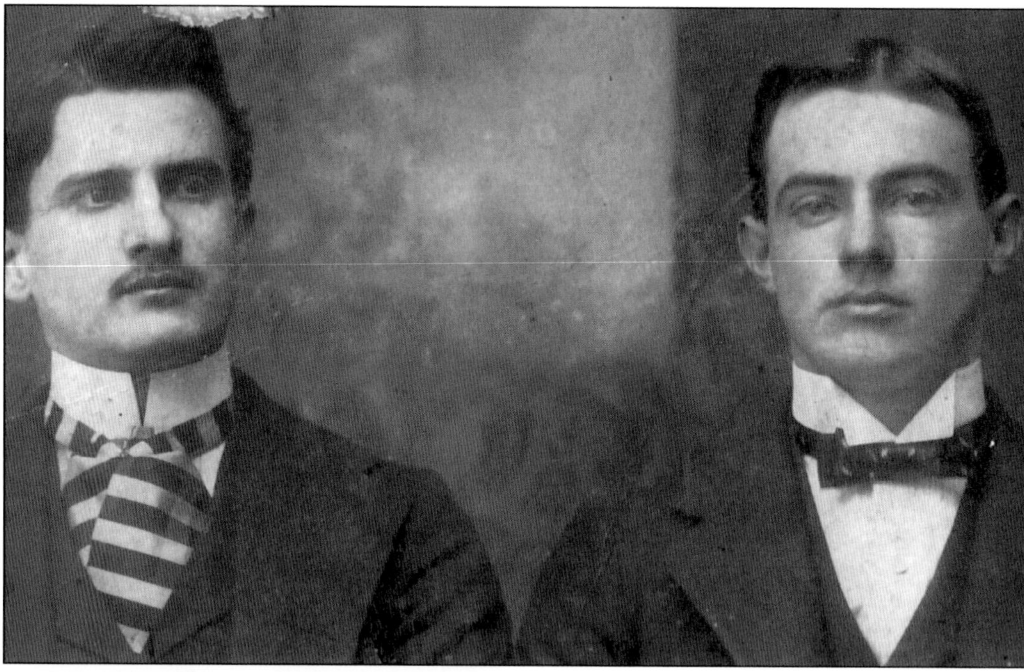

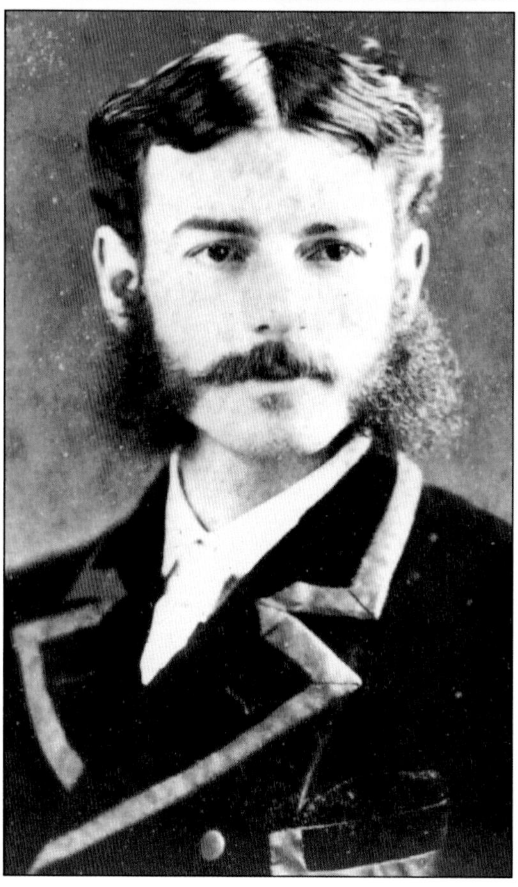

In 1765, two years after the French and Indian War, groups of Acadians began arriving unexpectedly in Louisiana, which had been recently acquired by Spain. Settling on Spanish land grants in the Poste des Attakapas, they made a remarkable adaptation to their new environment. Pictured are Paul Anthony Landry (left), a descendant of Acadian pioneers who became sheriff of Iberia Parish, and Louis Cyrus deBlanc. Both were prominent citizens of New Iberia who co-owned a general store.

According to a recently discovered letter written on April 20, 1766, by Jean-Baptiste Semar, an Acadian boy who was separated from his family during deportation, the Spanish provided the pioneer Acadians with weapons and food. It stated that their leader, "Beausoleil" Broussard, died in October 1765. By the 1770s, Acadians had settled along the Bayou Teche in Iberia Parish. Pictured in 1870 is John "Jack" Henshaw, a New Iberia planter who worked with the Acadians. Henshaw Street in New Iberia is named for his family, who resided on the future site of St. Peter's College. Today, it is the site of the Iberia Parish Library. (Courtesy of the Avery Island, Inc. Archives.)

Several unique cultural traits, such as the capacity to adapt to any given condition, gave Acadians the ability to endure and prosper in the new territory. Acquiring survival skills from the local Native Americans proved beneficial. They learned to treat illnesses with native plants, weave palmetto leaves into shelters, and farm local vegetables. Their strong Catholic faith also gave them the strength to endure hardships. Pictured are Antoine Reaux, Sr. and his second wife, Aurelia LeBlanc. Antoine Reaux, Sr. is the great, great grandfather of Ebrar Reaux and the great grandfather of Dr. Andy Reaux.

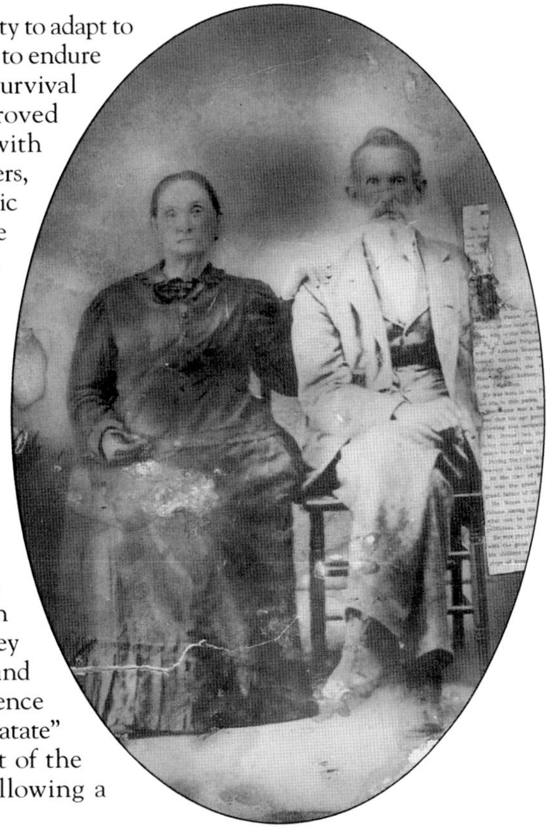

The largest group of Francophones came to Louisiana between 1820 and 1860, when 500,000 French immigrants—called "Foreign French"—came through New Orleans. They prospered because of their skills as tradesmen and craftsmen, and were responsible for the emergence of French education, opera, and newspapers. "Patate" Vincent and Arthur Derouen, a descendant of the "Foreign French," are pictured in 1950 following a successful bear hunt.

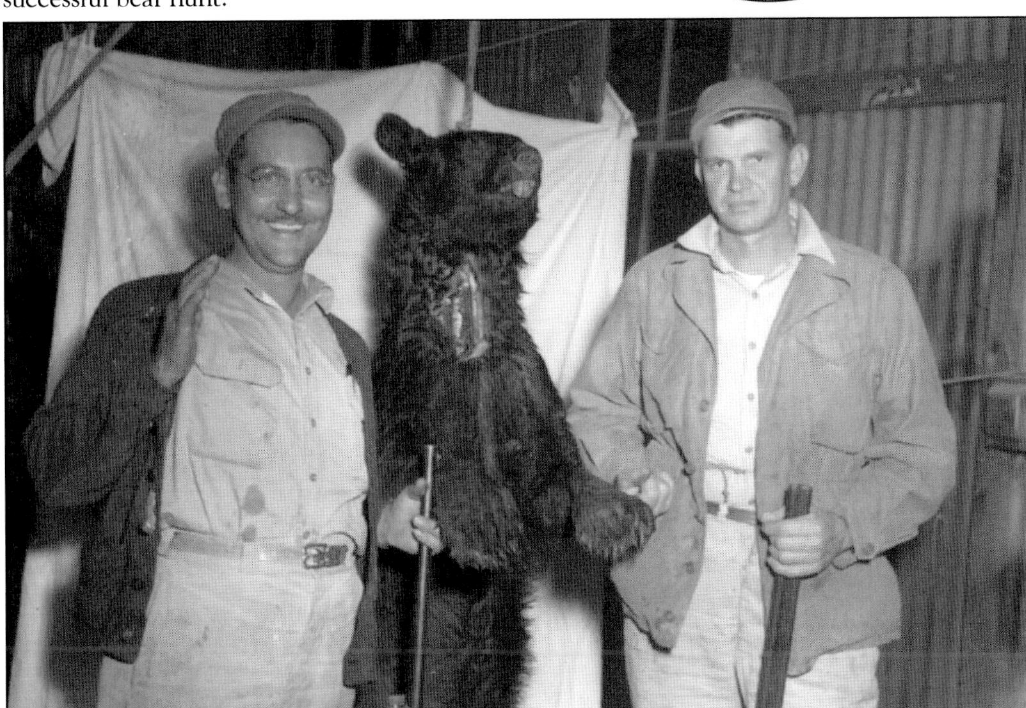

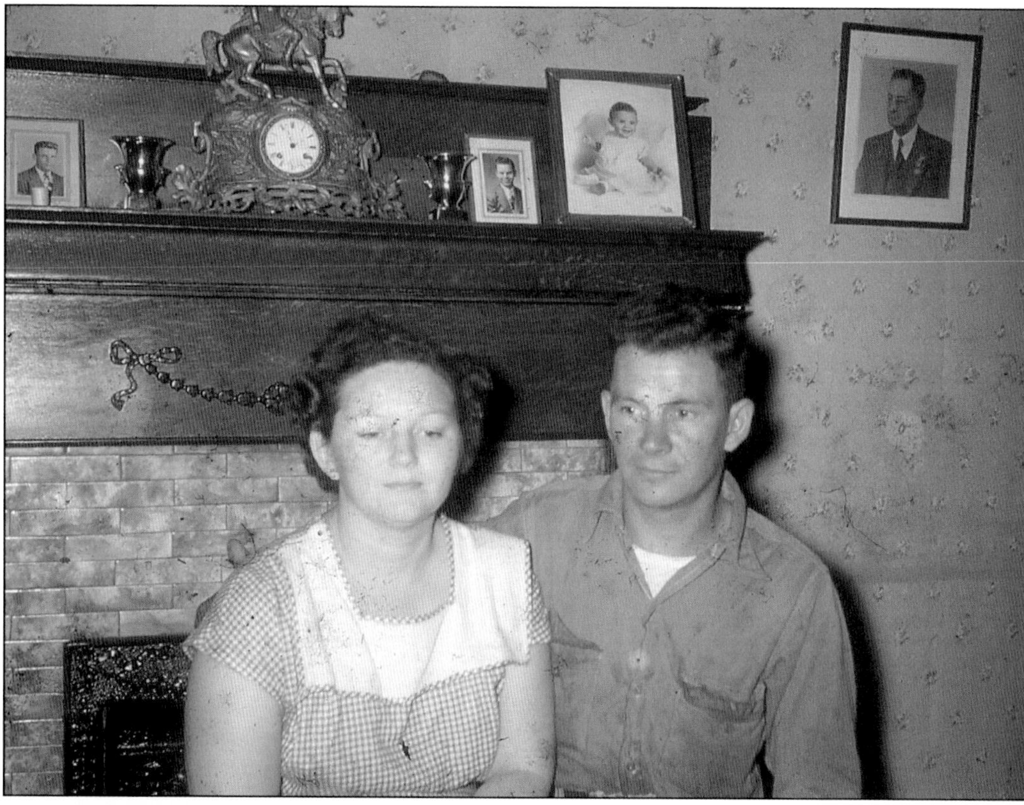

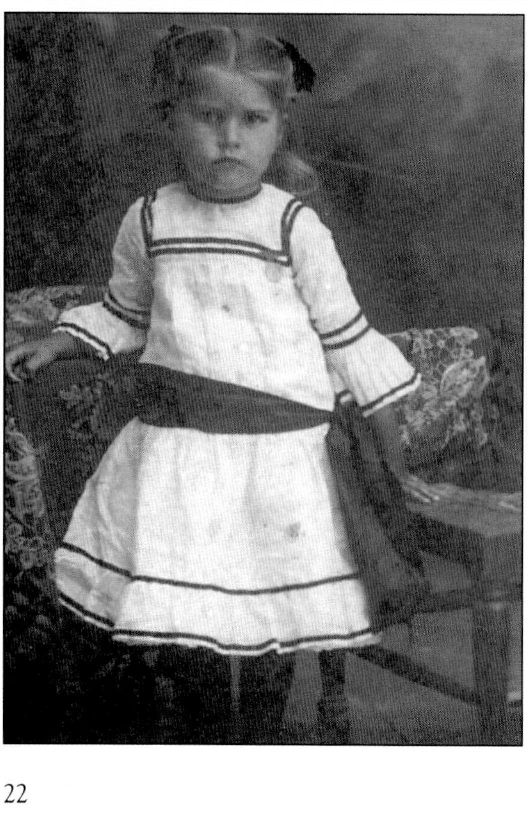

In the mid-1800s, many Europeans resettled in Louisiana, most of them craftsmen who could no longer adapt to the changes brought by the Industrial Revolution. In Iberia, these people and their descendants, such as Bessie and Jimmy Markham (pictured), became the new and progressive middle class. Others to come directly from France were the DeBlancs, delaHoussayes, Oliviers, St. Clairs, deClouets, Devezins, and the Gonsoulins, who were the young American nation's original surveyors.

By 1900, many of Iberia's new settlers were on the threshold of a sociocultural change that would create what is known worldwide as the Cajun culture, exemplified by Amedese Delcambre, photographed in the 1890s. Today, it is estimated that there are over two million Acadians dispersed throughout the world with 600,000 living in south Louisiana, the largest concentration in the world.

The unique Cajun culture consists of interesting characteristics that have been passed on to Acadian descendants, such as family cohesiveness, community commitment, self-effacement, friendliness, and the enjoyment of life. Today, it is admired throughout the country as one of the few thriving ethnicities. Pictured in 1930 at their family home on West St. Peter in New Iberia are, from left to right, (first row) Sammy Karnoski, Richard C. Sealy Jr., Dixie Lou Sealy, and Helen Gayle; (second row) Richard C. Sealy Sr.

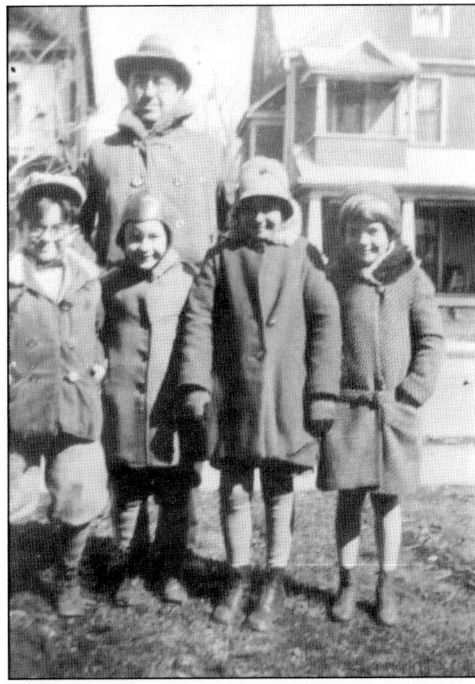

The parish's evolution was marked by many of its cultures being assimilated by the Acadians. This interaction, along with the palpable Spanish presence, contributed to its distinctiveness. Pictured on August 24, 1906, at Lake Dauterive are, from left to right, Delano Delcambre, Bee Delcambre, Cora Audibert, and Claire Dartez enjoying an outing in a skiff. The beautiful bayous were initially foreboding, but eventually proved to be nurturing.

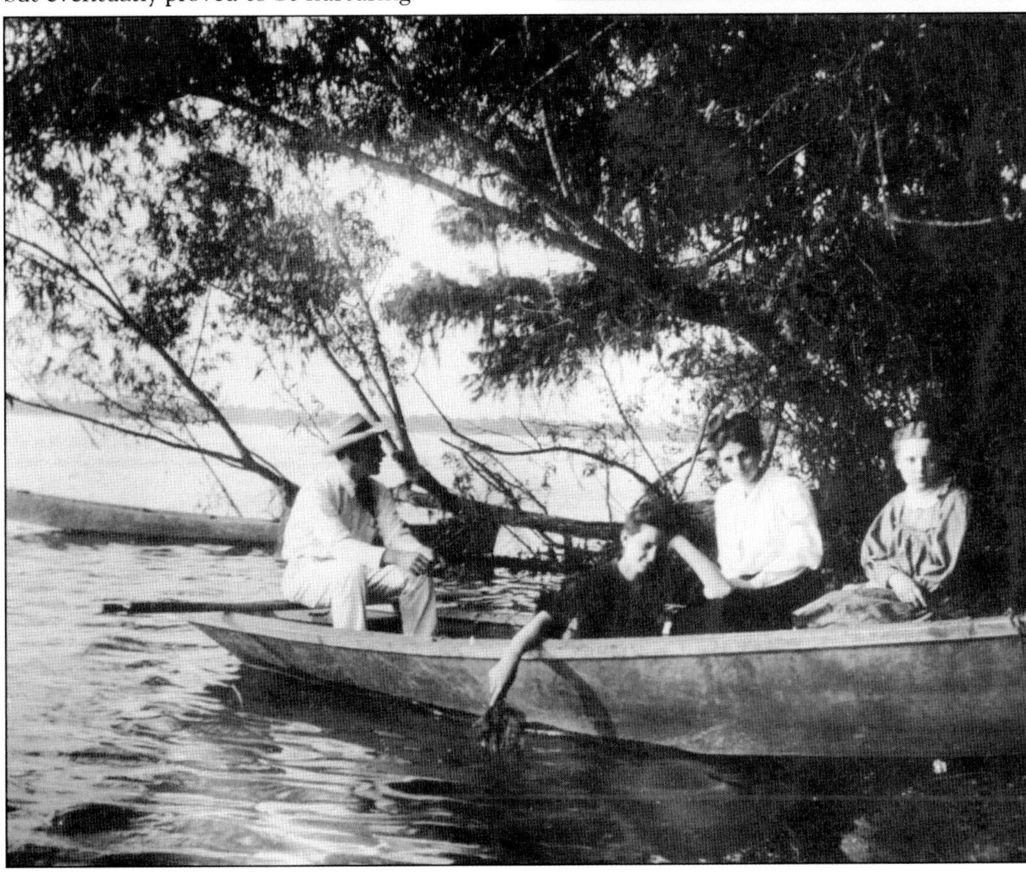

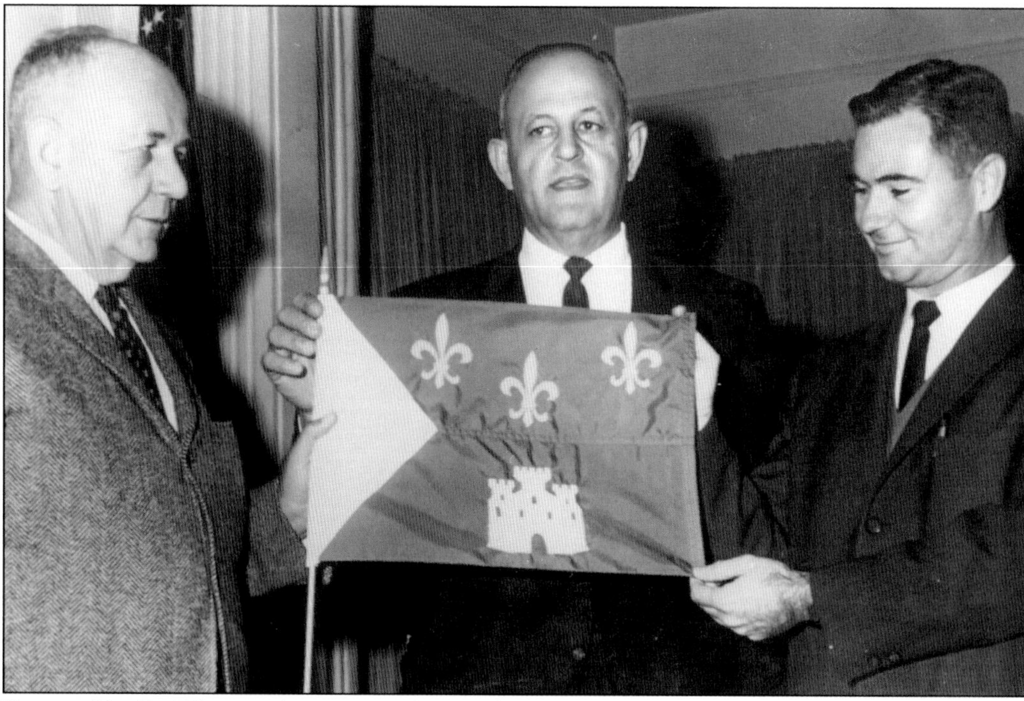

Designed by Dr. Thomas Arceneaux, the Acadian flag features three silver fleurs-de-lis on a blue field, which symbolize the Acadians' French heritage; a gold castle on a red field, which symbolizes Spanish rule; and a gold star on white, which represents Our Lady of the Assumption, patron saint of the Acadians. The flag was unveiled on February 22, 1965 (above), by, from left to right, Dr. Thomas Arceneaux, state comptroller Roy Theriot Sr., and Judge Allen Babineaux. The flag was made official by Louisiana in 1974. Below, on March 31, 2001, King Juan Carlos and Queen Sofia of Spain received a delegation from Louisiana in Jackson, Mississippi, which presented the royals with an Acadian flag. Shown from left to right are Ed Cailleteau, assistant sergeant-at-arms, Louisiana House of Representatives; Robert Shelton; Jolie Shelton; Warren Perrin, president of the Council for the Development of French in Louisiana (CODOFIL); Charles LeBlanc; King Juan Carlos; Queen Sofia; Bryce Breaux, representative of the Louisiana Children of the American Revolution; Mrs. Charles LeBlanc; Julia Chatam, Institute Cervantes; H. Lynn Breaux, a native of Lozes and ambassador to France for the Sons of the American Revolution; Dorothy Broussard; and Antoine J. LeBlanc, president of *Monde des Cadiens*. (Courtesy of Kermit Bouillion.)

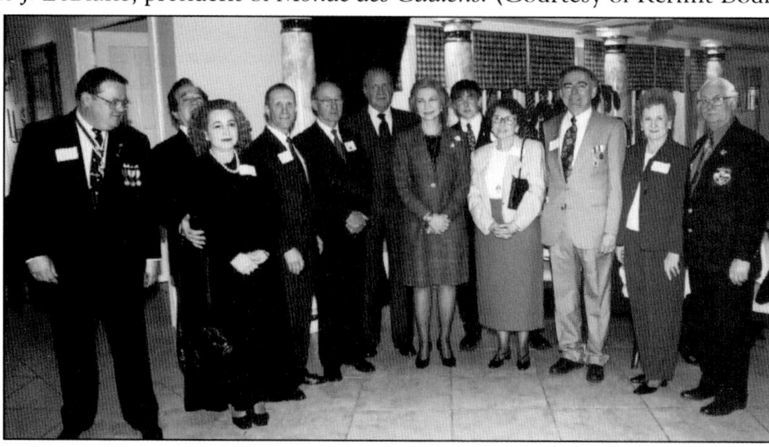

Three

Geography and Bounties of the Land

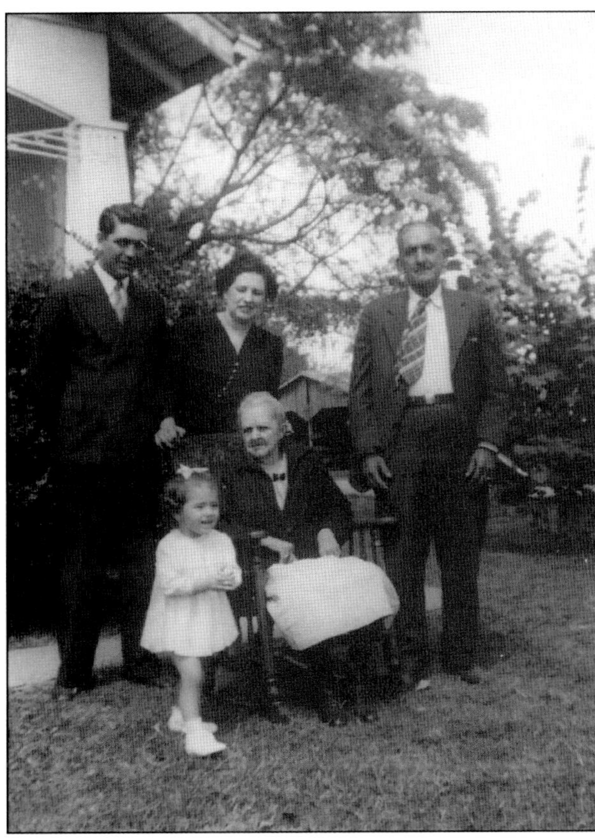

Pictured in 1941 are five generations of founding families. From left to right are (first row) Lynette Nicholson Gosnell (the child), fifth-generation descendant; Julie Althee Romero Lopez (seated), first-generation descendant of New Iberia founders Miguel Romero and Francisco Segura; (second row) Lloyd A. Nicholson, second generation; Eunice Lopez Nicholson, third generation; and Eugena Edouard Lopez, fourth generation, whose husband, Eusebe Edouard Lopez (not pictured), was a descendant of Lt. Col. Francisco Bouligny.

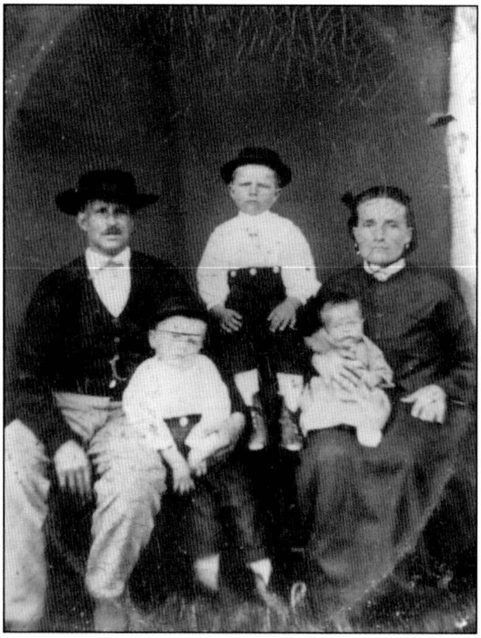

The family pictured here shows the common cultural occurrence of a French man marrying a German woman. From left to right are Charles Delcambre, Victor Delcambre, Amadee Delcambre (sitting on stool), Oleus Delcambre (baby), and Amy Himel Delcambre. In an article written for *Harper's* magazine in 1887, Charles Warner stated, "From New Iberia southward toward Vermilion Bay stretches a vast prairie that is absolutely flat and resembles the ocean. It would be monotonous were it not dotted with small round ponds and herds of scattered cattle."

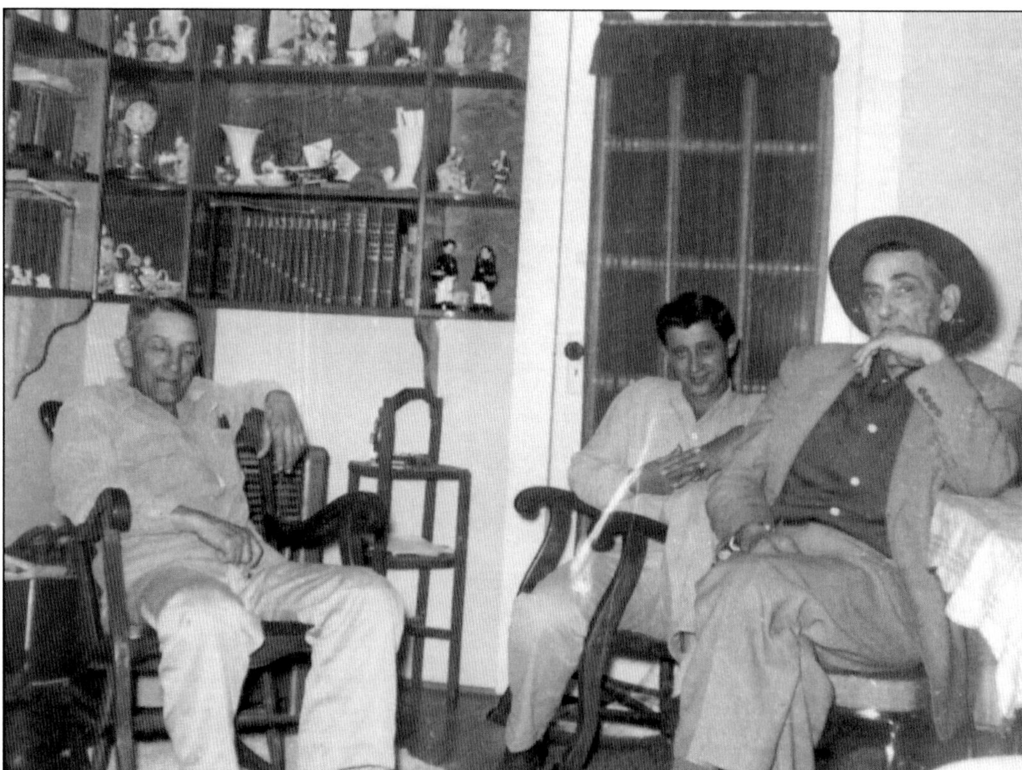

Pictured in June 1956 from left to right are Paul Miguez, his brother Neuville Miguez, and his brother-in-law Relius Derouen. Today, led by Pres. Ovey Viator and Vice Pres. Troy Broussard, Cajun culture and music are promoted by the local chapter of the Cajun French Music Association, *Les Cadiens du Teche*, which sponsors the Cajun French Music Festival.

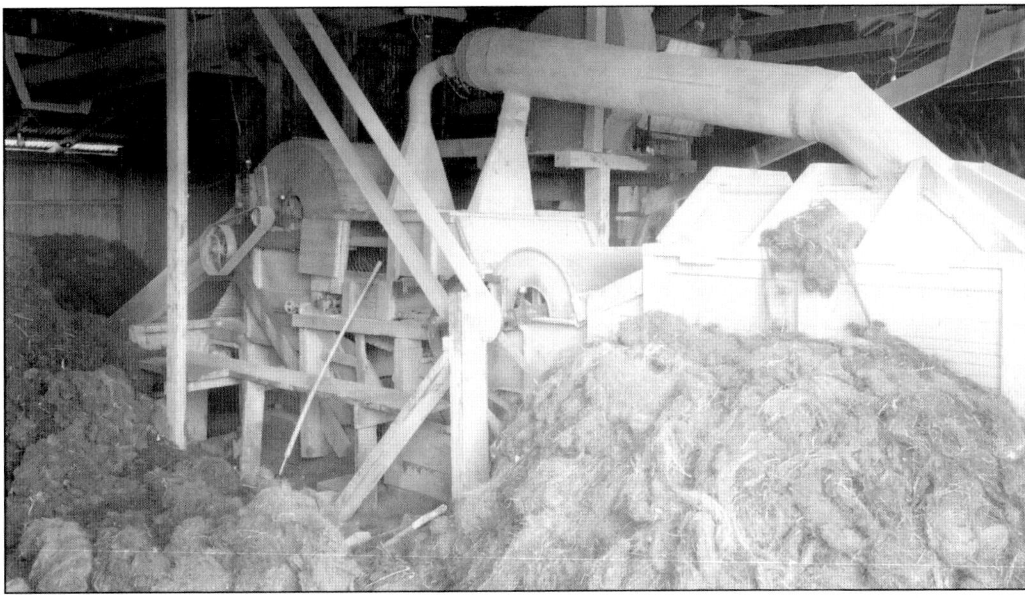

The town of Delcambre (named after Desiré Delcambre) has utilized its strategic location on Bayou Carlin, which leads directly to the Gulf of Mexico, to become a leader in the seafood industry. Its first settlers were the Geoffroy, Miguez, Viltz, Rodrigues, Viator, Goutierrez, Segura, Romero, Gary, and Nunez families, who were given Spanish land grants in 1790. Pictured is a Spanish moss mill near Delcambre. (Courtesy of Center for Louisiana Studies, University of Louisiana at Lafayette.)

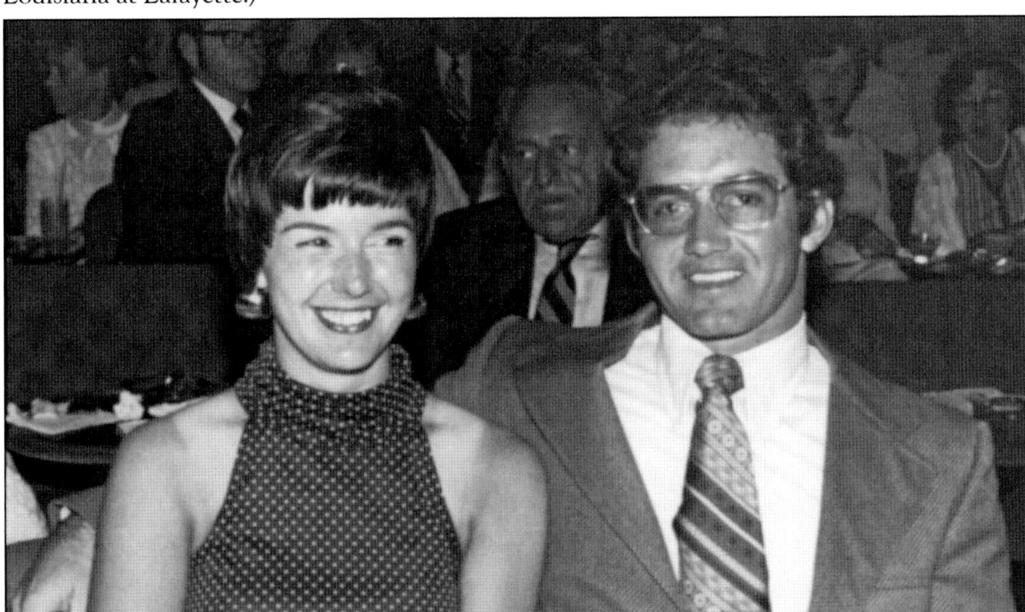

By the end of the 19th century, many Iberians sought livelihoods in fields like fishing, hunting, and trapping. Glen Viltz (right) is a native of Delcambre whose father, Preston Viltz, was a shrimper. He is pictured in 1974 with his wife, Garneth Barras Viltz, the 1962 New Iberia High School homecoming queen. They are the parents of Keri and Ross Viltz, who is the director of the Stadium Club, Louisiana State University.

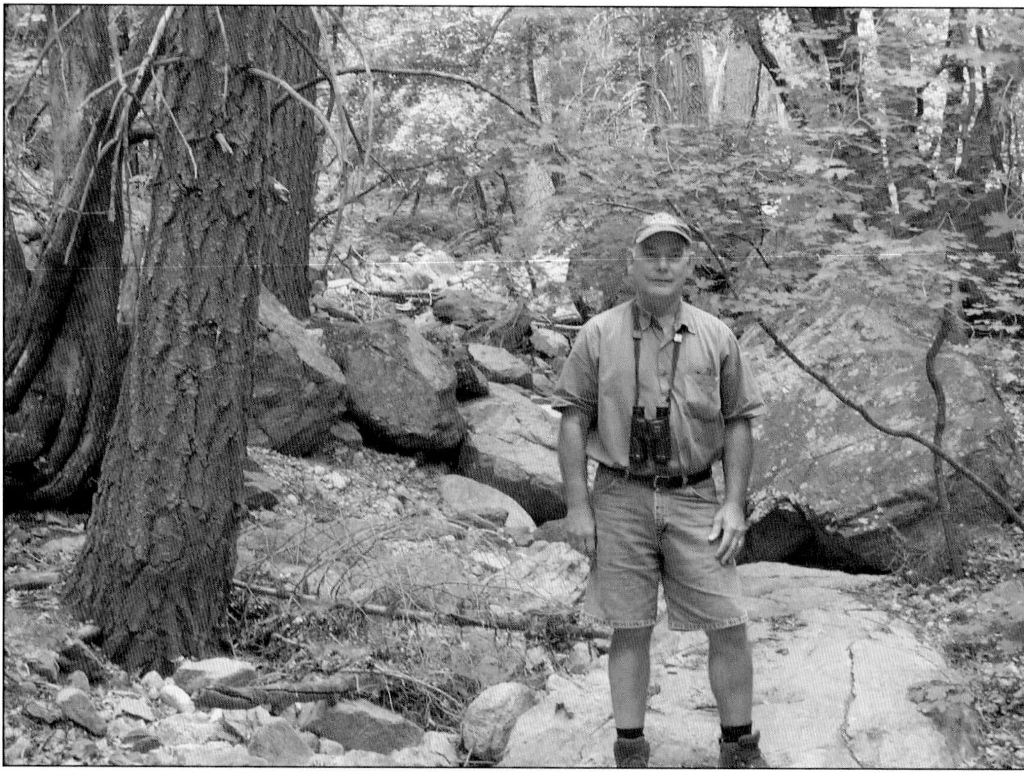

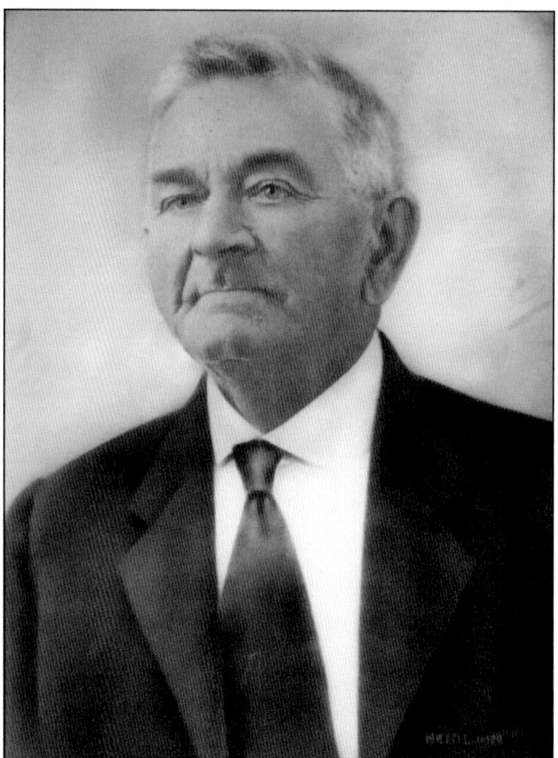

Michael Musumeche is a certified ornithologist, graduate of Catholic High School, and retired biology teacher who has recorded bird species around the world. This photograph was taken on a birding expedition to Arizona and Belize. He has written many pamphlets, including *Birds of Iberia Parish—Birds of Spanish Lake—A Seasonal Checklist*, which is available at the Iberia Parish Convention and Visitors Bureau. He is the son of Vince Musumeche, a second-generation Italian American. Rocco Musumeche, the son of Vincent Musumeche, was a prolific writer nationally known for his short stories.

Pictured is Oscar Viator, husband of Amanda Huval and father of Abra, Lloyd, Dudley, Wilson, Roosevelt, J.C., Roy, Ordley, William, Lillian, and Lois. In 1891, Bayou Teche was lined with plantations and farms nearly the entire distance from its entrance into the parish east of Spanish Lake to the line where it leaves the parish, below Jeanerette.

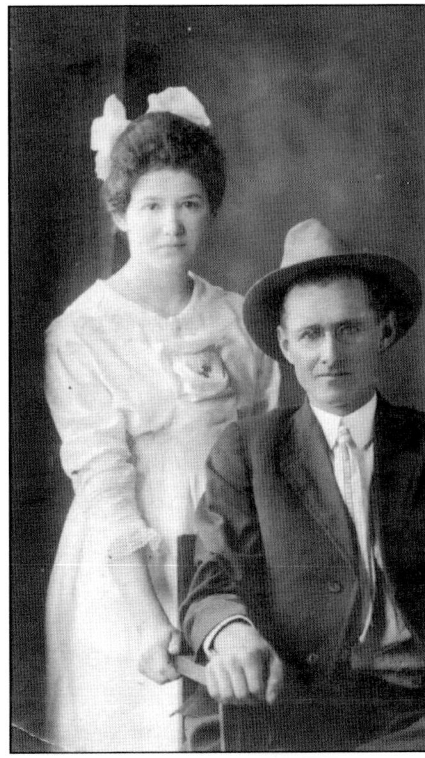

In 1948, Pure Oil Company discovered natural gas while drilling one of the first offshore oil wells near Marsh Island. At right, Elian Derouen Bonin (left) and Deluke Bonin are pictured in 1919. Pictured below in 1945 in New Iberia are the Bonins' eight children. From left to right are Rita, Gernice, Una, Elina, Luke, Irene, Gussie, and Claude. Like many families in the parish, several in this family worked in oil-related jobs.

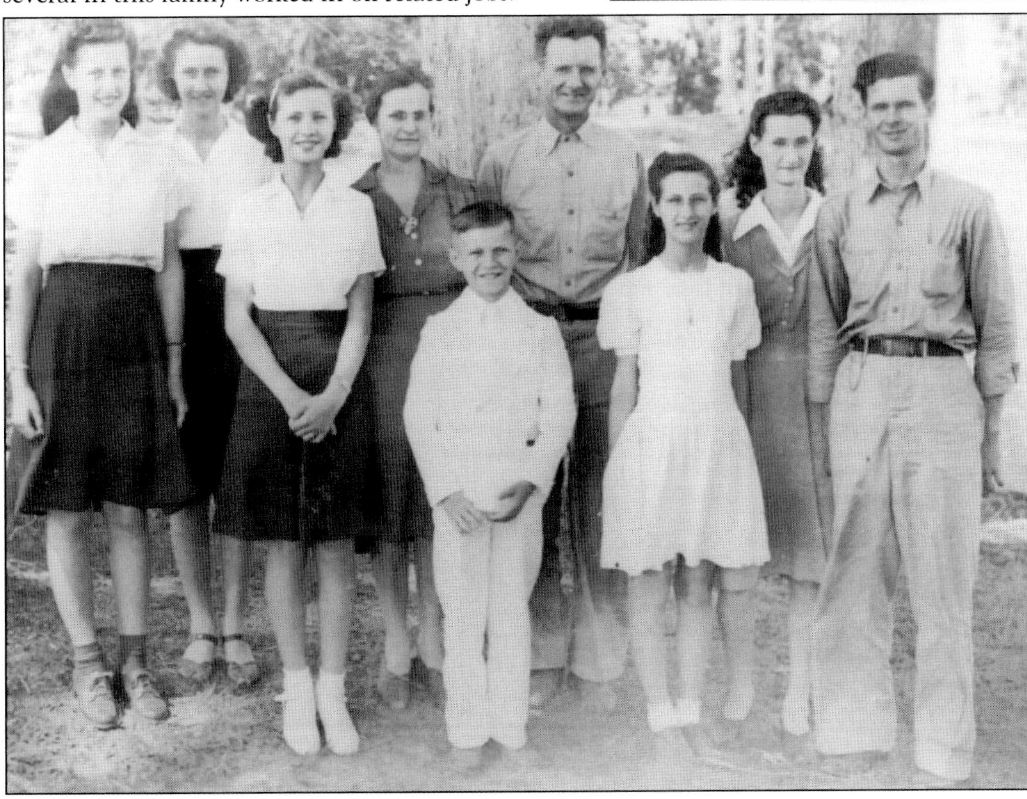

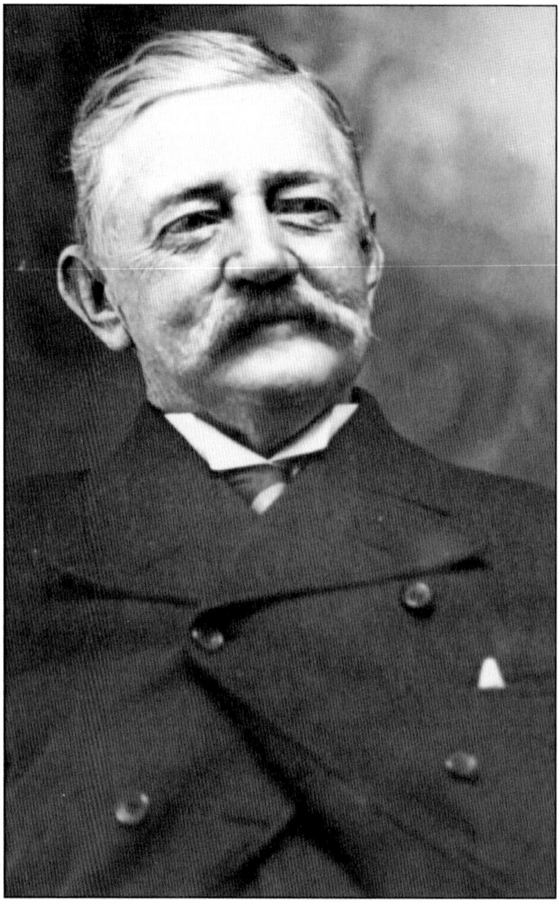

American pioneer settlers who came from the eastern United States included the Bakers and Wilkins from Virginia, and the Smiths and Youngs from Maryland. Pictured around 1900 is Dudley Avery, son of Judge Daniel D. Avery of Avery Island. Dudley Avery served as an officer in the 18th Louisiana Regiment, CSA, during the Civil War and was shot in both knees at the Battle of Shiloh. After several months, he recovered from his wounds and returned to duty. (Courtesy of the Avery Island, Inc. Archives.)

In 1920, the largest industry in New Iberia was the Charles Boldt Paper Mill, which used rice straw to make paper for shipping boxes. Beneath the one remaining brick tower are passageways leading to former rice and sugar mills. There are boilers and copper pipes in the wall underneath the parking lot, making one wonder if rice wine was made here during prohibition. In 1880, world famous actor Joe Jefferson (circled) is pictured near the mill with the Robertson family of New Iberia. (Courtesy of the Avery Island, Inc. Archives.)

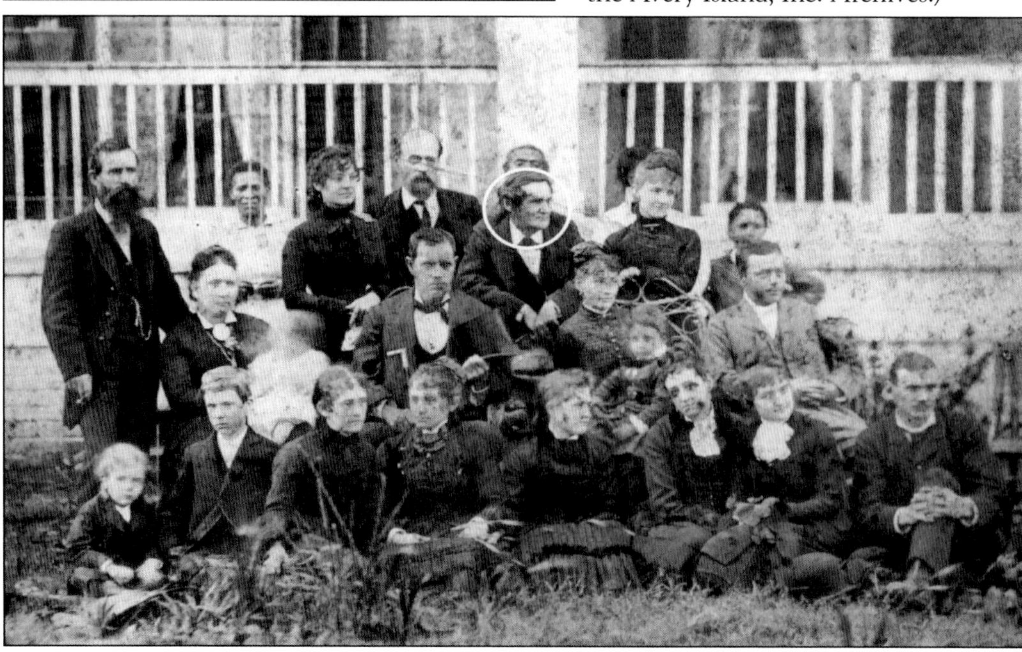

Four

Communities

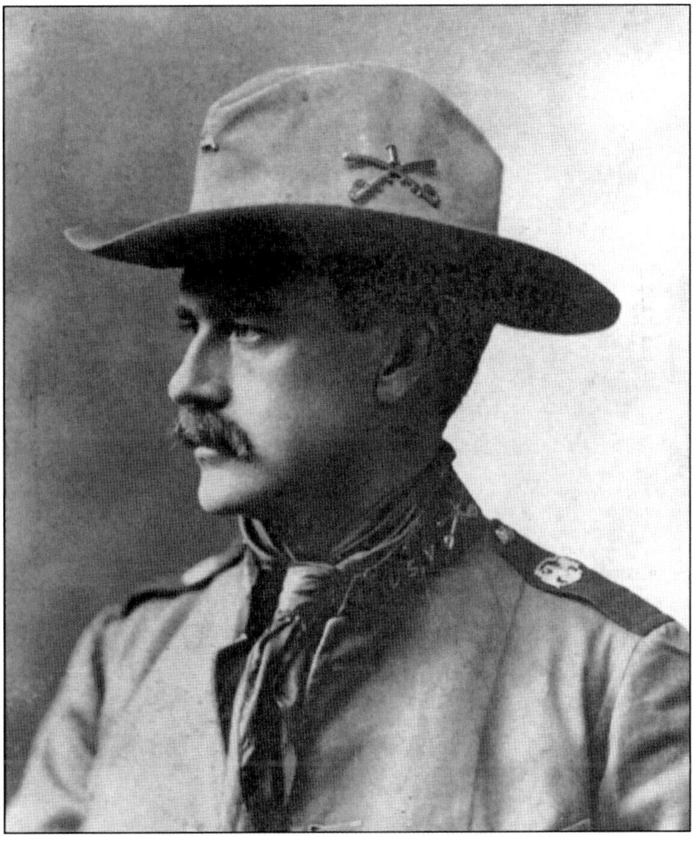

The society that emerged following the Civil War bore little resemblance to stratified antebellum society. The postwar community essentially became a two-tiered society in which social status and wealth were polarized between a small, educated landed gentry and a large lower class. Soldier, politician, and businessman J.A. McIlhenny of Avery Island is pictured in 1898 in his Rough Rider uniform. McIlhenny stepped down as president of McIlhenny Company to join Theodore Roosevelt's famed cavalry regiment during the Spanish-American War. (Courtesy of the McIlhenny Company Archives.)

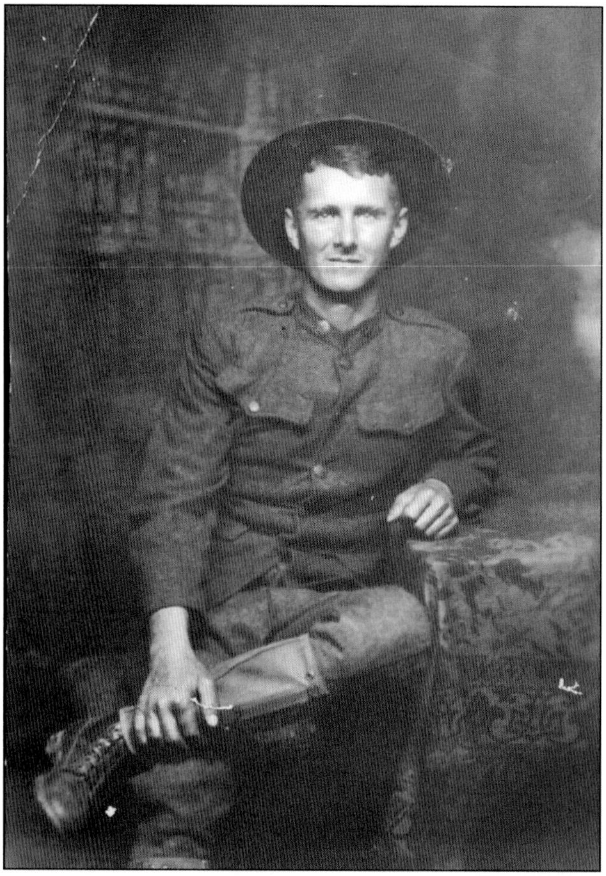

At the turn of the 20th century, many Iberians were able to obtain work in local industries. Others worked as tenant farmers, where they would remain in poverty as *engagés* (indentured workers) until the discovery of oil and the industrialization of Texas's Golden Triangle of Port Arthur, Orange, and Beaumont in the 1910s. Deluke Bonin is pictured in 1918 wearing his World War I army uniform.

In 1891, William Henry Perrin wrote, "The Negroes here take much interest in public education. The colored school of New Iberia is in the charge of a Miss Mitchell." This 1927 photograph of the sixth grade class at Loreauville High School was taken when schools were segregated. In the late 1960s, Federal Judge Richard J. Putnam adopted the desegregation plan, which resulted in the integration of local public facilities. From 1976 to 1980, Iberia historian and African American Wilbert Lemelle served as US ambassador to Kenya and Seychelles.

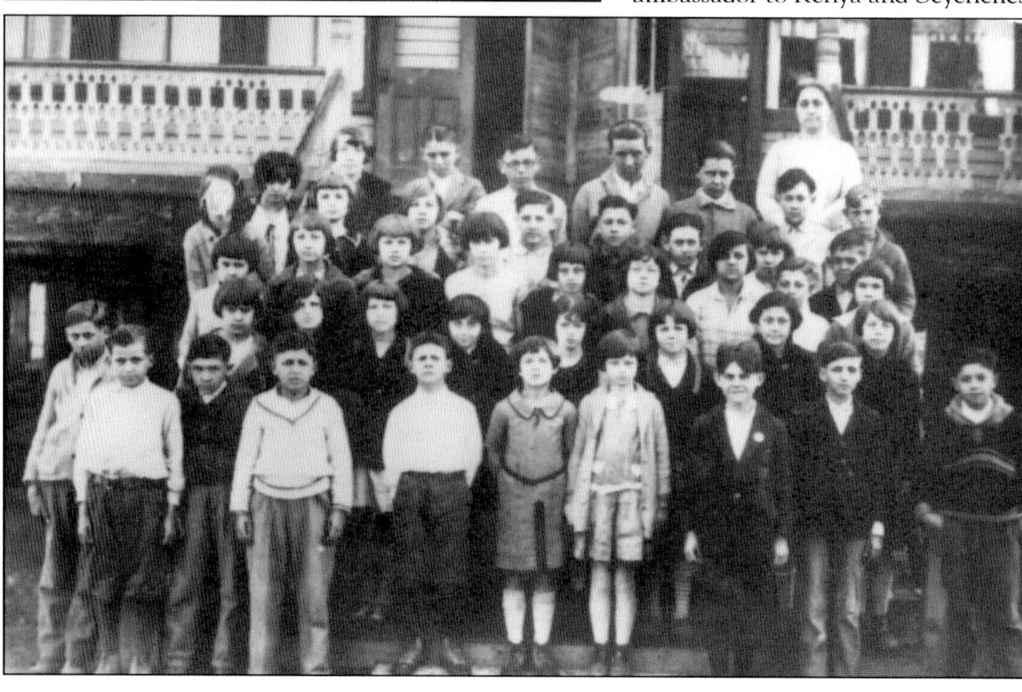

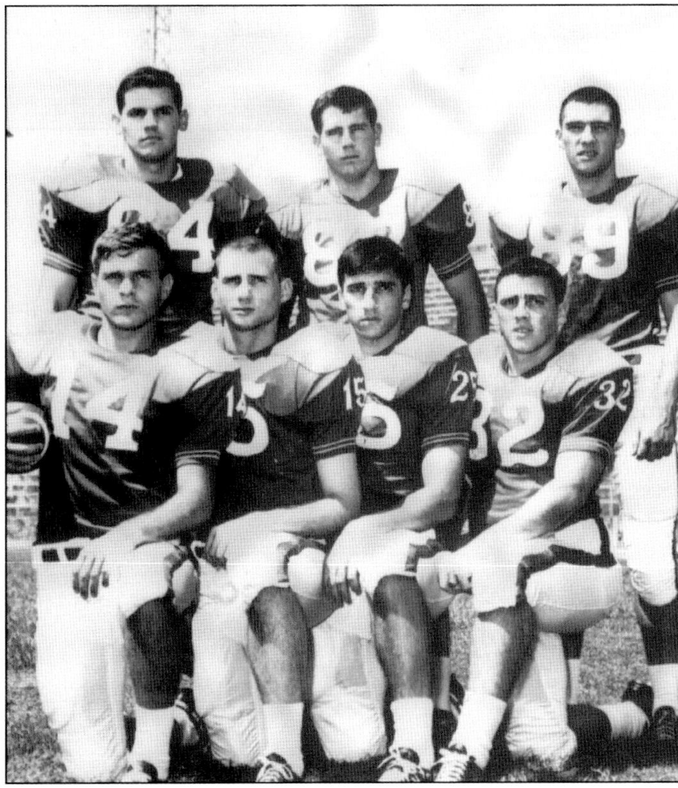

In 1918, the Christian Brothers arrived in New Iberia and opened a school for boys called St. Peter's College, located in the Henshaw home on East Main Street. Today, a grotto to Our Lady of Lourdes is all that remains. In 1957, land was purchased on Forty Arpent Road (now Admiral Doyle Drive) and a new facility was built. Shown in 1964 from left to right are (first row) Bill Bayard, Edward Pratt, Chester Gosnell, and Miles Gosnell; (second row) Kenny Greig, John Conery, and Ray Scott. All were members of the University of Southwestern Louisiana (USL) football team who had played for Catholic High School.

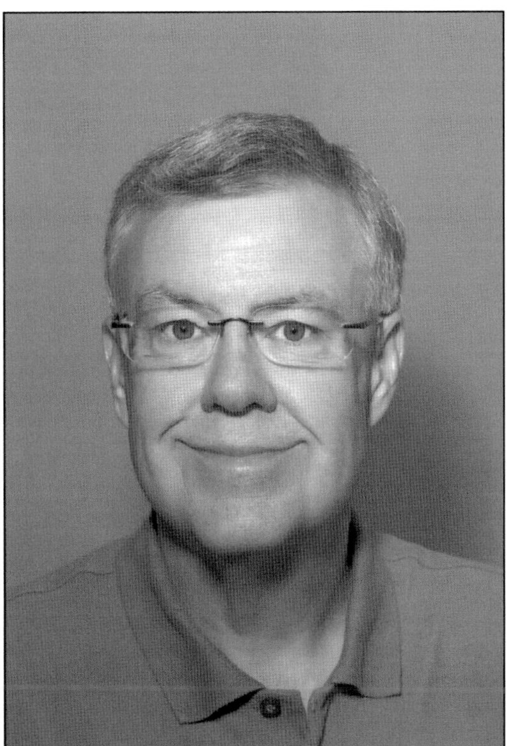

In 1920, the parish had two newspapers: the *New Iberia Enterprise* and the *Iberian*. Today, the *Daily Iberian* is published under the direction of Will Chapman, who followed his father and both of his grandfathers into the business. In 2001, he was inducted as a Living Legend by the Acadian Museum. In 1979, Chapman married Gladys Hentz of Spain. They have two sons, Adam (the fourth generation of his family to work in the newspaper business) and Daniel.

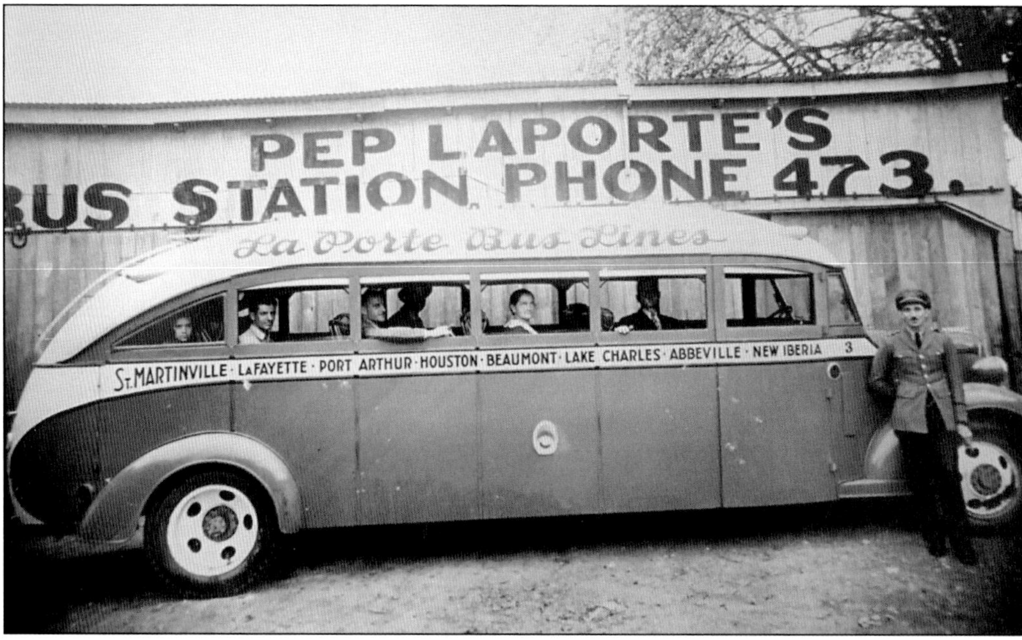

Steamboats once plied the waters of the Bayou Teche, serving as the method of transporting goods to and from New Orleans. Initially, overland transportation was by horses or mules. In 1880, the Southern Pacific Railroad completed its line from Texas to New Orleans. In 1892, the extension of rails from New Iberia to Abbeville became a reality. The railroad brought rapid change to the prairie landscape, with an influx of farmers from the Midwest, the beginning of the oil industry, and agricultural mechanization. On the main line, New Iberia was 125 miles west of New Orleans. Locally, the Laporte Bus Line (pictured) provided regional service.

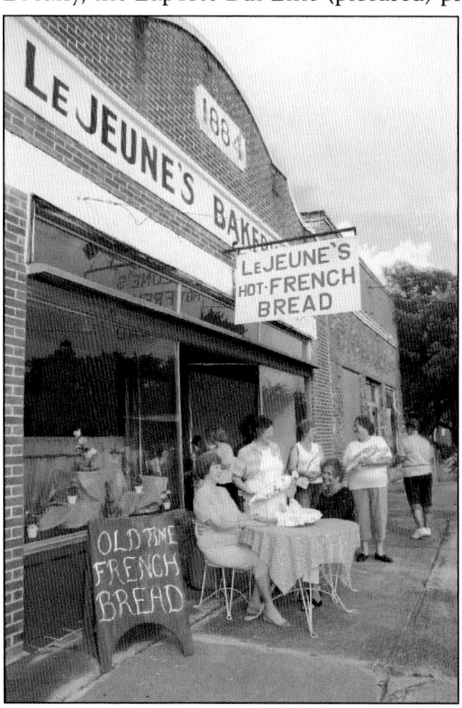

Over the past four decades, the parish has felt the highs and lows of business trends dictated by the oil industry, yet some things do not change. LeJeune's Bakery has been baking French bread in Jeanerette since 1884. It has remained a family business and is currently being run by the fifth generation. Everyone knows that when the red light is blinking, it is time for some hot French bread. Pictured are, from left to right, Ramona Hebert, Ruth Eldridge, her granddaughter Nicole Affaunt (in doorway), Janet Robicheaux, Kathy Rosamond, Patricia Broussard Migues (seated), and Elizabeth Bourgeois Sovine. (Courtesy of Iberia Parish Visitors and Convention Bureau.)

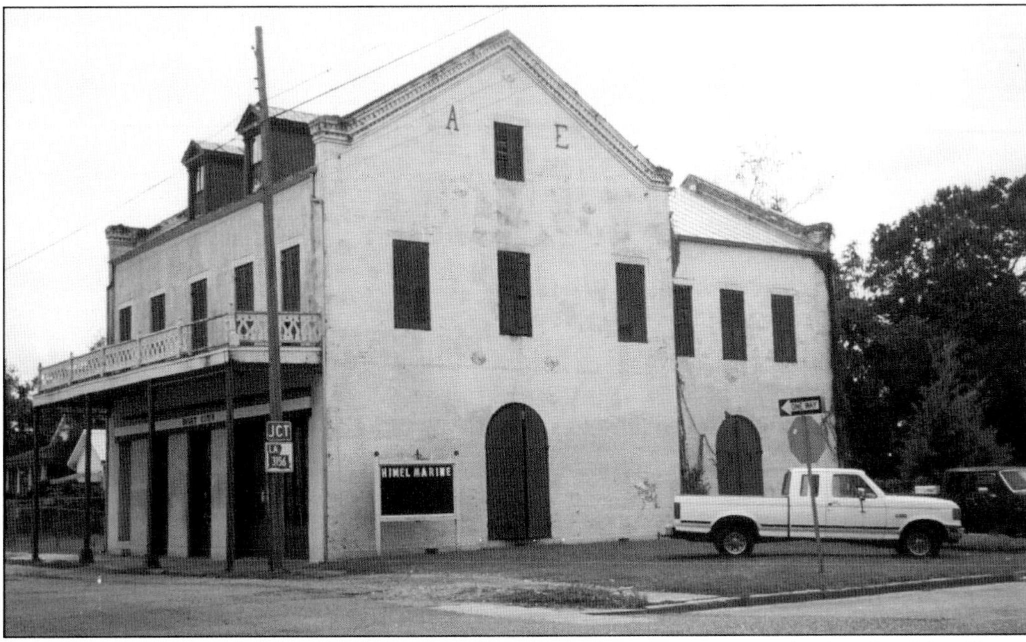

In 1899, Auguste Erath founded the town of Erath. A Swiss immigrant who lived in New Iberia, Erath was also the owner of Erath Bottling and Ice Works. This building, originally the Auguste Erath home on East St. Peter and Railroad Streets, was later converted to the Duplantis Store and then to Himel's Supply Store. Note Erath's initials, "A.E.," on the building. Today, it is owned by Himel Marine and houses the A and E Art Gallery.

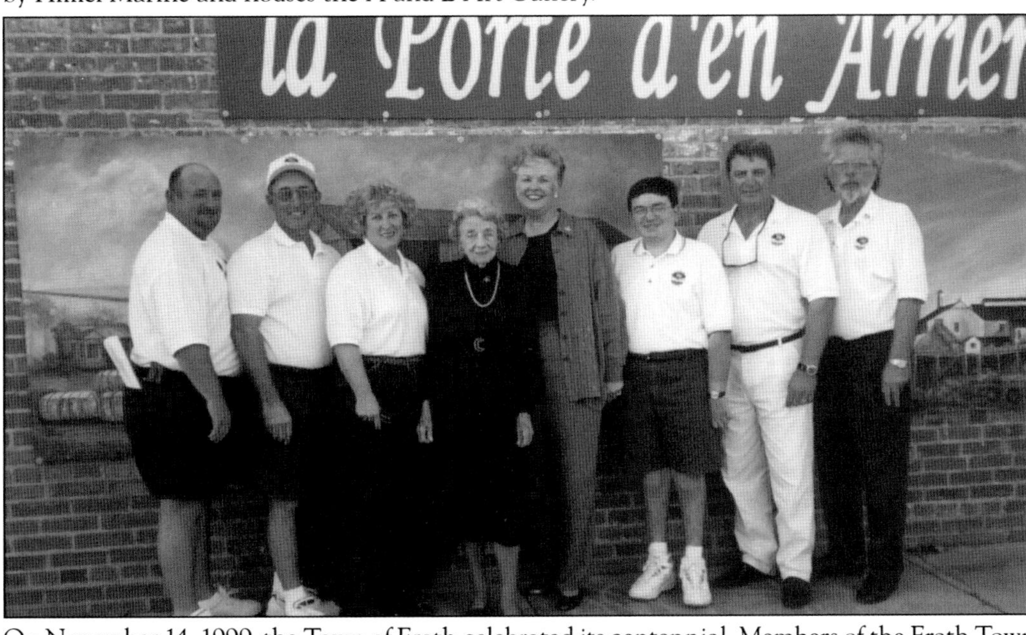

On November 14, 1999, the Town of Erath celebrated its centennial. Members of the Erath Town Council are shown with the descendants of Auguste Erath, the namesake of the town. From left to right are Carl "Coco" Broussard, Mayor Keith Arceneaux, Claudette Lacour, Willa Guidry (granddaughter of Erath), Lynette Loewer (great-granddaughter of Erath), Mayor pro tem Robert Vincent, Robert "T-Bob" Domingues, and John Earl LeBlanc.

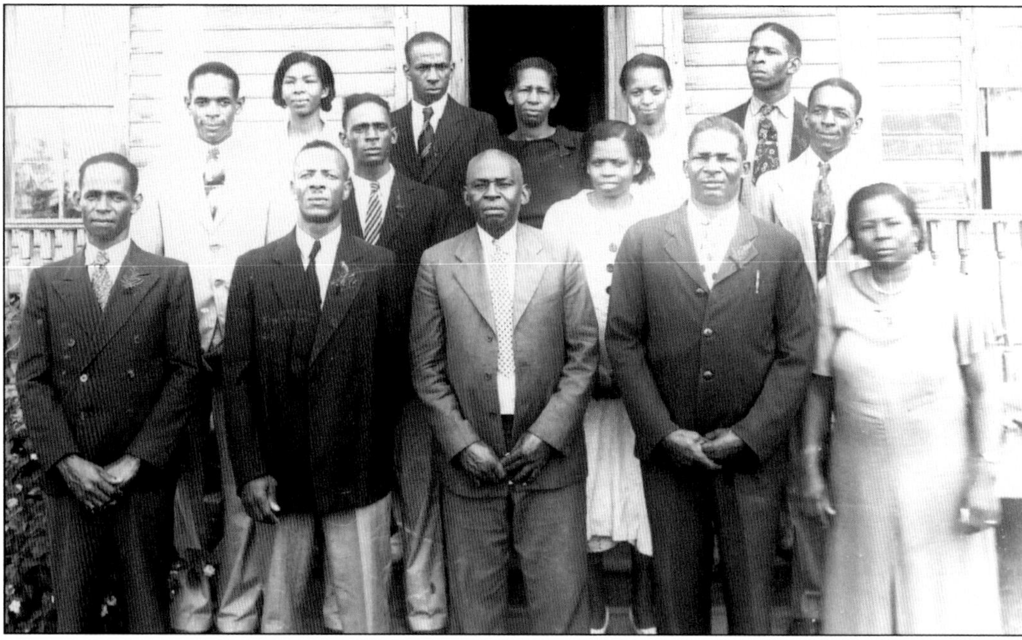

Prior to the civil rights movement in the mid-20th century, segregation was maintained by repressive Jim Crow laws. Although they contributed significantly to local culture in areas like music and cuisine, African Americans who dared to transcend racial barriers often faced violent extralegal retribution. Pictured is the Noah family of New Iberia. (Courtesy of Center for Louisiana Studies, University of Louisiana at Lafayette.)

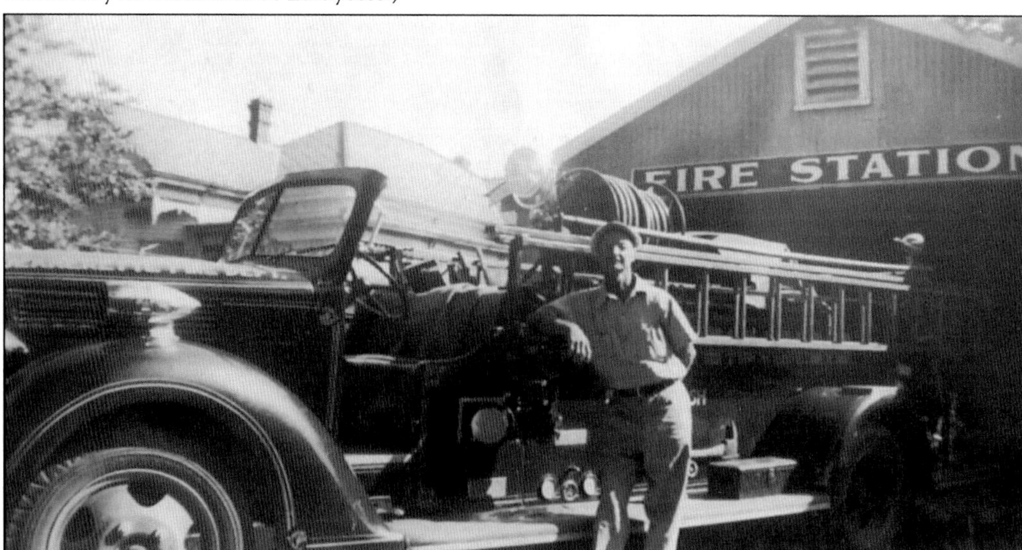

Fire Chief Carmen Rene Mequet, husband of Hilda Bernard, is pictured at the Jeanerette fire station on Main Street (present-day city hall), where he served 42 years with the volunteer fire department. Mequet, Jeanerette's 1958 Outstanding Citizen, was a charter member of the Rotary Club and its president in 1945. He was on the Jeanerette City Council under four mayors, served as president of the Jeanerette Chamber of Commerce, and was superintendent of the Waterworks Department.

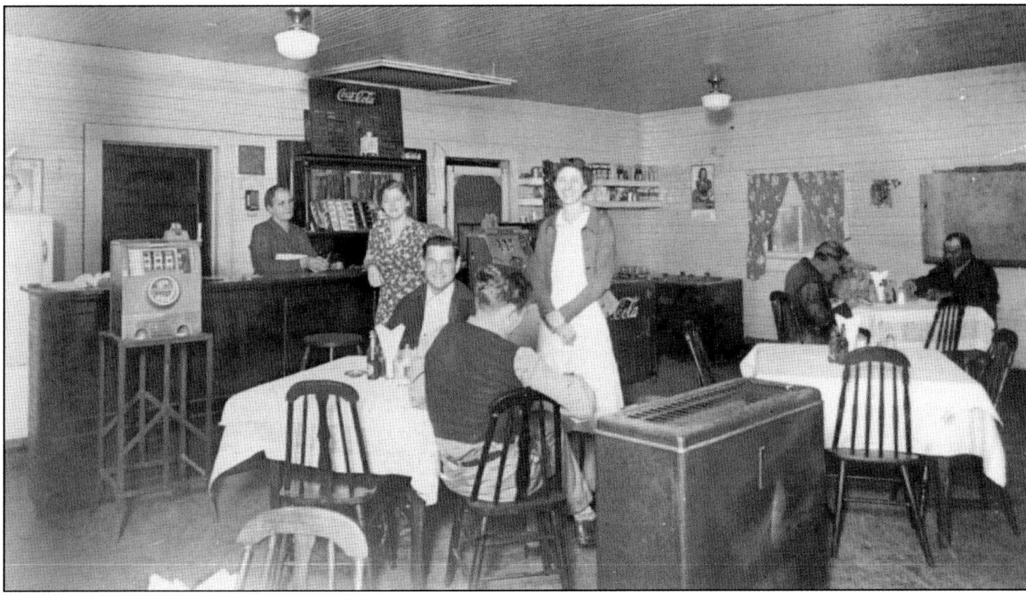

Gov. Huey P. Long, who was assassinated on September 9, 1935, dominated state politics in part because there was no civil service system. From the late 1930s until 1958, politicians often gathered at Mother Deare's Café, where two Texaco employees are pictured seated in the foreground. Mother Deare (left) and Ola Kelley Deare are shown behind the counter. Waitresses Verna Faulk Williams and Iva Faulk are standing nearby.

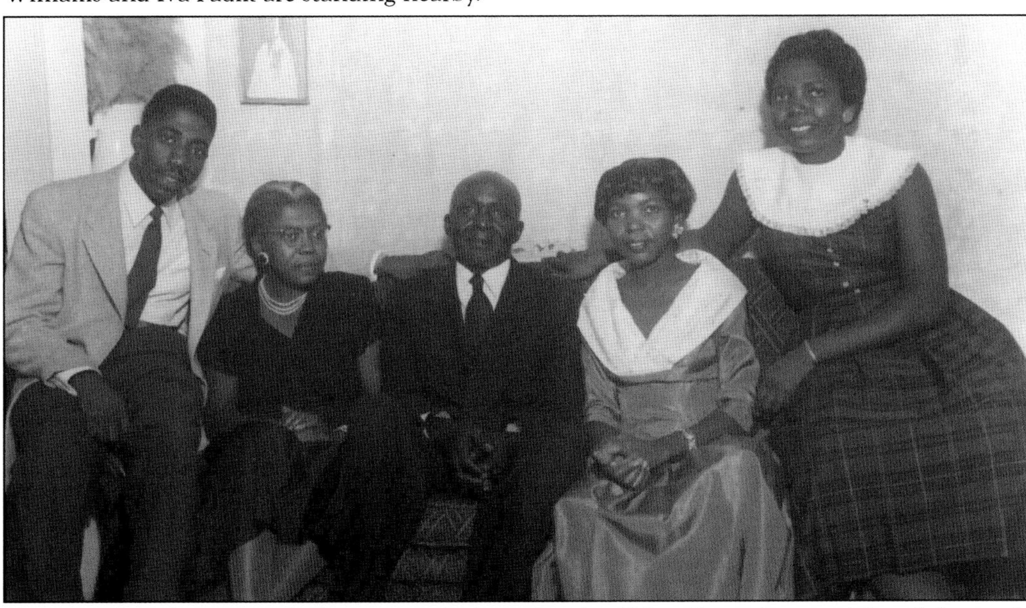

Shown is the Clarence and Clara Manuel Moore family of New Iberia. Pictured from left to right are Harold Moore, Clara, Clarence, Ruby Archon Moore, and Sedonia Moore. Clarence worked for Southern Pacific Railroad for 48 years. Clara was a graduate of Howe Institute, founded by African American Baptist churches in Iberia and St. Mary Parishes and headed by Jonas Henderson. Clara taught school, but after marrying, had to resort to being a domestic. Nevertheless, all of Clarence and Clara's descendants are college graduates—three having earned PhDs, and one in the process of doing so.

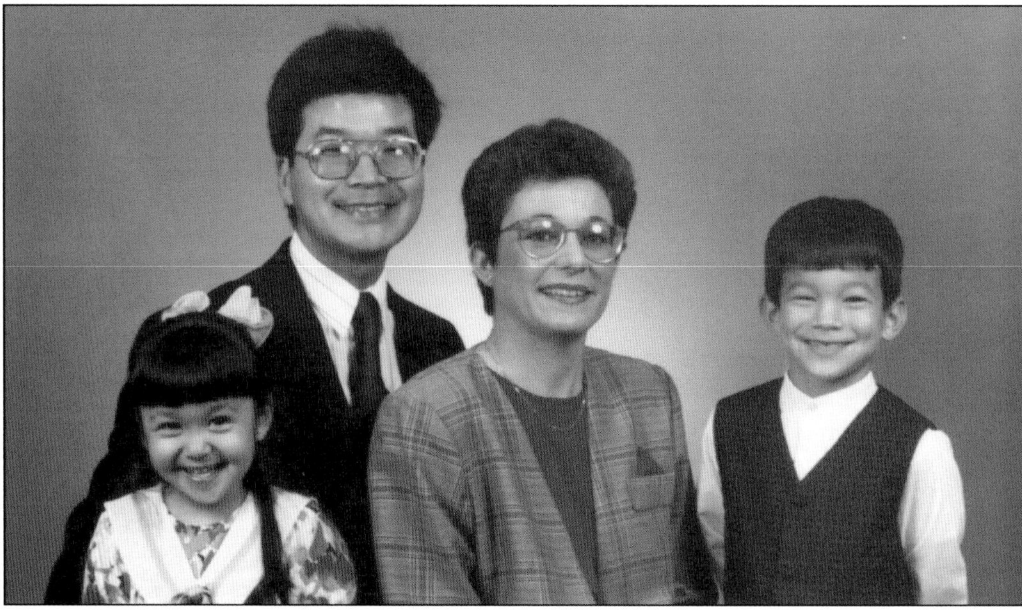

Iberia is a melting pot of cultures. After the Vietnam War, many Vietnamese immigrated to Iberia Parish since Vietnam, like Louisiana, had been a French colony. Learning of available jobs, Laotians and other Asians began moving to Iberia and today make up about three percent of the population. The Sun family is pictured from left to right: Emily, Tai (from Taipei, Taiwan), Elaine Delaune (from Jeanerette), and Wesley. Tai and Elaine met as pen pals and married after several years of correspondence.

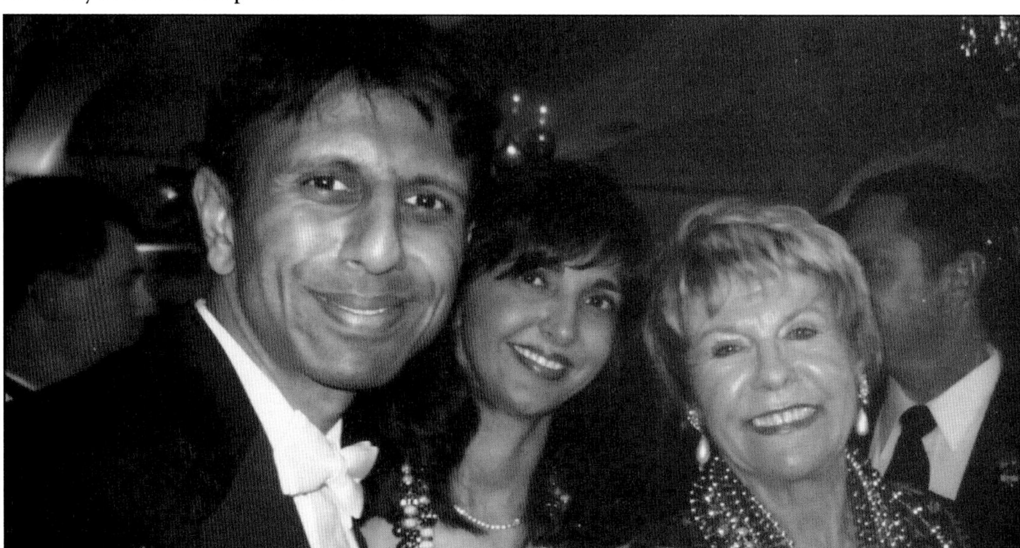

The parish has lost much of its wetlands due to man-made erosion, and low-lying areas of the parish remain vulnerable to storms. Hurricanes Rita in 2005, when Kathleen Blanco was governor, and Ike in 2008, when Bobby Jindal was governor, brought many difficulties for Iberians. New Iberian Nancy Mixon attended the Washington, DC, Ball of the Mystick Krewe of Louisianians and is pictured with Louisiana's first family. From left to right are Gov. Bobbie Jindal, Supriya Jindal, and Mixon.

Five

Major Attractions and Affairs

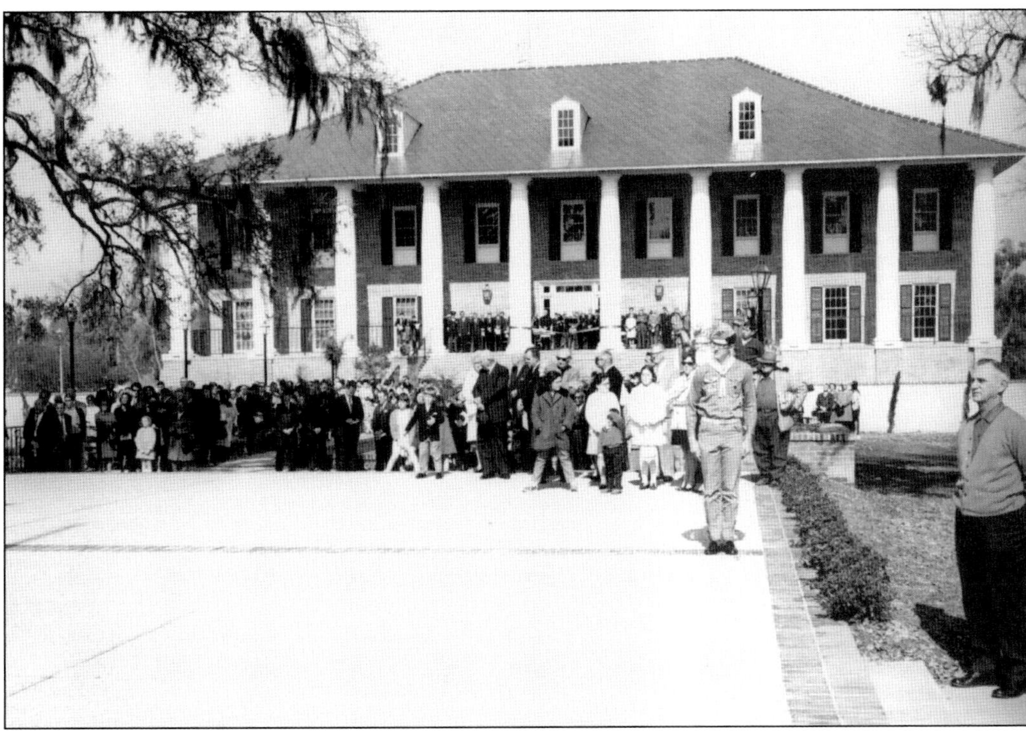

Citizens and officials are pictured attending the dedication of the New Iberia City Hall. This facility has been used on many occasions to host visitors, including international guests from New Iberia's twin cities of Woluwe St. Pierre, Belgium; St. Jean d'Angely, France; and Alhaurin de la Torre, Spain.

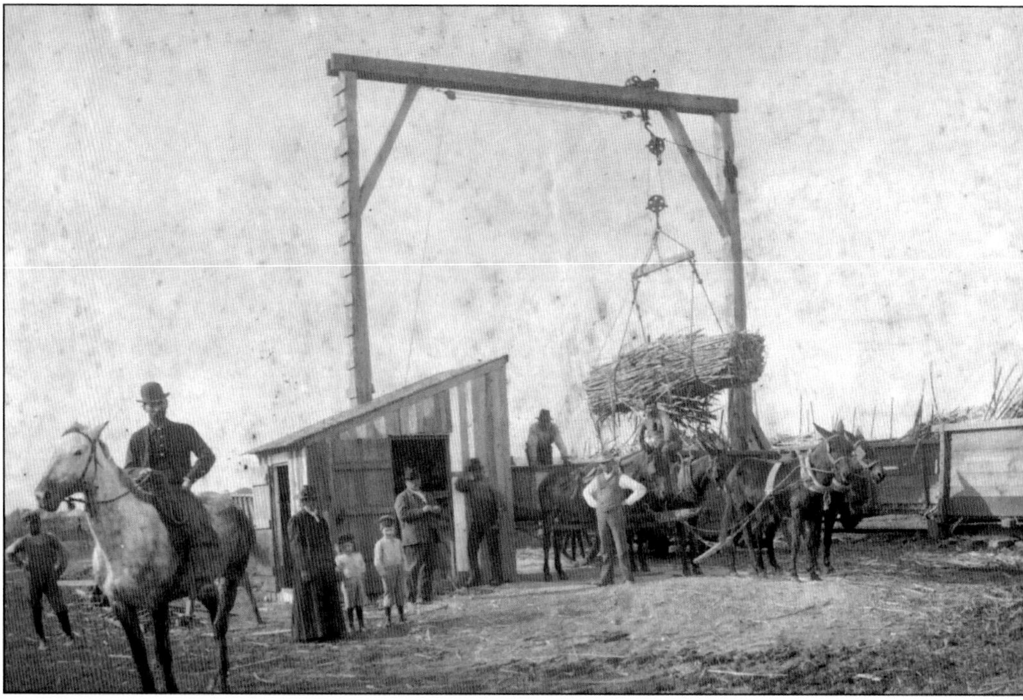

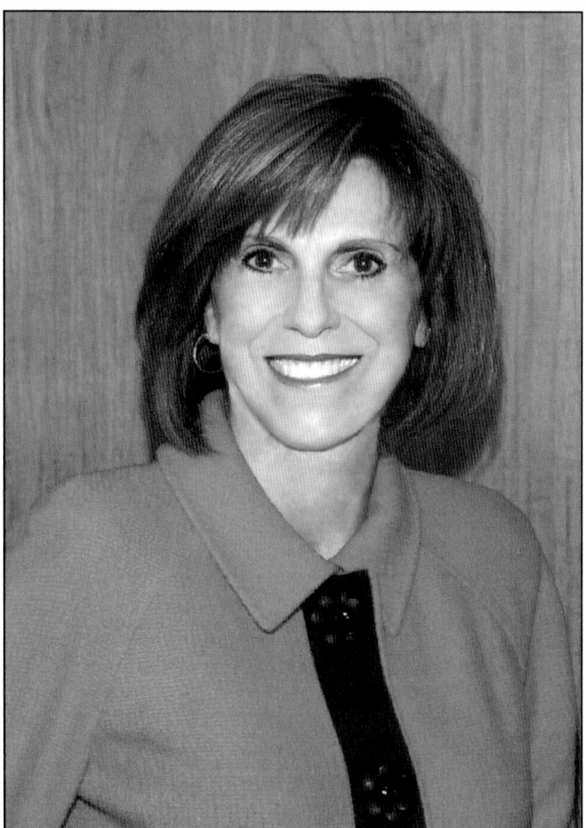

Pictured in 1905 at Solitude Plantation in Lozes are overseer Terville Landry Jr. (on horse) and Leon and Aurelia Theriot Lozes (center). Between them are their grandchildren Henry and Paul Chastant. Laborers are shown loading sugarcane onto the narrow gauge rail tram to be hauled to Segura Sugar Mill near Spanish Lake. In 1911, Franklin and Abbeville Railroad constructed a second rail line. In 1930, L.C. Soileau built a sugar grinding operation that was sold in the 1970s to Bruce Foods.

Hilda Daigre Curry, the 26th mayor of New Iberia, grew up in a family where public service was a way of life. Both her grandfather Joseph A. Daigre and father, J. Allen Daigre, served as the city's mayor. When the opportunity came to enter the political arena, Curry's first role was on the city council, where she served for five years. Currently, she is first vice president of the Louisiana Municipal Association.

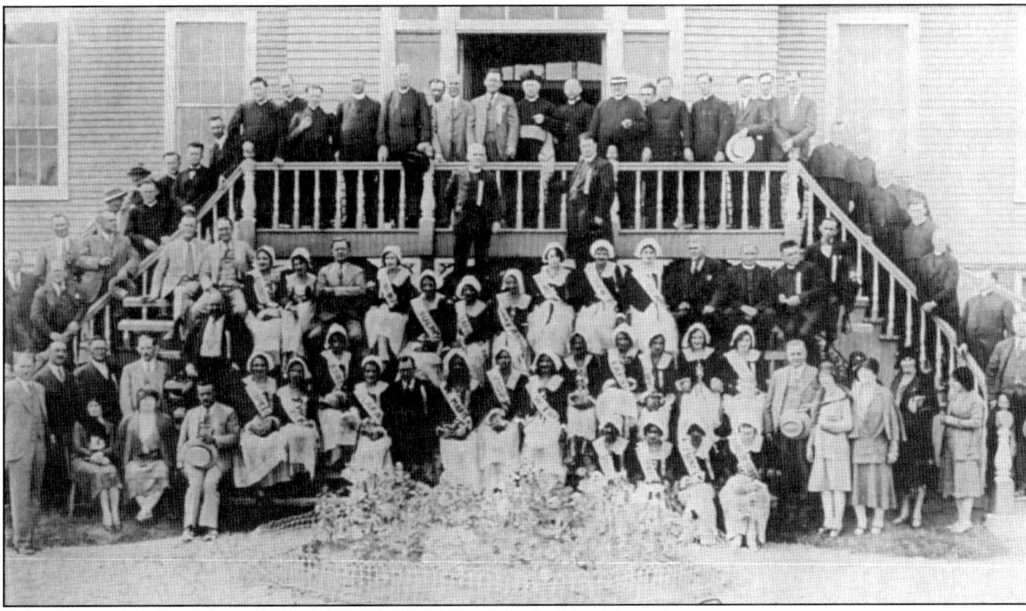

In the 1940s and 1950s, Sen. Dudley J. LeBlanc invented and was purveyor of a popular elixir, Hadacol, which was first produced at Lake Peigneur. In 1930, LeBlanc organized an excursion of Louisiana Acadians, including some Iberians, to Grand Pré, Nova Scotia. In this photograph of the group in Nova Scotia, LeBlanc is standing to the left of the monsignor in the center at the top of stairs. In 1927, he wrote *The True Story of the Acadians*. Under LeBlanc's leadership, the revival of the Cajun and Creole cultures is considered one of America's great ethnic success stories.

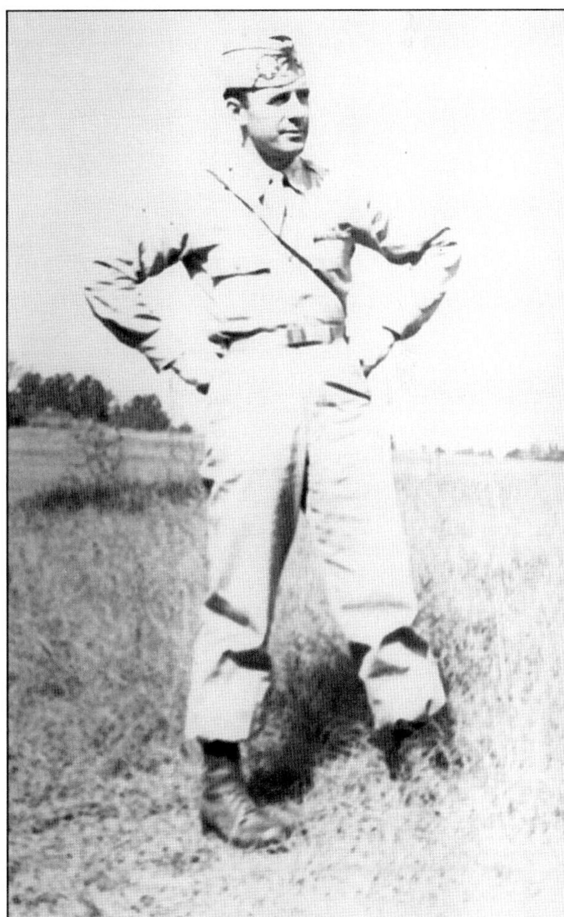

French speakers sought to stem the tide of Americanization, so under the leadership of Sen. Sam Broussard (pictured), State Representative "Dickie" Breaux, and Congressman James Domengeaux, the Council for the Development of French in Louisiana (CODOFIL) was created in 1968. Broussard was a member of the Office of Strategic Services (OSS), World War II Special Forces, and played a major role in the Normandy campaign as a French-speaking operative, coordinating activities with the French Resistance behind enemy lines.

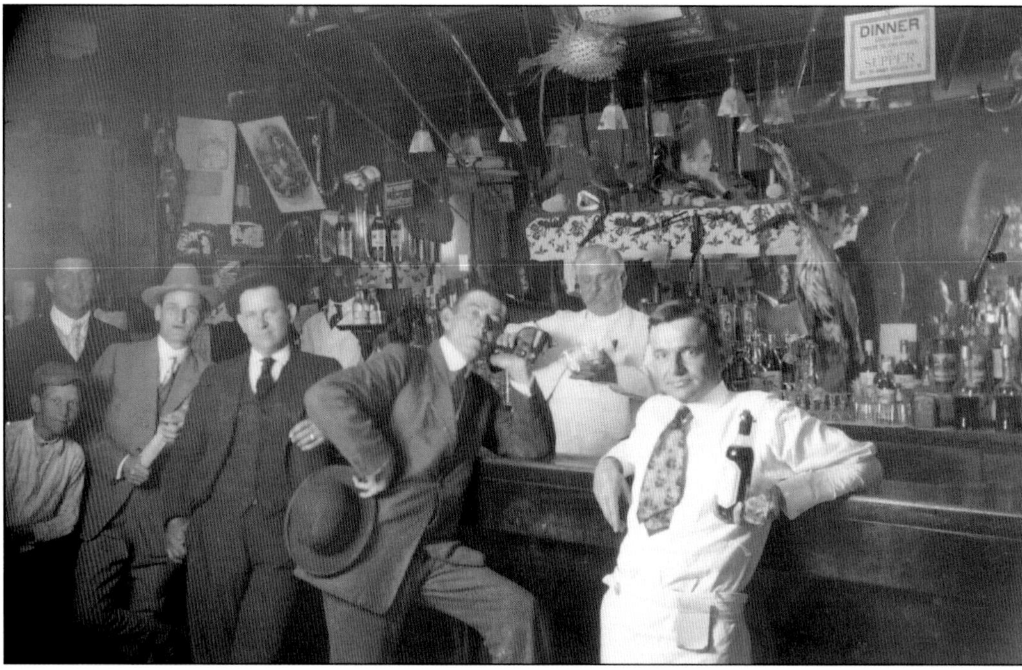

In an effort to end the saloon culture and its devastating effect on families, the 18th amendment to the US Constitution, banning the sale of intoxicating beverages, was enacted in 1919. For 13 years before its repeal, the era known as Prohibition created many unintended consequences, including the use of Iberia Parish's bayous by bootleggers to illegally import alcohol. A group of men are pictured in a saloon in New Iberia. (Courtesy of Center for Louisiana Studies, University of Louisiana at Lafayette.)

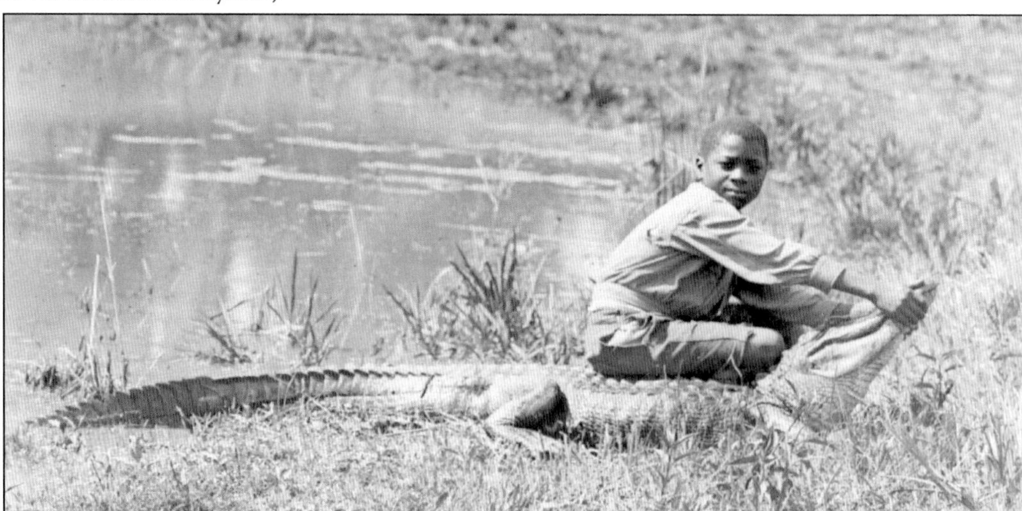

Alligators were so abundant during the 1920s that hunting them was encouraged in order to safeguard the important fur industry. Later, however, alligator skins became so desirable in the fashion industry that they were nearly hunted to extinction. Currently they are protected, and landowners are issued a limited number of tags for harvesting. This 1920 photograph, taken in lower Iberia Parish, shows a child holding an alligator's mouth closed. (Courtesy of the E.A. McIlhenny Collection, Avery Island, Louisiana.)

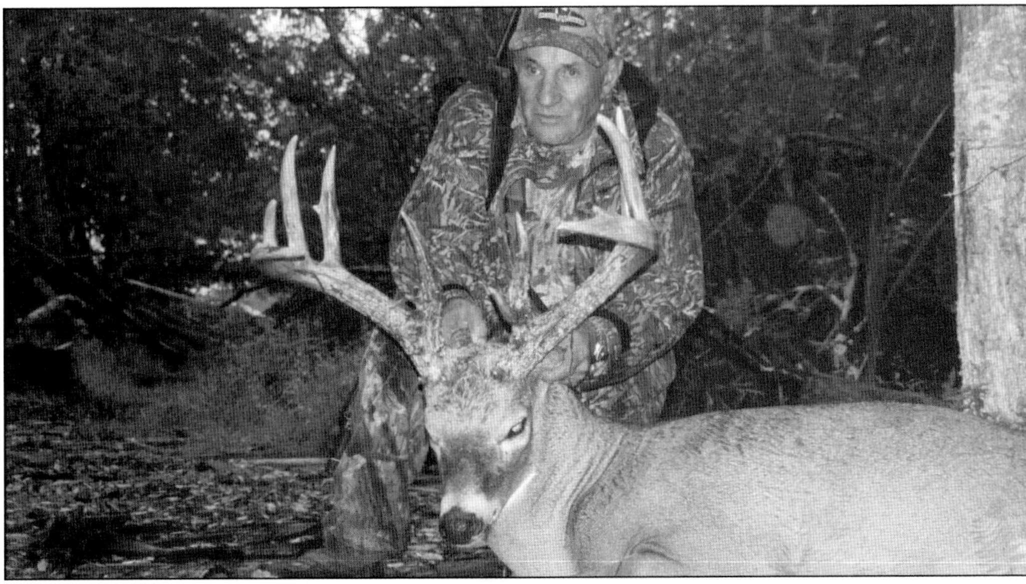

Perry J. Segura shows off a trophy deer he has just bagged. Parks and recreation have great meaning to civic-minded Segura, who donated a tennis facility complete with eight courts, dressing rooms, an administration building, land for a driving range, and soccer fields to his hometown of New Iberia. Segura, founder of the architectural firm Perry Segura, Inc., is also past chairman of the United Givers Fund, recipient of a multitude of awards, and a board member of the Evangeline Area Council of the Boy Scouts of America.

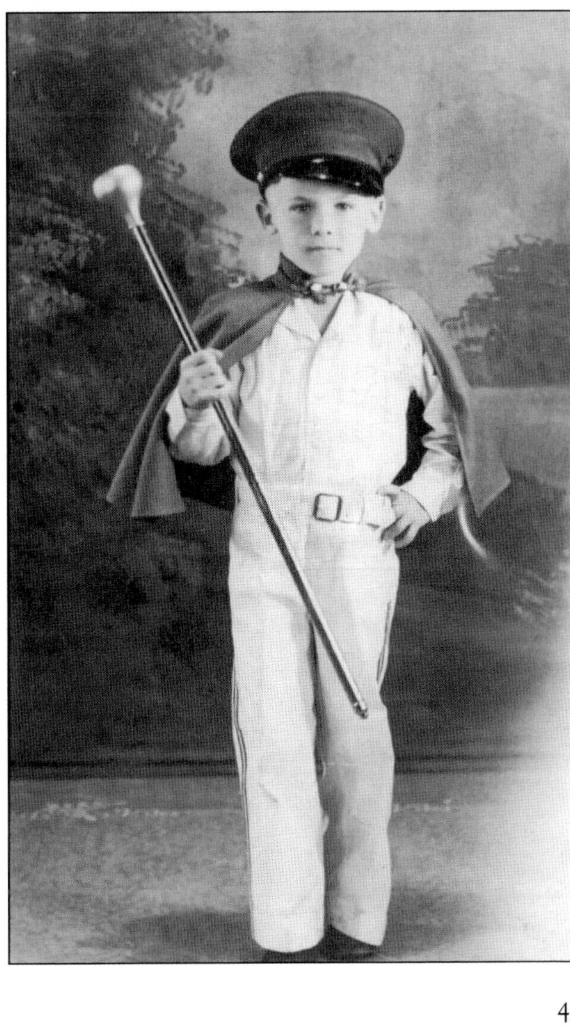

Frank George "Boogie" Mixon Sr. is pictured in 1935 in his St. Peter's College band uniform. He married Elise Scroggin and they had six children: Frank Jr., Henry, Virginia, Stephanie, Eugenie, and Elise. Boogie lettered in football and track at Southwestern Louisiana Institute (now the University of Louisiana at Lafayette) and, in 1953, was named an All-Gulf States Conference halfback. After the death of his father, Tynes, Mixon and his wife ran the Mixon Lumber Company.

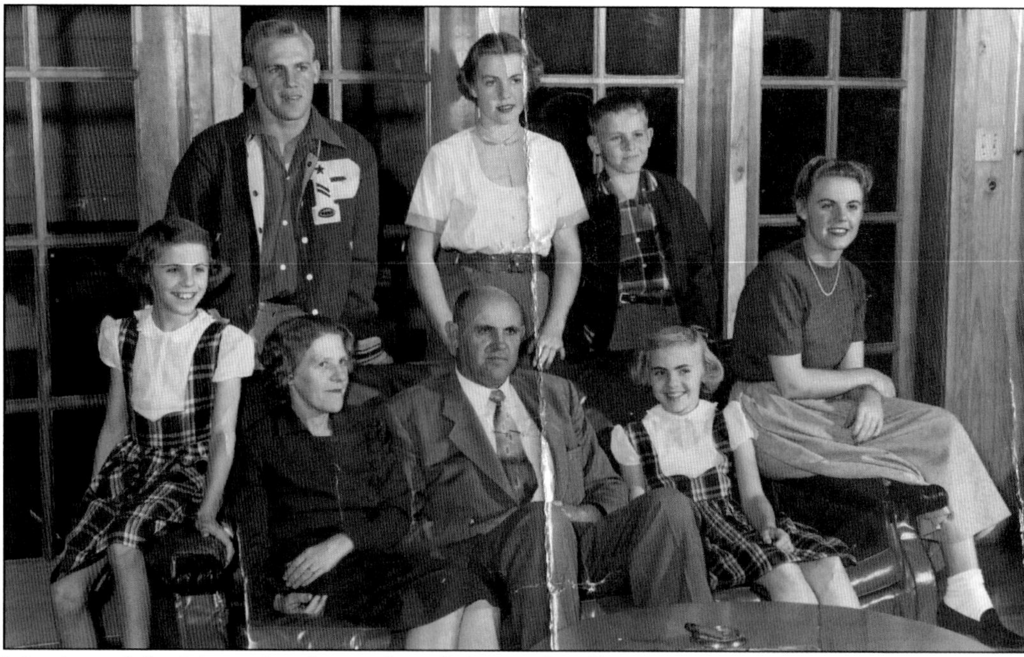

Members of the Mixon family are, from left to right, (first row) Nancy Patricia Mixon, Eugene "Pim" Decuir Mixon, Tynes Emery Mixon, Margaret Mixon Trahan, and Louise Mixon Pederson; (second row) Frank George "Boogie" Mixon, Myrtis Blanch Mixon, and Tynes Emery "Bros" Mixon. The Mixons worked to develop the West End of New Iberia.

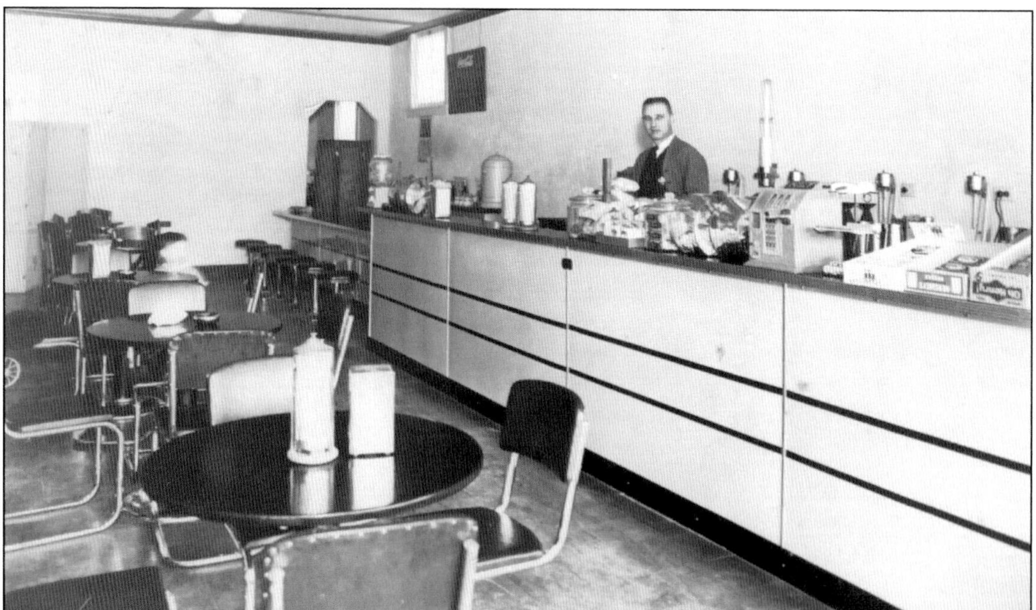

In 2012, Louisiana's Bicentennial Commission organized the launch of the 200th anniversary of its statehood. The statewide event commemorating Louisiana's 1812 admission into the Union attracted tourists to all areas of the state to enjoy its cultural treasures, including Iberia's unmatched Cajun and Creole cuisine. This 1937 photograph was taken inside Veazey's Café in New Iberia, well known for its local cuisine.

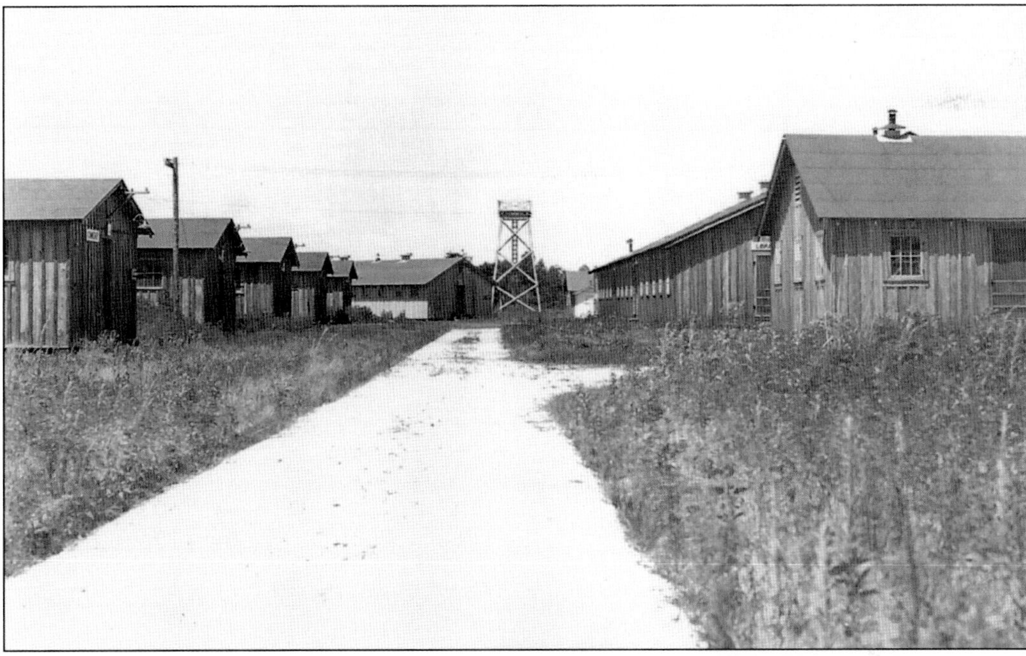

During World War II, a prisoner of war camp was located near Jeanerette. Most prisoners were members of the German Afrika Korps, led by Gen. Erwin Rommel, the "Desert Fox." In 2010, the son of Johannes Thieme, a prisoner at the camp, visited the Jeanerette Museum. Upon his return to Germany, his father wrote a letter to the museum, saying that prisoners had been dumbfounded by the almost cordial reception they received in the area. Prisoners worked the sugarcane fields of Duhe and Thibodeaux. (Courtesy of Jeanerette Museum.)

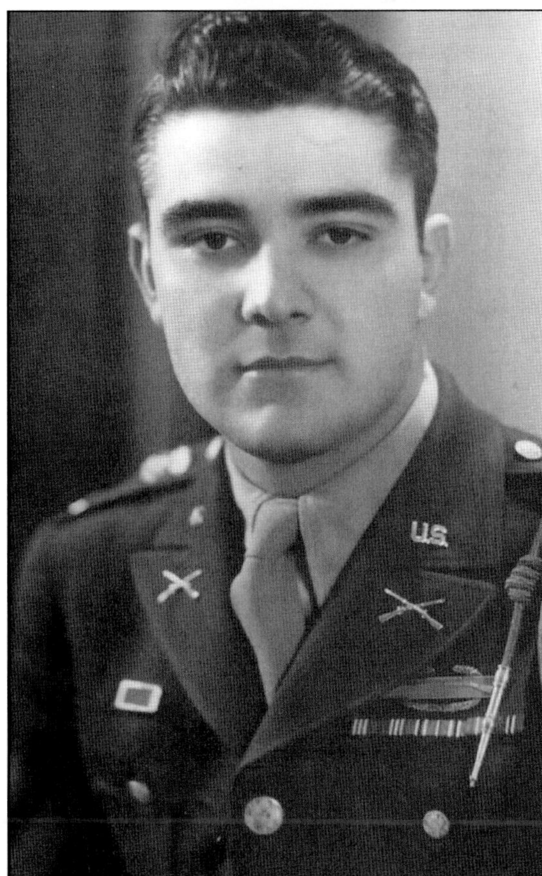

During World War II, Elton Barras was a first lieutenant in the US Army in the Ardennes-Alsace campaign. On December 24, 1944, he was sent into combat in the Ardennes Mountains of France near Phillipsbourg. From that date until February 16, 1945, the lieutenant had little sleep or food and suffered frostbitten feet. His company encountered fierce fighting as the army marched toward Berlin. He fought in five major battles as infantry unit commander, for which he subsequently received a battlefield commission.

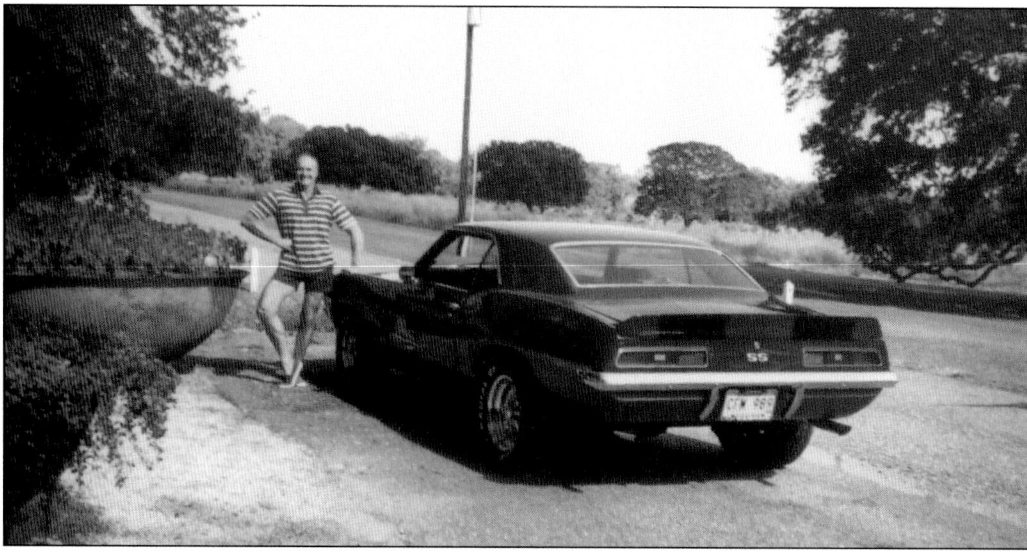

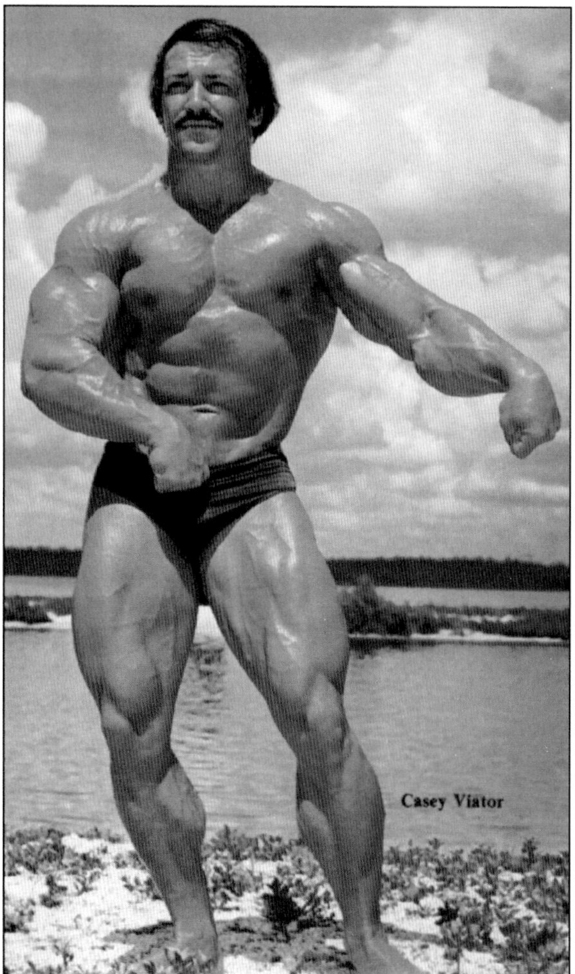

This 2001 photograph (above) of Ken Broussard and his 1969 Camaro SS was taken in Live Oak Gardens on Jefferson Island. Born in 1941, Broussard graduated from New Iberia High School in 1959 and from the University of Louisiana in 1963. Subsequently, he taught at his alma mater where he met Casey Viator, a future Mr. America. Having obtained a master's degree in 1973, Broussard counseled at New Iberia and Belle Place junior high schools. With assistance from Lloyd Geoffroy Jr., Broussard trained Viator, pictured in 1978, in bodybuilding and led him to an unmatched career. Viator won the Mr. Gulf States title at 16, and at 18, became Mr. Teen America. At 19, the iconic muscleman became the youngest person ever to win the coveted title of Mr. America. After turning professional and training with greats like Arnold Schwarzenegger, he won several other major titles. Today, Viator resides in Florida and advises clients on health training. Currently married to Mary Lois Leleux, who taught English and business at New Iberia Freshman High and Westgate High for 30 years, Broussard now manages his own gym adjacent to his home near Jefferson Island. He continues to enjoy his favorite pastimes of helping others and collecting classic cars.

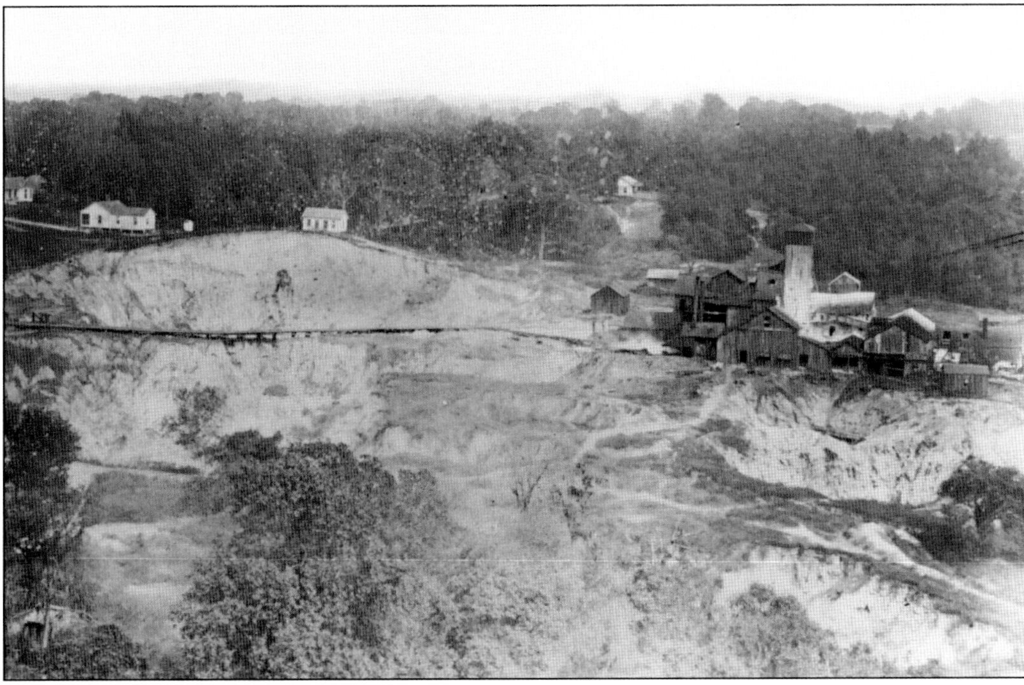

The largest salt deposits in the western hemisphere are found beneath Jefferson, Weeks, and Avery Islands. Pictured here is Salt Mine Valley on Avery Island after the collapse of its original subterranean mine around 1893. The two depressions seen in this photograph (one on each side of the railroad tracks leading to the mine buildings) are now ponds known as the Blue Hole and Brown Hole. (Courtesy of the Avery Island, Inc. Archives.)

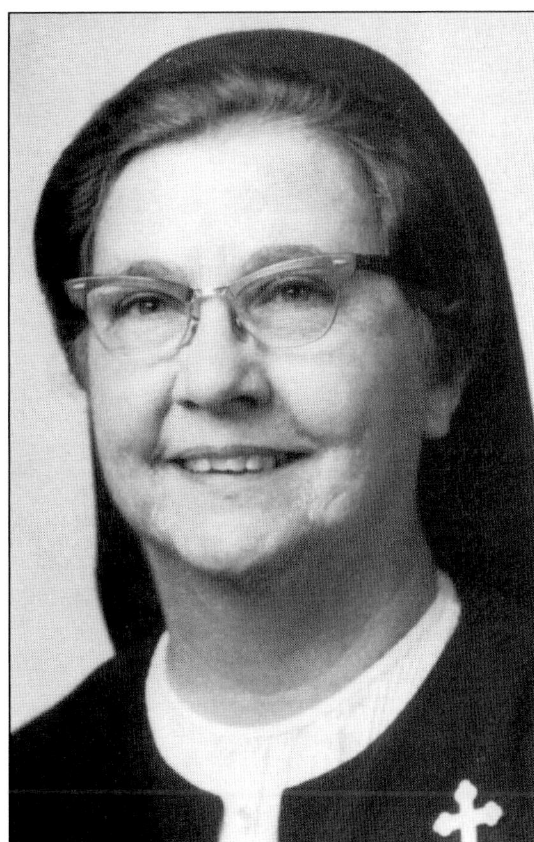

The Sisters of Mount Carmel arrived in 1870 and opened a day and boarding school for girls in 1871. In 1872, the sisters purchased the Duperier House and moved into Mount Carmel-on-the-Teche. They maintained and expanded Mount Carmel Academy until their departure from New Iberia in May 1988. Sr. Ann Carmel Segura's father was Albin Segura, who owned property on Spanish Lake. A sister of Mt. Carmel, Ann Carmel Segura was an artist known for her paintings. Her murals can be seen in several schools in Iberia Parish as well as the Delcambre Shrimp Festival building.

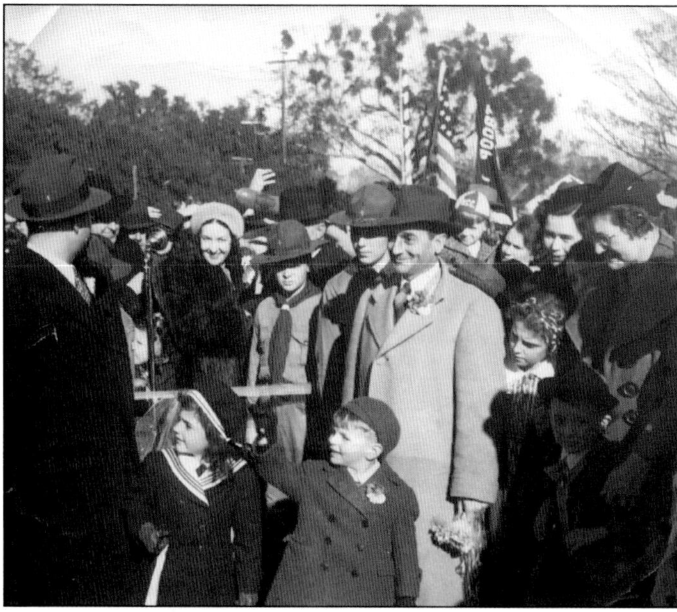

In 1891, historian William Henry Perrin wrote, "New Iberia, the thriving mart of the region, is a village mainly of small frame houses, with a smart court house, a lively business street, a few pretty houses, and some old-time mansions on the bank of the bayou." Pictured from left to right are New Iberia Mayor William Lourd, his daughter Clara Elizabeth Lourd, and his nephew Leon Roy Jr. Holding the little girl and wearing the MCC cap is Billie Gates Hitter. The child is her daughter Betty Hitter Lee.

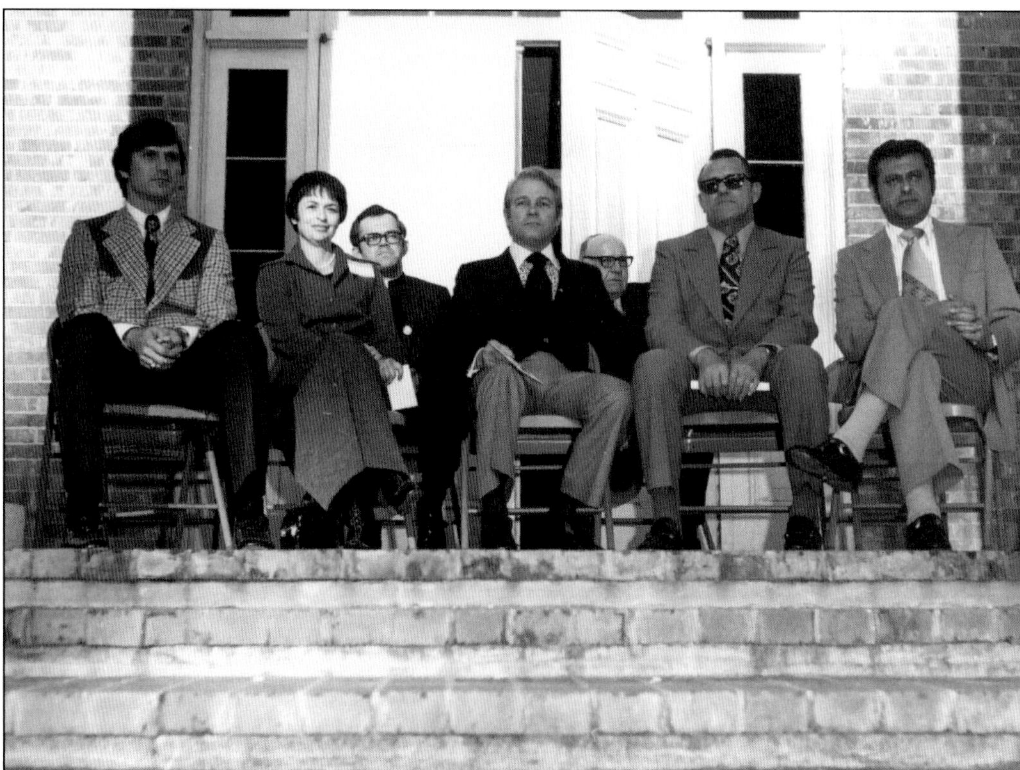

Pictured at the 1974 dedication of trilingual plaques for historic buildings and sites in New Iberia are, from left to right, (first row) Sen. Paul Hardy, Jacqueline Voorhies, Gov. Edwin W. Edwards, Mayor J. Allen Daigre, and Rep. Elias "Bo" Ackal; (second row) Fr. Gary Schexnayder and S.J. "Sos" Segura. The Iberia Cultural Resources Association, founded in 1969, continues the dedication of trilingual plaques.

Six

Cultures and Customs

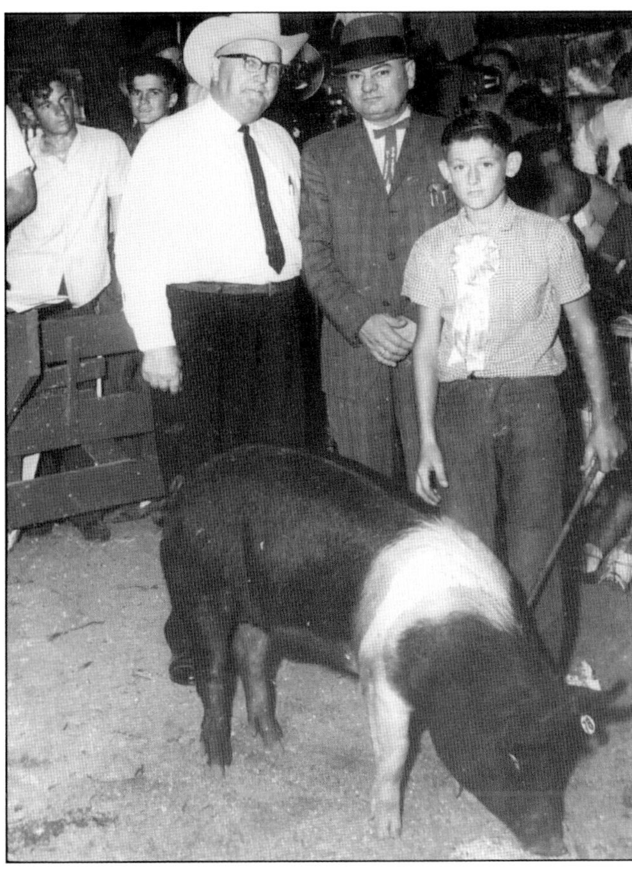

The *boucherie* (slaughter) joined families together to provide meat for the week and was a tradition developed out of necessity before the advent of refrigeration. When a pig was slaughtered, *fricassé*, a roux-based stew, was prepared. Hansel Borel owned this Sugar Cane Festival Livestock Show reserve champion pig. Pictured from left to right are agriculture commissioner Dave Pearce, auctioneer Eldridge Theriot, and Borel.

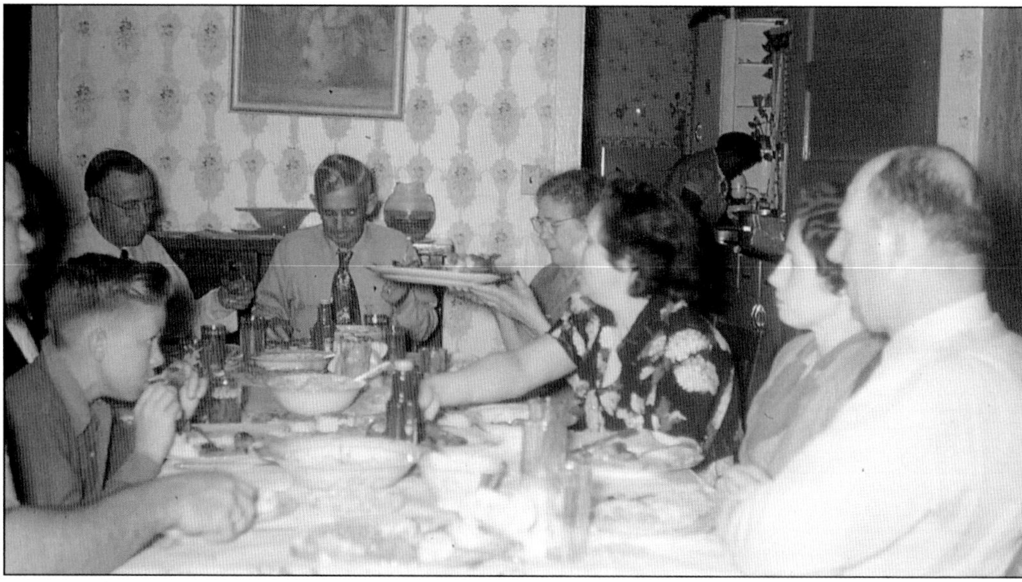

Women played an important role in shaping the culture of Iberia. They were influential landowners responsible for maintaining not only the family unit, but also in many cases the farm, finances, and religion. Pictured enjoying a meal are, from left to right, Leroy Haycock, Chester Haycock, Roland Denison Sr., Paul Denison, Blanche Migues Denison, Dot Markham, Ruth Denison Eldridge, Oswald "Frisco" Eldridge, and Eloise ? (in kitchen), who prepared the meal.

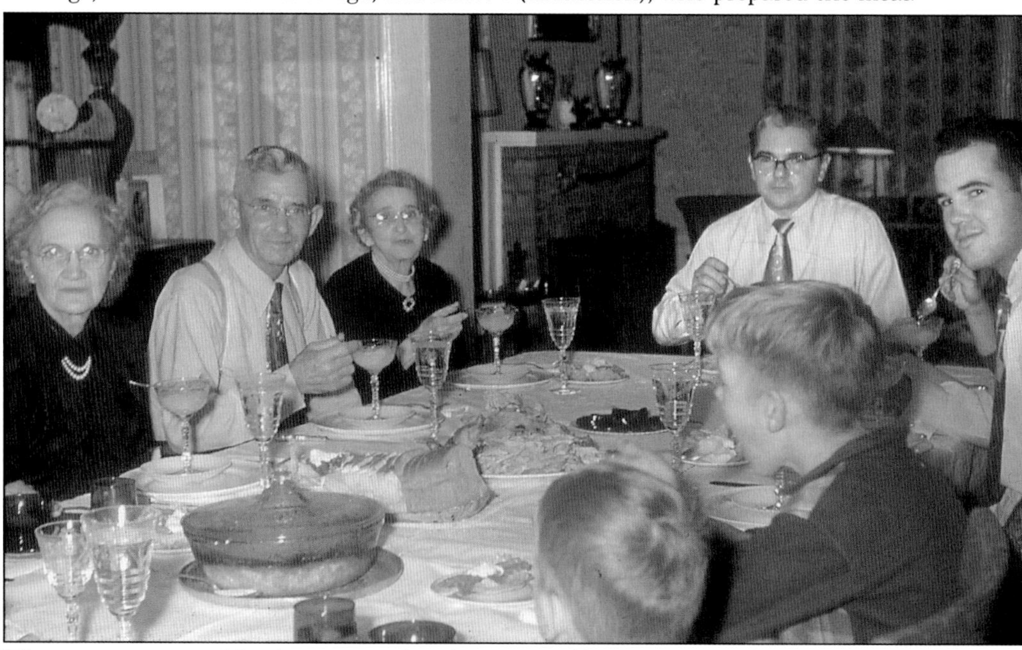

The consumption of food was considered an enjoyable pastime for Iberians. *Roux*, a browned mixture of flour and oil, provided the thick, robust body for gumbo and *sauce-piquante*, a highly seasoned stew. The Malaguénos brought with them the process of smoking meats, and paella, a dish that evolved into jambalaya. Enjoying a meal from left to right are Pearl Denison Markham, Paul Denison, Claudia Denison Laperouse, Jimmy Delcambre, Lynn Landry, Tam Delcambre, and Wayne Delcambre.

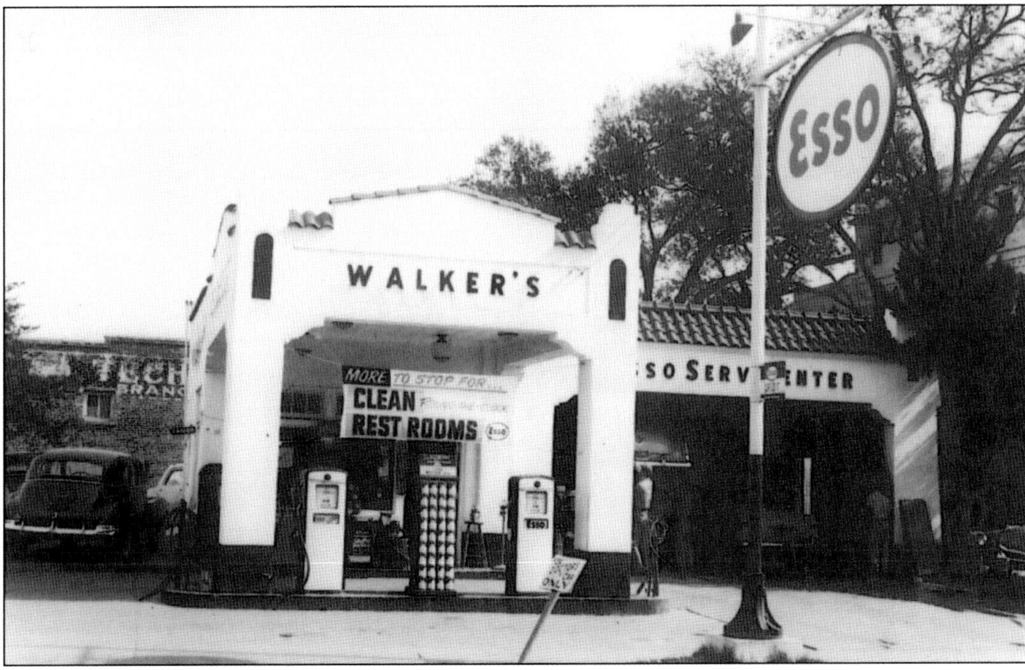

According to the *Abbeville Meridional*, on October 23, 1902, R.S. McMahon and W.E. Satterfield drove from New Iberia to Abbeville to deliver the first automobile in Vermilion Parish to Dr. Francis Fenwick Young. In the late 1940s, Walker's Esso Service Station, now Bouligny Plaza, was on the corner of Main and Fisher Streets. It was owned by Bob Walker, who died in May 1950.

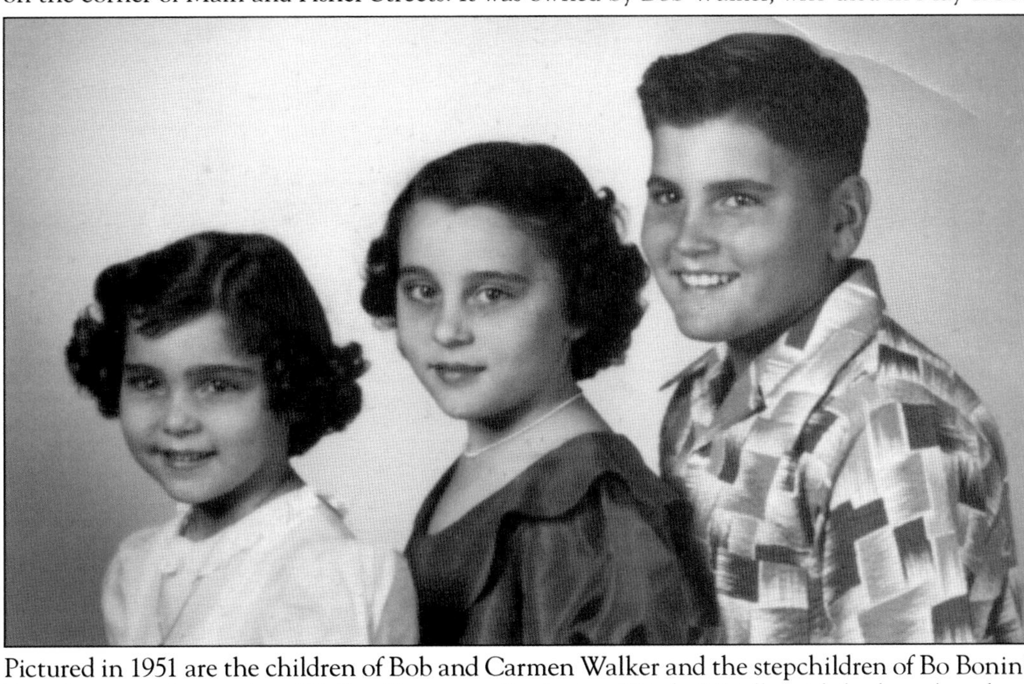

Pictured in 1951 are the children of Bob and Carmen Walker and the stepchildren of Bo Bonini. From left to right are Jane Walker Barringer, Katherine "Kathy" Walker Thibodaux (paralegal to author Warren Perrin), and Robert J. "Bobby" Walker Jr. The Thibodauxs are the 11th largest family in the parish.

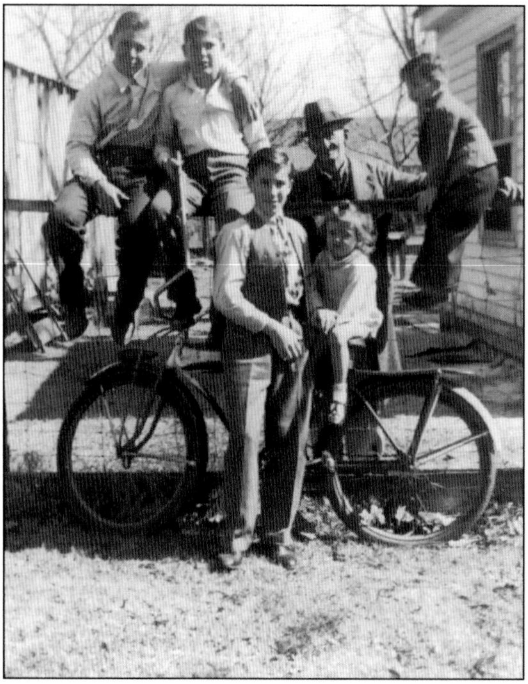

People often worked together in communal events called *coups de main* (helping hands). When better employment opportunities presented themselves elsewhere, some locals reluctantly moved away. In 1917, Elie Romero, a native of Iberia Parish, moved his family to Biloxi, Mississippi, to work in the developing seafood industry. Pictured in 1939 are, from left to right, unidentified, Floyd Primeaux, Rexall Romero (standing), Emily Sanders (sitting on bike), Elie Romero (with hat), and Rogers Romero (sitting on the fence).

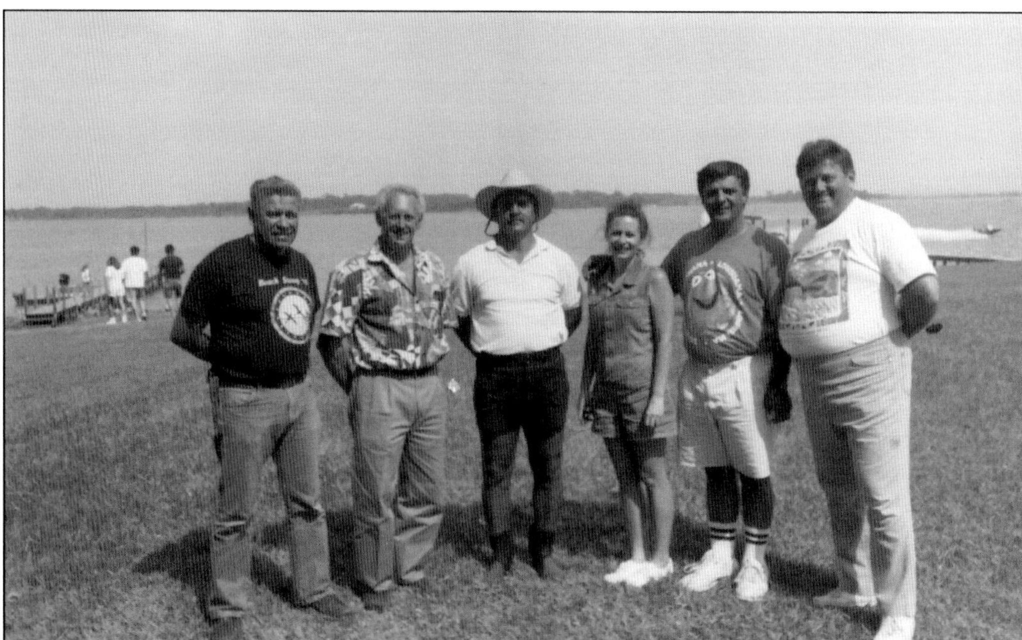

In 1994, Lake Peigneur residents unsuccessfully contested natural gas storage under the lake. Kermit Bouillion, leader of the opposition, was honored with the Woodmen of the World Conservation Award. Shown in this 1990 photograph are, from left to right, Harold Schoeffler (president of the Sierra Club), Noicy "Red" Langlinais, two unidentified, Bouillion, and Rep. Sammy Theriot. Currently, opposition to additional development has received widespread support. Primary concerns include contamination of the Chicot Aquifer, the quantity of water required to expand caverns, subsidence, and explosion.

In 1891, historian William Henry Perrin commented on New Iberia, writing, "The population is mixed—Americans, French, Italians, now and then a Spaniard, and even a Mexican, occasionally a basket-making Attakapas, and the all-pervading person of color." Paul Schwing, pictured in his Navy uniform during World War II, is the owner of Paul's Flower Shop and affectionately known as the "Mayor of Main Street" in New Iberia. He is the son of Anna Blanchet Schwing and John Elmer Schwing.

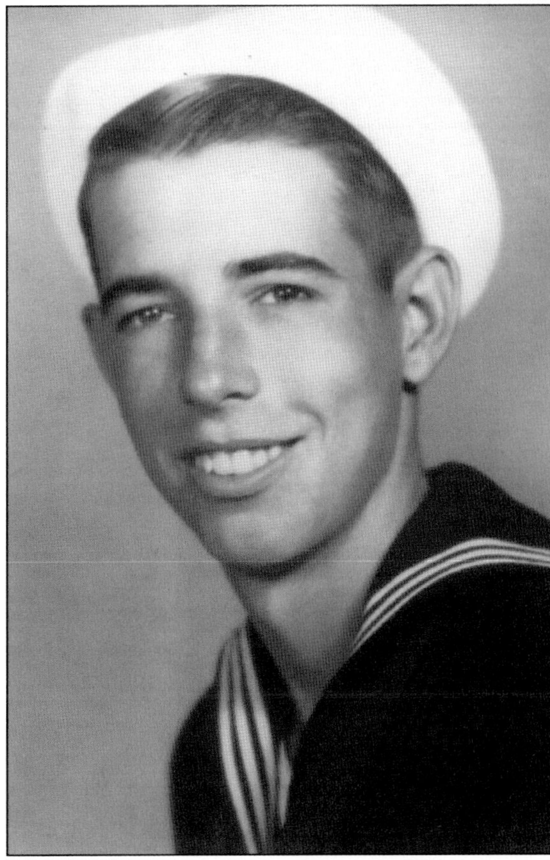

After the flood of 1927, the US Army Corps of Engineers built the Atchafalaya Basin Protection Levee. This caused diminished flow of water to the Bayou Teche, but exacerbated pollution. Today, the creation of the Teche-Vermilion Fresh Water District has improved water quality. Pictured at its dedication are, from left to right, unidentified, Carrol Fuselier, Gov. Dave Treen, Paul Begnaud, Dr. Harold Travasos, and executive director Donald Sagrera.

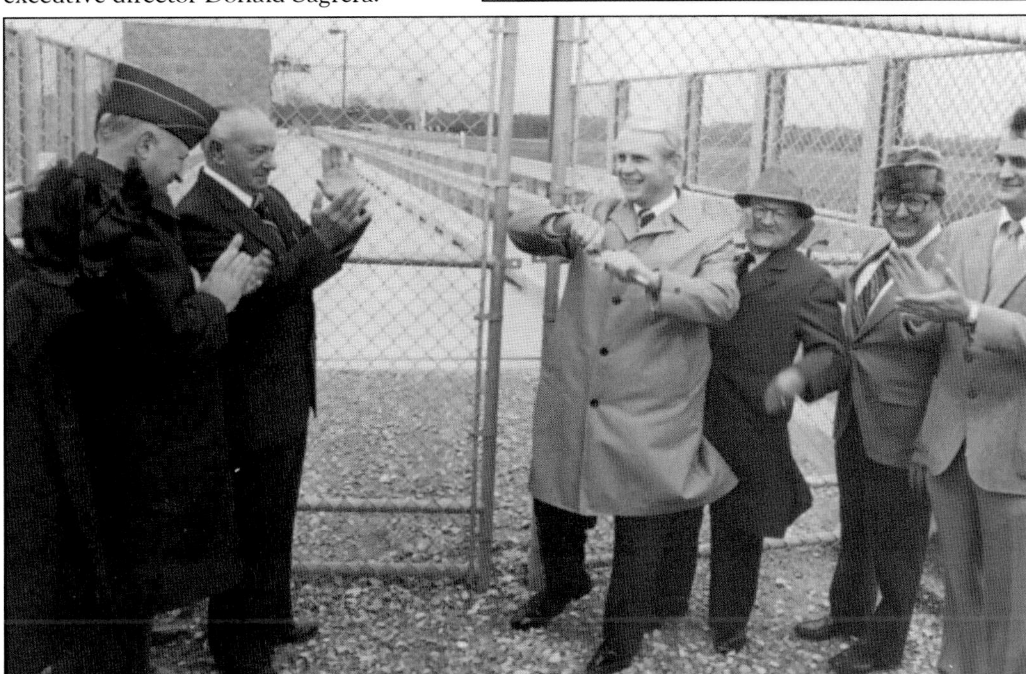

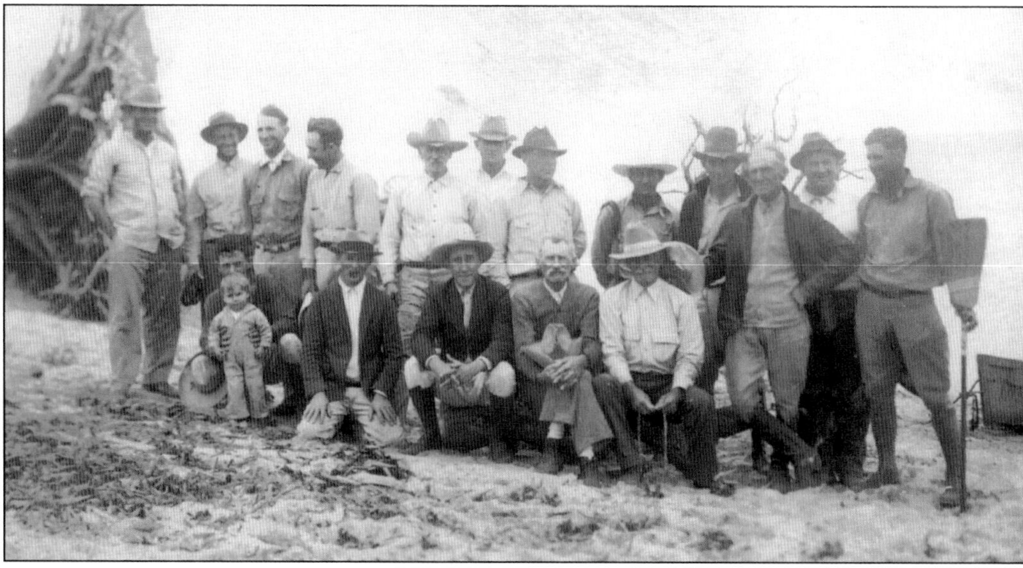

In the 18th century, 3,000 Acadians arrived and adapted well to the marshes, helping to develop the cattle industry. Families wintered cattle on Marsh Island, where they shared a camp. The cattle were transported to the island on the *Mae West*. Pictured in 1925 on the island are, from left to right, (first row) three unidentified, Ulysse Marceaux, Leodice Hulin, and Aristide Broussard; (second row) Emile Thibodeaux, unidentified, Lastie Broussard, Edmond Dugas, unidentified, Clairville Hulin, Fils Broussard, Willis Hulin, Jay Rodrigue, unidentified, Owen Williams, and René Leblanc.

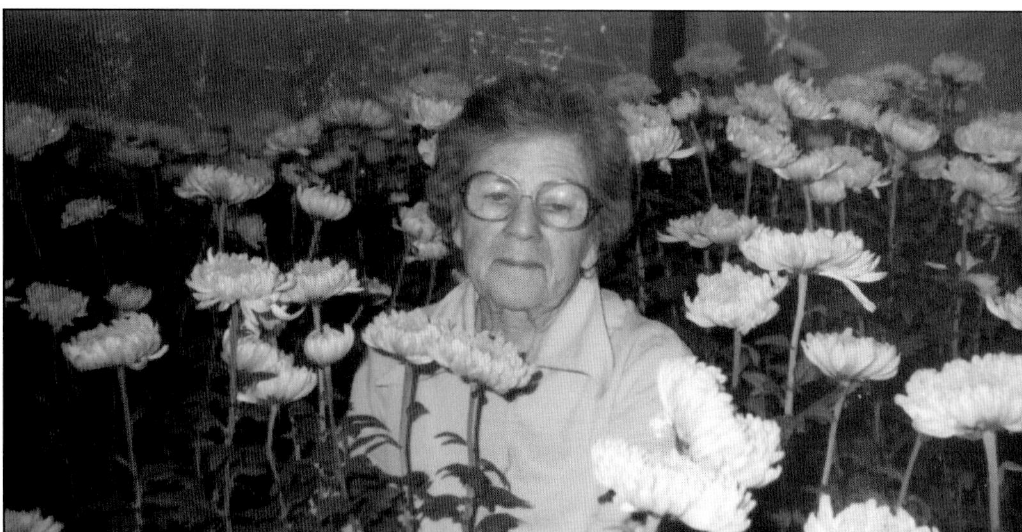

On November 1st, the whitewashing of tombs brought families together for *la Toussaint* (All Saints' Day). Although the purpose was to maintain the tombs, it also involved graveside communal meals. Arthur Hebert and Eunice Blanchard Hebert (pictured) grew chrysanthemums at their home near Patoutville and every year delivered over 10,000 blooms for All Saints' Day. Eunice was born in the Amant Broussard house in Loreauville. When it was moved to Vermilionville in Lafayette, she was consulted on the renovations to maintain its authenticity. In August 2011, she celebrated her 104th birthday.

Seven

MAJOR EVENTS

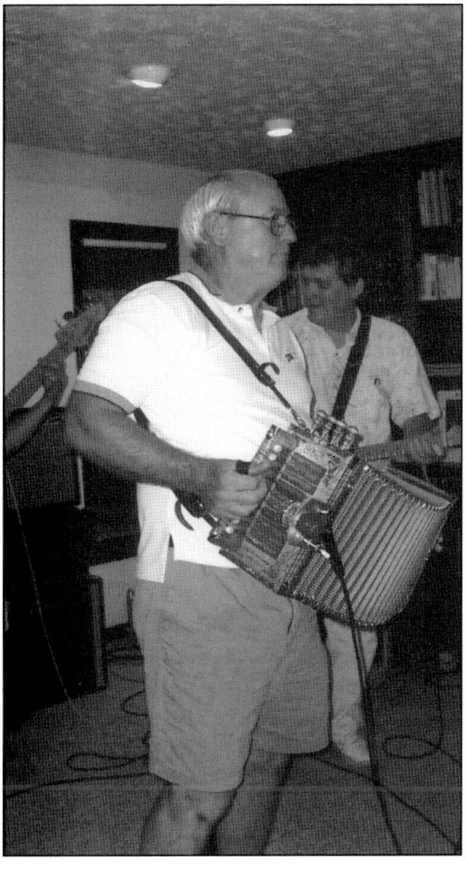

The *bal de maison* (house dance) was an early tradition. The accordion is the main instrument of Cajun bands today, but it did not appear until German-Jewish retailers introduced it in the late 19th century. By the early 20th century, a stock repertoire of music developed based on French, Acadian, German, Spanish, Native American, Scots-Irish, African American, English, and American traditions. Pictured is Pat Campbell, former principal of Delcambre Elementary, playing the accordion.

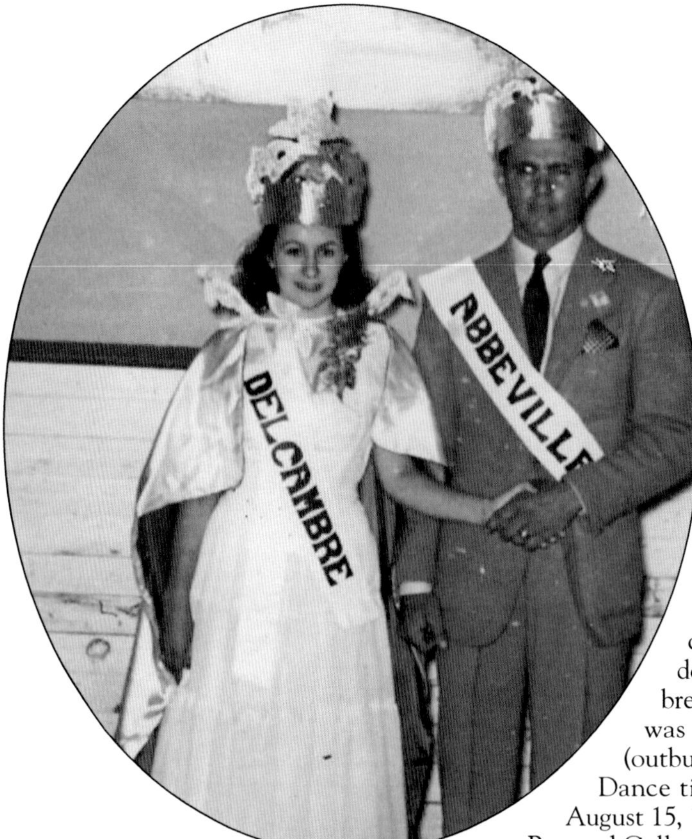

Dance clubs, such as the Belvedere, La Louisiane, and the Oriental, were popular in the mid-20th century. Pictured at left are unknown contestants from Delcambre and Abbeville competing in a Coronation Dance in Delcambre. Families also enjoyed inviting their *voisins* (neighbors) to a *veillée* (social gathering). Guests were served cakes, pies, *tarts à la bouillie* (sweet dough pies), lemonade, and home-brewed beer. *Bourré* (a card game) was played by the men in a *cabine* (outbuilding). Below is a Coronation Dance ticket to the Belvedere Club for August 15, 1957. (Courtesy of the Shane K. Bernard Collection.)

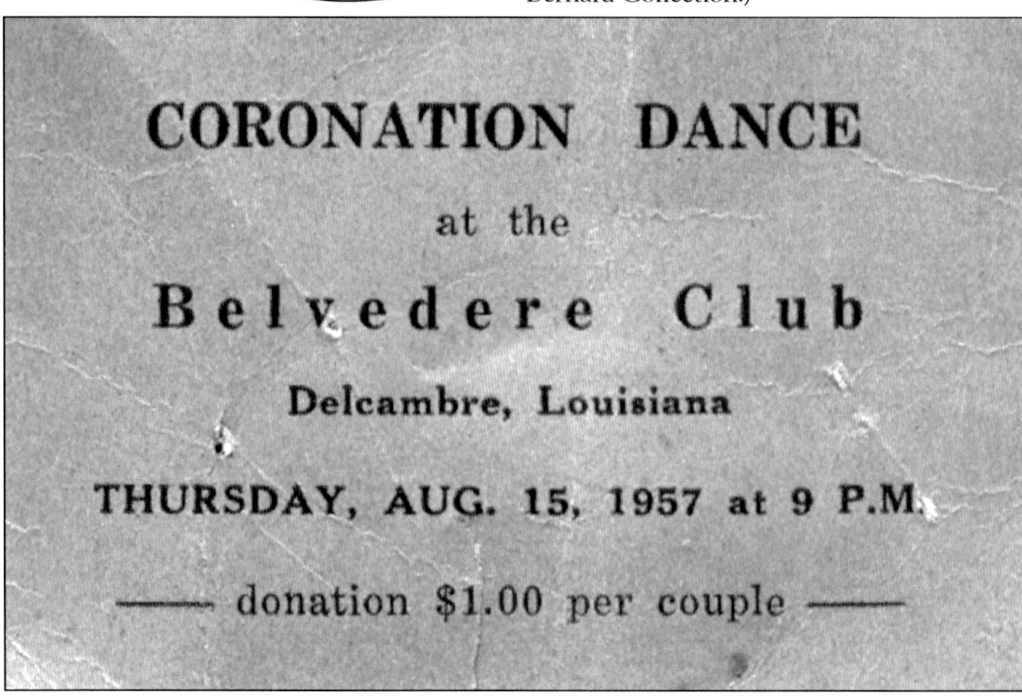

CORONATION DANCE

at the

Belvedere Club

Delcambre, Louisiana

THURSDAY, AUG. 15, 1957 at 9 P.M.

— donation $1.00 per couple —

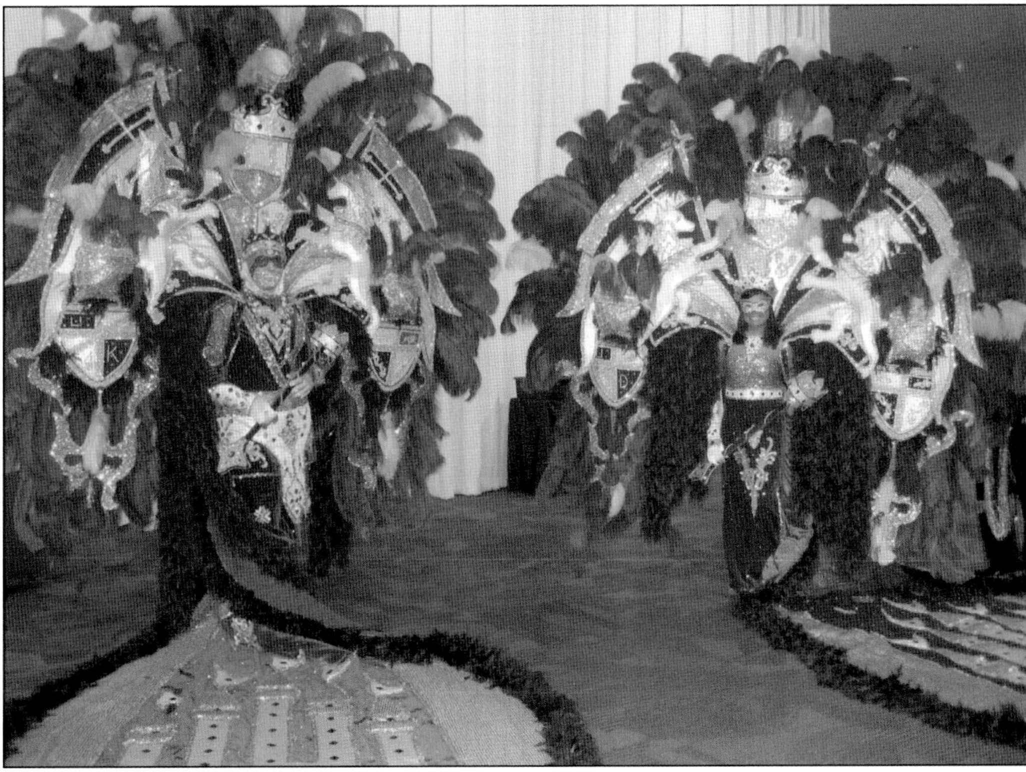

Mardi Gras brought communities together. Today, Grand Marais, a Creole community, carries on the carnival spirit in a rural setting with zydeco music, which evolved from 19th-century La-La (Creole) music, which itself heavily influenced rhythm and blues. These celebrations represented one way a community survived when there was a poor harvest. The celebrations ended in a dance, and food collected communally was used to provide a meal—usually chicken and sausage gumbo. (Courtesy of Creole Heritage Center at Northwestern State University in Natchitoches, Louisiana.)

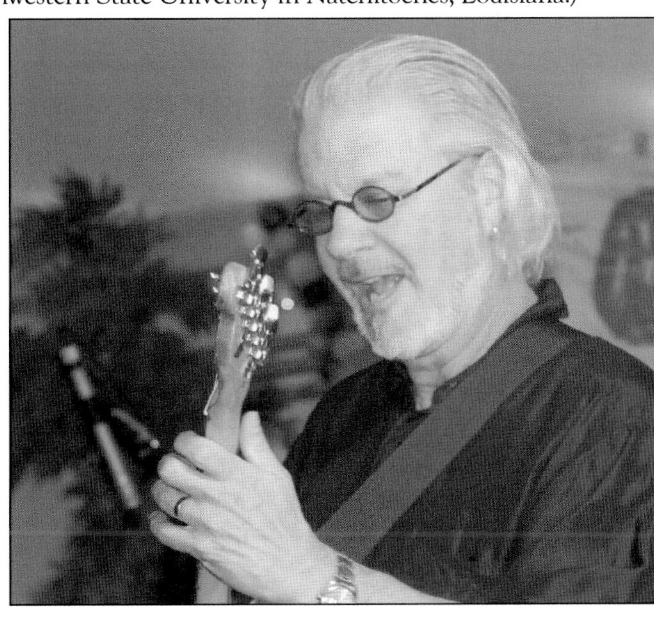

The guitar was Spanish in origin. Sam Broussard (pictured) plays with the Cajun band Steve Riley and the Mamou Playboys, who are four-time Grammy nominees. Broussard is the great-grandson of Sheriff T. Lazaire Broussard and the son of Alton Broussard, former journalism professor at USL. His great-uncle James Broussard, professor of romance languages at Louisiana State University (LSU), published *Louisiana Creole Dialect*, the first book of its kind. Sam Broussard has written music around the poems of Pierre, a slave from the 1860s, found in James Broussard's book.

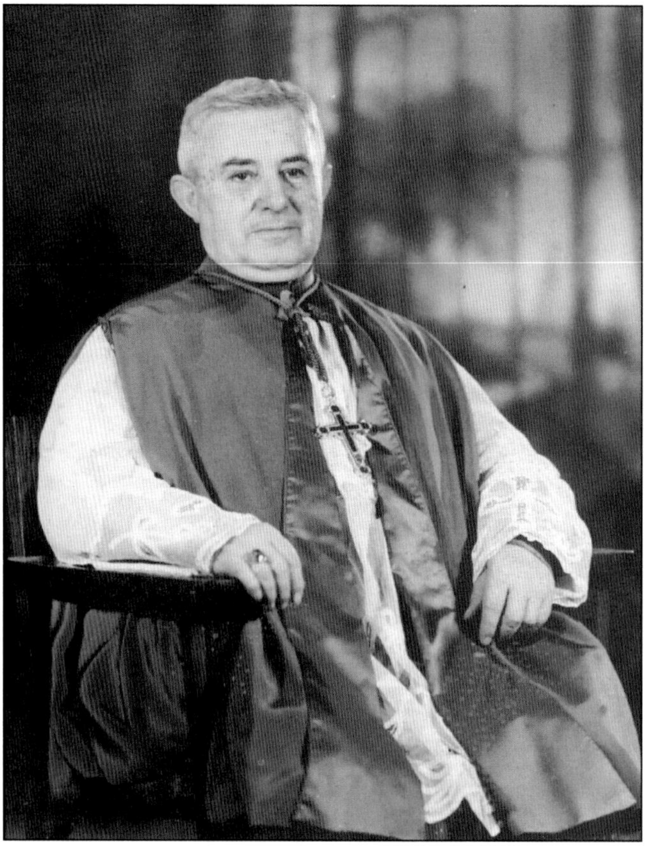

Msgr. Jean Marie Langlois, former pastor of St. Peter's Catholic Church, served for 39 years. Some of his accomplishments were the founding of Catholic High School, the Rynella Chapel, St. Edward's Church, and the Knights of Columbus Council 1208. He also established a new rectory, built Mt. Carmel Convent, and founded the Society for the Propagation of the Faith.

Hunting has always been a favorite local pastime. Most rural families had dogs for flushing and retrieving game during the hunt. Flooding from Hurricanes Rita in 2005 and Ike in 2008 took a heavy toll on the wildlife population. The duck and goose population, however, later returned to the local wetlands. Pictured in the 1920s is Paul Emile Voorhies (left) following a duck hunt with friends.

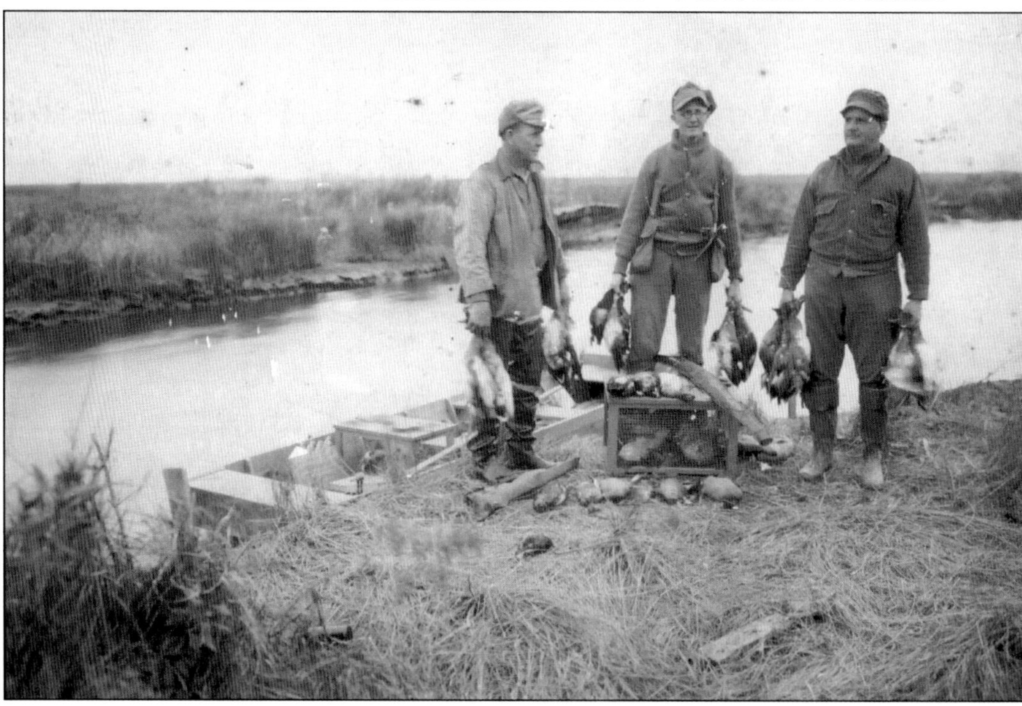

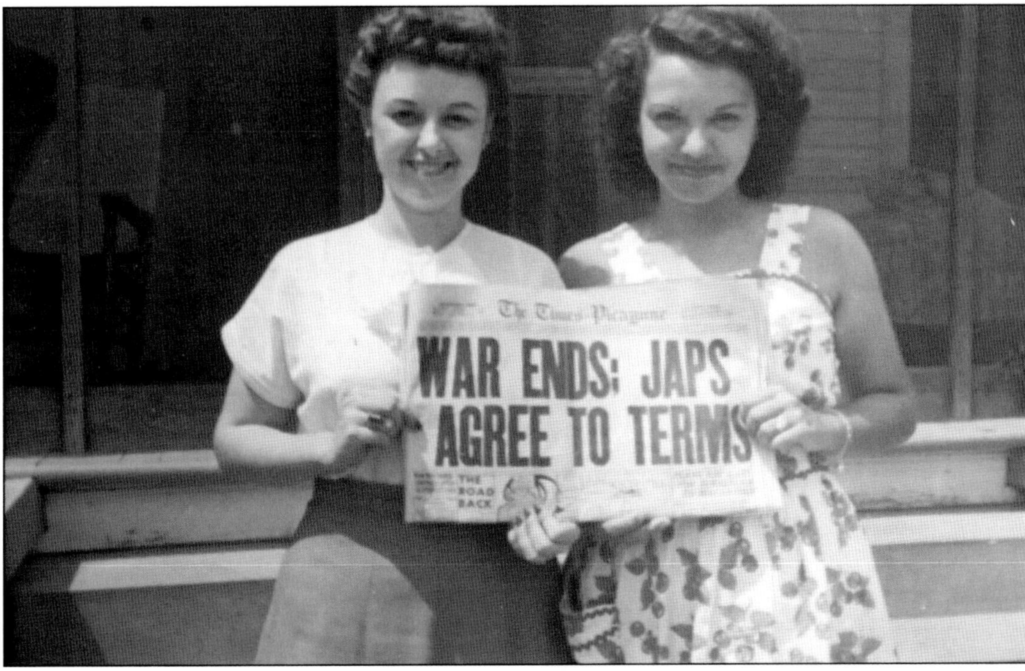

Pictured above are Dixie Lou Sealy (left) and Betty Mae LeBlanc St. Dizier, happily displaying a newspaper's front page announcing that World War II had ended on August 15, 1945. Iberian John "C.D." Lopez (right) served as a corporal in the Pacific theater. On February 19, 1945, he was among the first Marines to hit Yellow Beach on the volcanic island of Iwo Jima, where he spent 25 days. Lopez, now deceased, was one of only a few in his platoon who survived the fierce battle. He was married to Rosie Simon and was the father of Charlotte Lopez Segura and Juanita Lopez Romero. With the soldiers returning after World War II, Cajun music—a combination of old French songs, swamp pop, and blues—emerged as a symbol of ethnic pride.

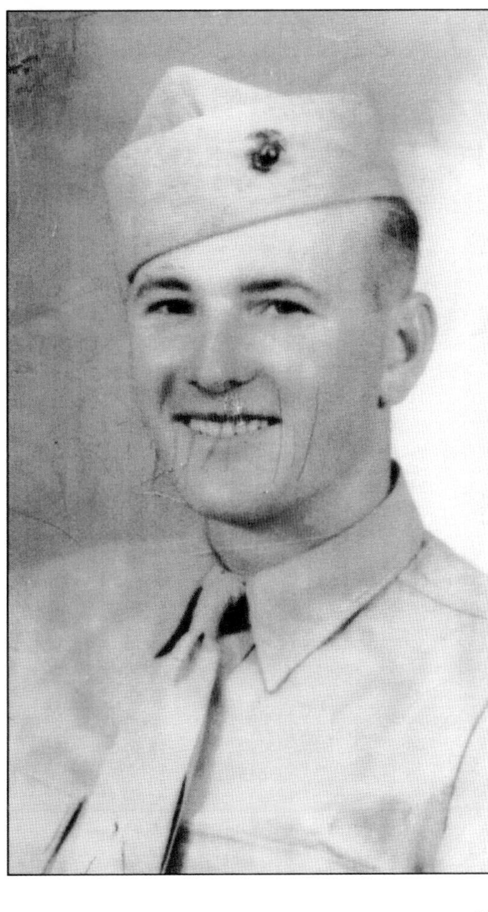

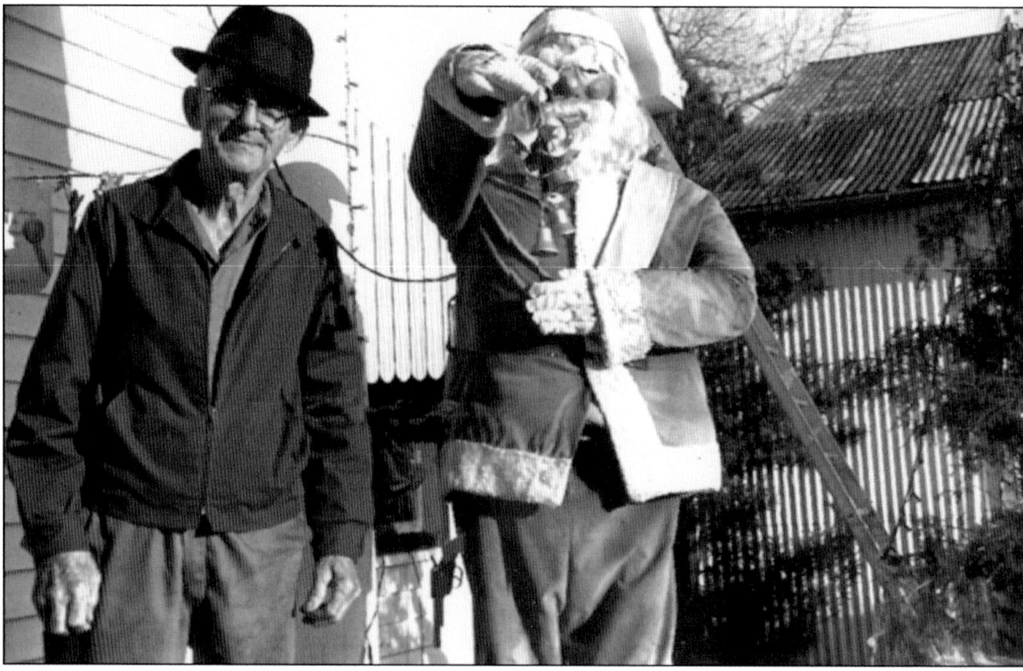

Gail Garcia took this 1986 photograph of Joseph Borel and his mechanical Santa when she was researching a news article. During Christmastime for over 35 years, Borel spread seasonal joy to the residents of Jeanerette. He was an inventor who made the walking mechanical Santa from old lawnmower and car parts. Borel took pride in his inventions and in the rare and amazing fact that he saw Haley's comet twice in his lifetime.

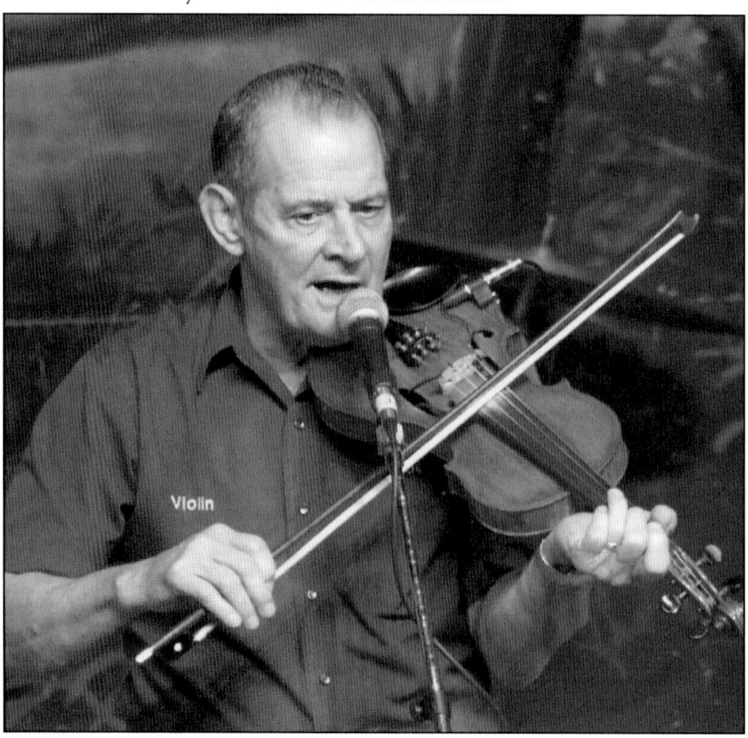

Joseph "Joe" Lopez learned to play the fiddle at New Iberia High School. The first band Lopez joined was Tee Denise and the Iberia Playboys, and later Badeaux and the Louisiana Aces. They recorded D.L. Menard's famous hit song, *The Back Door.* Lopez worked for Morton Salt Company and is married to Dorita Bonin. In 2001, *Les Cadiens du Teche* honored him with a lifetime achievement award. (Courtesy of David Simpson.)

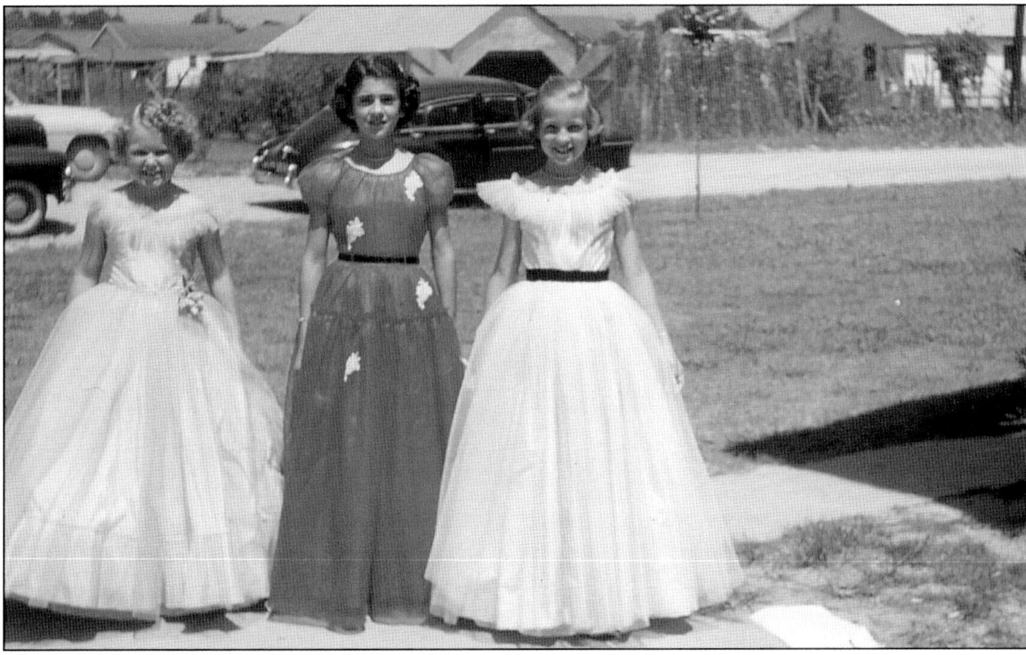

Pictured from left to right in their party dresses are Lillie "Buggy" Emmer Smith, daughter of Dr. Andrew and Miriam Derouen Emmer; Lyndel Laperouse Renoudet, daughter of Darby and Mildred Landry Laperouse, owners of Laperouse Insurance Agency; and Diane Laperouse Angers, daughter of Lionel and Helen Landry Laperouse Jr., former members of the Louisiana House of Representatives.

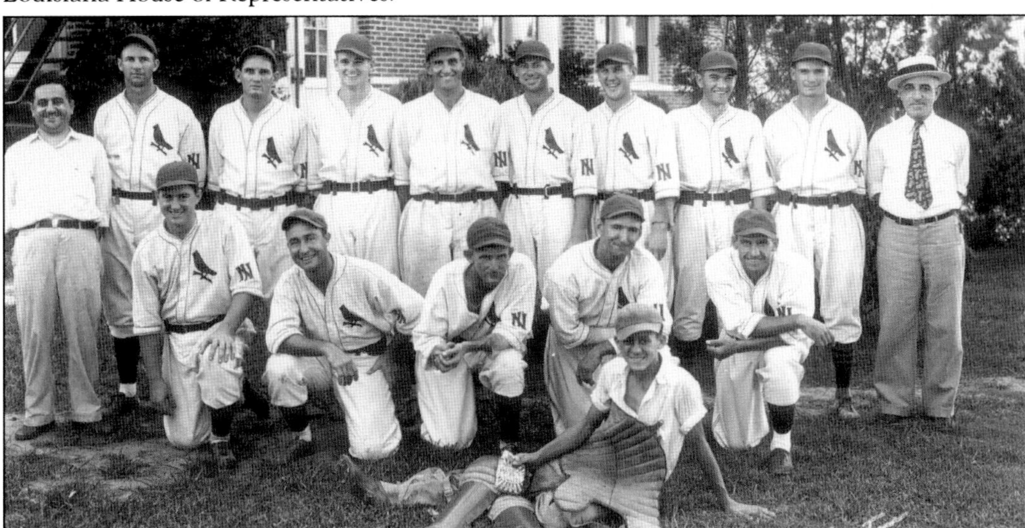

Shown here is the 1934 New Iberia Cardinals baseball team. The Cardinals were in the Evangeline League from 1934 to 1953. They were affiliated with the St. Louis Cardinals from 1935 to 1941 and the Boston Red Sox in 1946. Pictured from left to right are (sitting) Sam Drago; (first row) Paul Bruno, Sam Camalo, Hank Doty, Heby Pourciau, and Edwin "Lefty" Gore; (second row) "Nootsie" Jennaro (manager), Ray "Moon" Mullins, Pete Bourgeois, ? Baker, Milton Dalmas, two unidentified, Averette Thomspon, Roy Smith, and Luca Jennaro (manager). (Courtesy of Center for Louisiana Studies, University of Louisiana at Lafayette.)

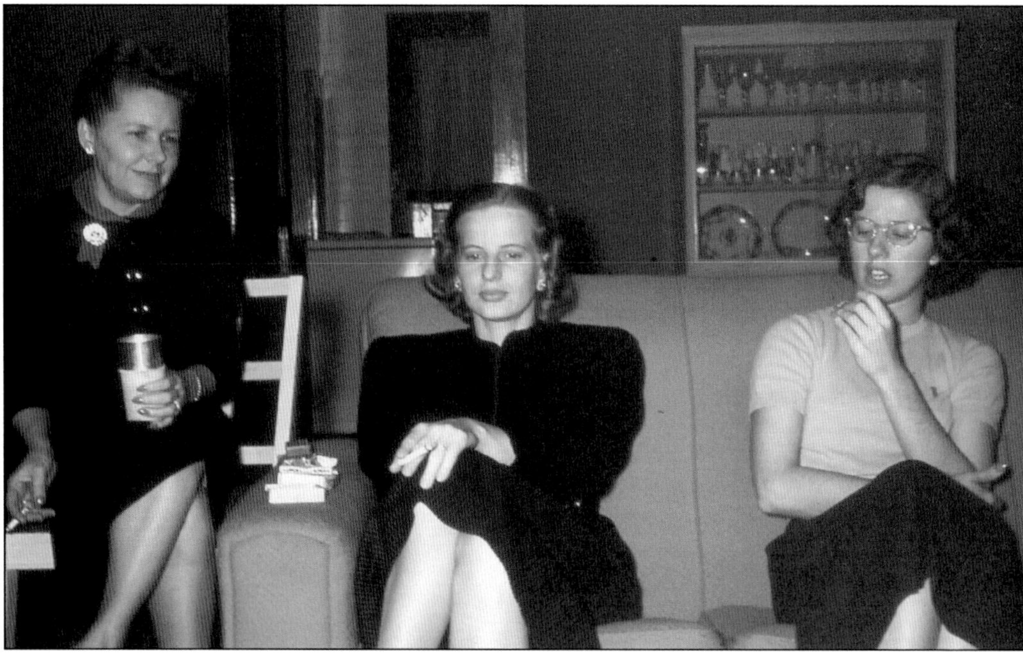

Shown during a Sunday social are, from left to right, Miriam Emmer, Margaret Smith Denison (wife of Roland Denison Jr.) and Elynordel Eldridge.

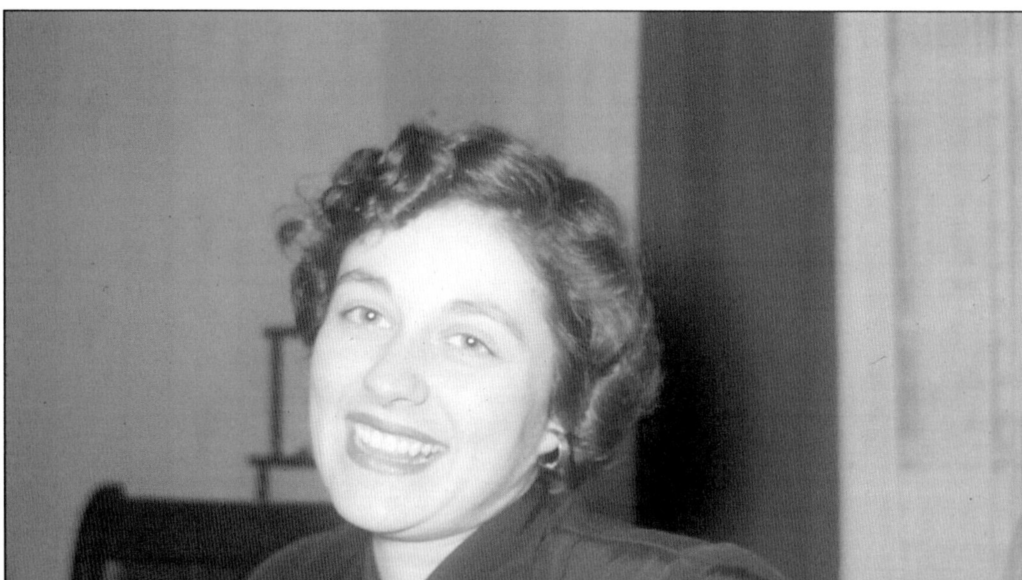

In the 1950s, the Teenage Center at City Park held many enjoyable activities, such as roller-skating, ping pong, and private parties, and was a safe place for young people to "hang out." Aimee Gates ran the concessions stand, Nassim Sarkies was the security guard, and Herb Pourciau was in charge of the general activities. There were also six movie theaters in New Iberia: the Essanee, the Evangeline, the Palace, the Colonial, the Musu, and the NILA theater on St. Jude Street. Pictured here is Armine Denison Bonin of New Iberia, wife of Donald Bonin, who like many, participated in these activities.

Pictured from left to right at Camp Blanding, Florida, on December 7, 1941, are Oswald Ronsonet, Ed Broussard, John Mestayer, and Green Stansbury. The four became well-known New Iberia National Guardsmen. Broussard and Mestayer were awarded Silver Stars for bravery. Oswald Ronsonet was killed in Europe, and the National Guard armory is named in his honor.

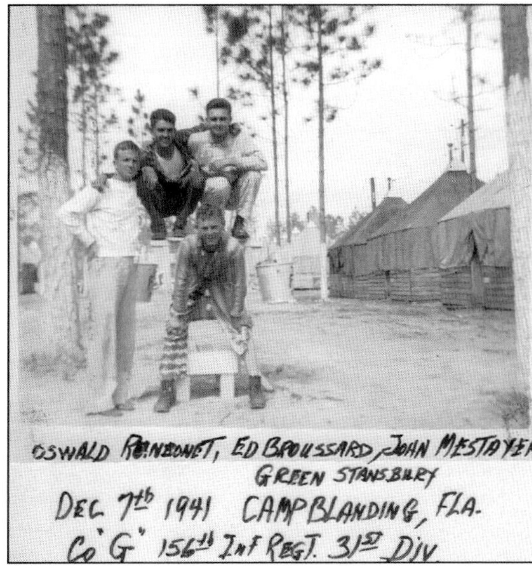

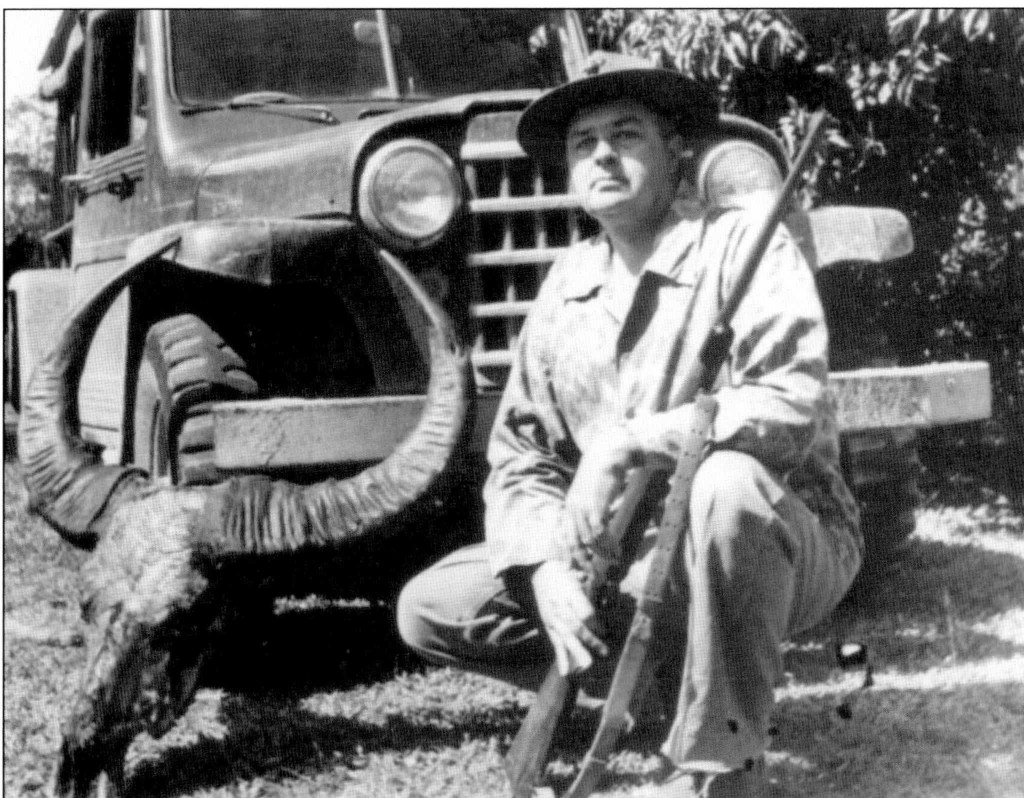

Pictured around 1955 is US Marine, businessman, and big-game hunter Walter S. McIlhenny. Although born in Washington, DC, McIlhenny resided on his ancestral home of Avery Island from 1940 until his death in 1985. He served 31 months in Pacific-theater combat during World War II, and rose from the rank of private in 1935 to brigadier general in 1959. He was awarded two Purple Hearts, the Silver Star, and the Navy Cross. He ran Tabasco operations for 35 years. (Courtesy of the McIlhenny Company Archives.)

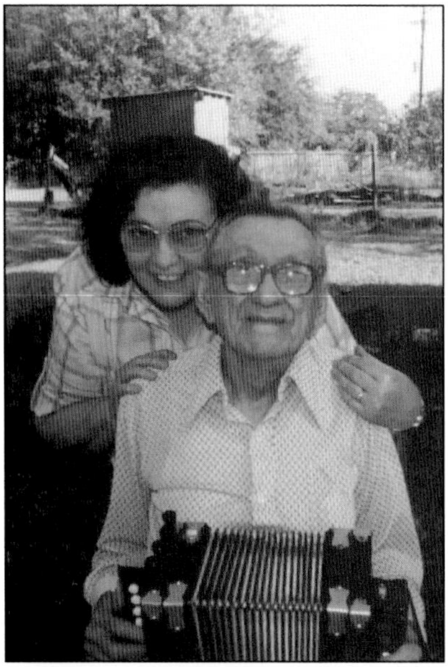

Dewey Segura of Delcambre was the second artist to record a Cajun song. In 1928, he and his brother Eddie of New Iberia performed as the Segura Brothers and recorded the classic "Bayou Teche Waltz (la Valse de Bayou Teche)," written by Dewey for Columbia Records in New Orleans. When he was asked the name of the song, he responded in his poor English and was misunderstood. Sadly, the company put the name of the song incorrectly on the record as "My Sweetheart Run Away," so others have claimed the authorship. In the 1980s, Segura played music on the *Bayou Queen*, which cruised the Bayou Teche. Segura, born on February 12, 1902, was one of 12 children. His father was of Spanish origin and his mother was French. Segura's wife, Euphemie, often accompanied him on guitar. Pictured at left are Segura and his daughter Irene Segura LaSalle. On August 5, 2011, Shannon LaSalle (below), granddaughter of Segura and daughter of LaSalle, is pictured in Branson, Missouri, performing on the *Karen Berka Radio Live, Branson* show.

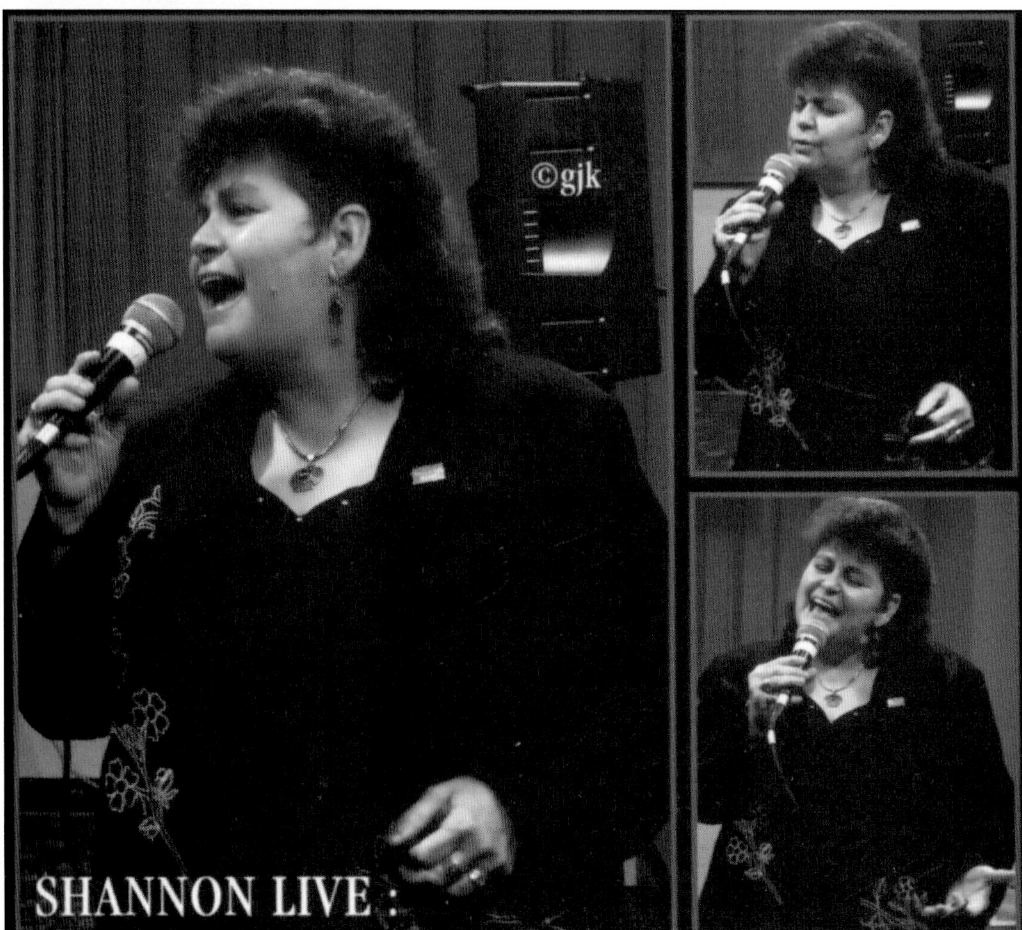

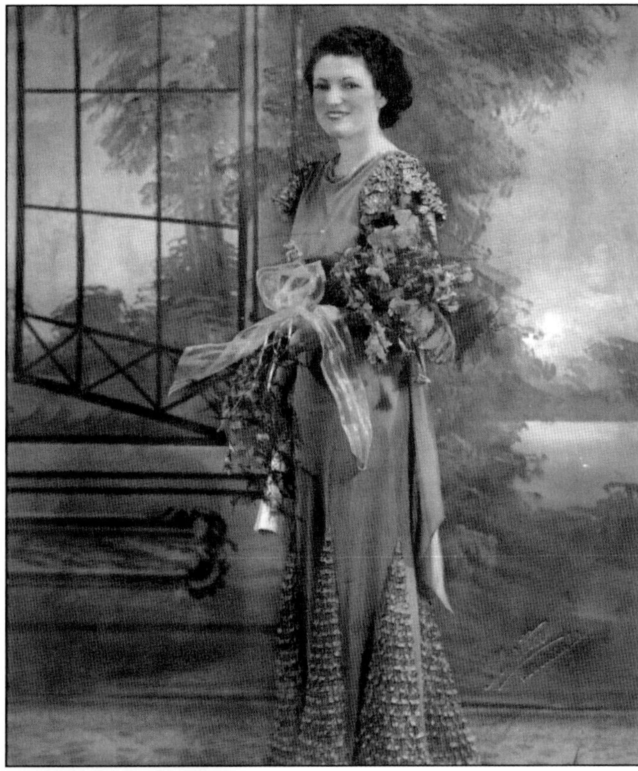

In 1877, William R. Burke was elected superintendent of schools in Iberia Parish and made the school system one of the best in south Louisiana. In 1891, historian William Henry Perrin wrote, "The town of New Iberia has an excellent public school, with the best of teachers, and a magnificent school building, complete in all its components. It is held up as a model school throughout the surrounding country, and it well deserves the credit and popularity it has attained." Pictured in 1937 is Lessie Babineaux preparing for her graduation from New Iberia High School, a typical graduation photograph of the time.

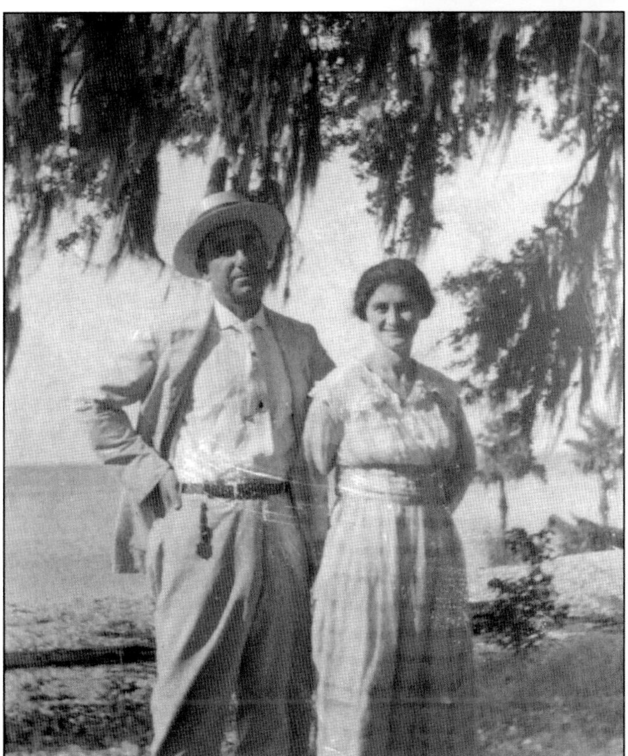

The relationship that Iberia Parish has with the Gulf of Mexico is unique; it is sometimes pleasurable, but at other times, it is devastating. The BP tragedy was a stark reminder that the technology of drilling offshore has far surpassed the technology of protecting the workers or the environment. On September 16, 2011, funerals were held for Nicholas Reed and Craig Myers, New Iberia natives who died working in the Gulf of Mexico. Pictured in 1919 are Richard C. Sealy Sr. and Lucille LeBlanc.

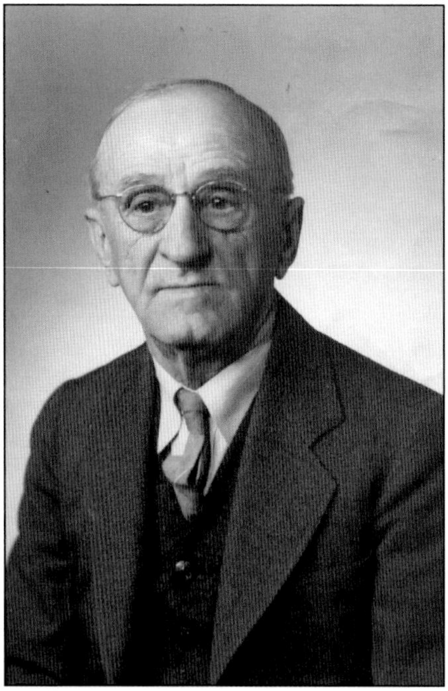

As the fifth most common surname in Iberia, the LeBlancs are widely distributed over the southern part of the state with concentrations in the Teche country. The LeBlancs of southwest Louisiana began with two members of the Acadian clan, Simon and René, who were listed in the Attakapas census of 1766. In 1912, Joseph Gabriel "Gabe" LeBlanc Jr. (pictured), in partnership with his cousin Henry Broussard, opened a car repair shop in New Iberia. Two years later, it became one of the first Ford automobile dealerships in the South.

Mary Avery McIlhenny (left), later Mrs. Sidney Bradford, and her older sister Sara Avery McIlhenny of Avery Island were daughters of Tabasco developer Edmund McIlhenny. They took an interest in Chitimacha Indian baskets, which were crafted in nearby Charenton. They encouraged Chitimacha women to pass down their traditional basket-making skills, helped to sell samples of their wares, and also worked to save the tribe's land. (Courtesy of the McIlhenny Company Archives.)

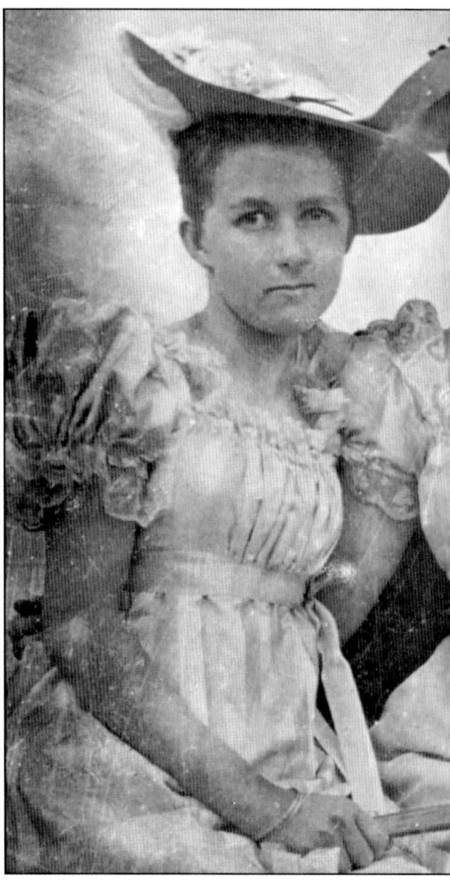

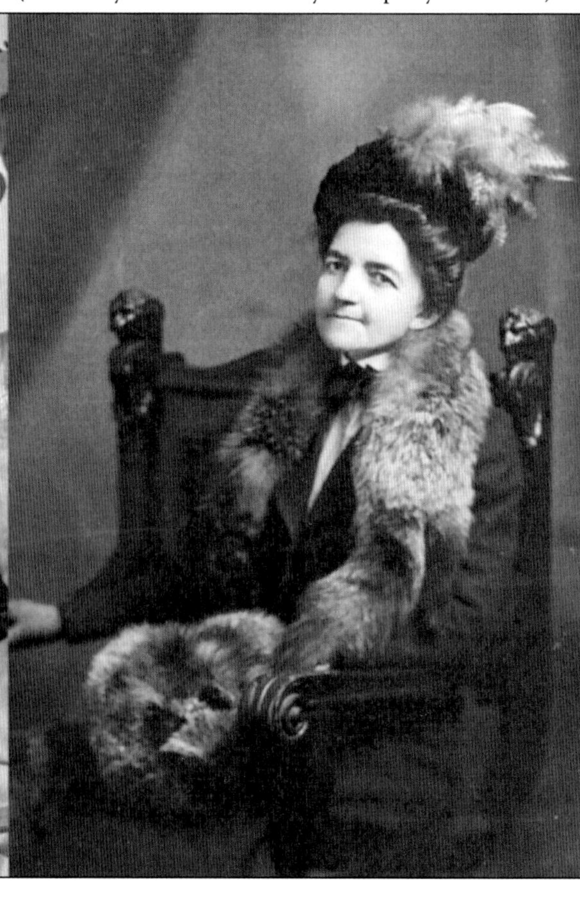

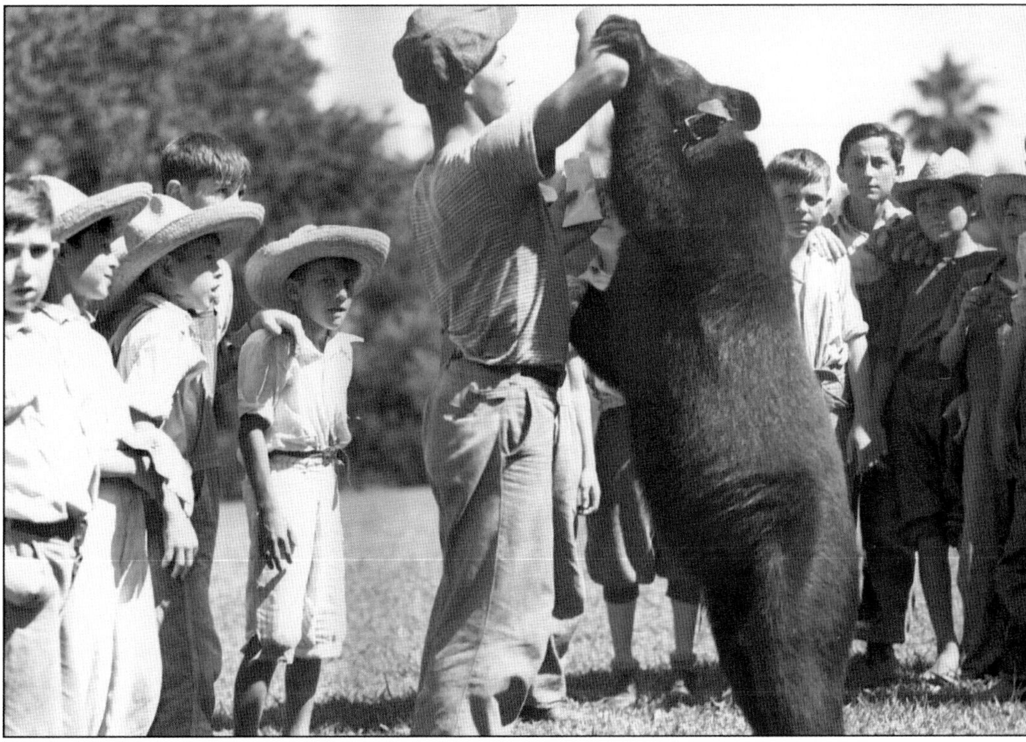

In 1891, historian William Henry Perrin wrote of Avery Island, "This island is one of the most interesting spots in Iberia Parish. It contains about 2,200 arpents of upland and 1,200 arpents of timber—cypress, gum, and oak." In this c. 1930 photograph, Cajun children on Avery Island are entertained by Tubby, a Louisiana black bear, a threatened species now federally protected. In October 2011, an elusive 300-pound black bear destroyed two traps and ravaged trash cans near Lydia. (Courtesy of the E.A. McIlhenny Collection, Avery Island.)

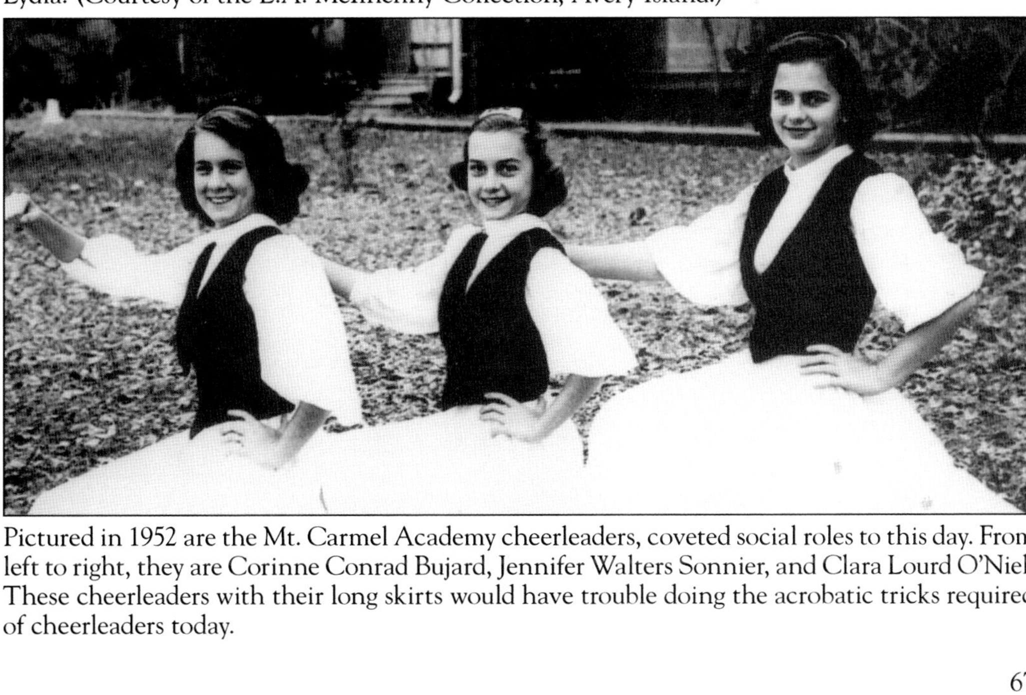

Pictured in 1952 are the Mt. Carmel Academy cheerleaders, coveted social roles to this day. From left to right, they are Corinne Conrad Bujard, Jennifer Walters Sonnier, and Clara Lourd O'Niel. These cheerleaders with their long skirts would have trouble doing the acrobatic tricks required of cheerleaders today.

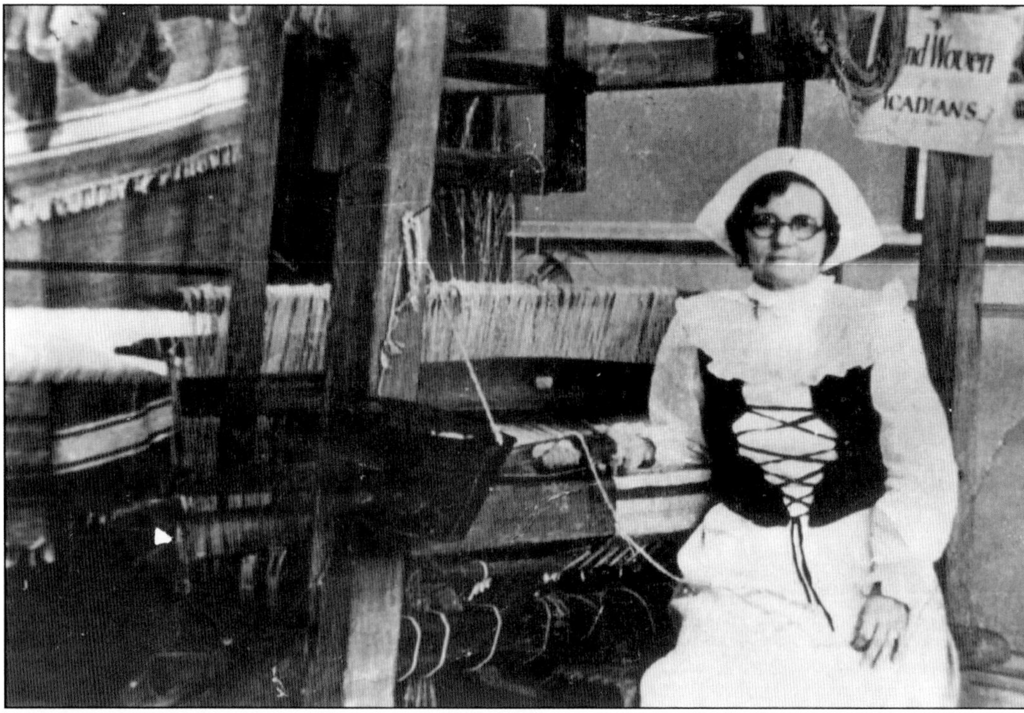

In 1942, André de La Varrés filmed *Cajuns of the Teche* as part of his Columbia Pictures series *Quaint People*. The film, an early documentary about the Teche area, was discovered in the US National Archives by historian Shane K. Bernard. Pictured is Thérèse Meyers Dronet, who was filmed weaving *la cottonade* along with her mother, Anaise Landry Meyers. Dronet was aided by Sarah Avery Leeds, who sold Acadian homespun cloth through the Christian Women's Exchange.

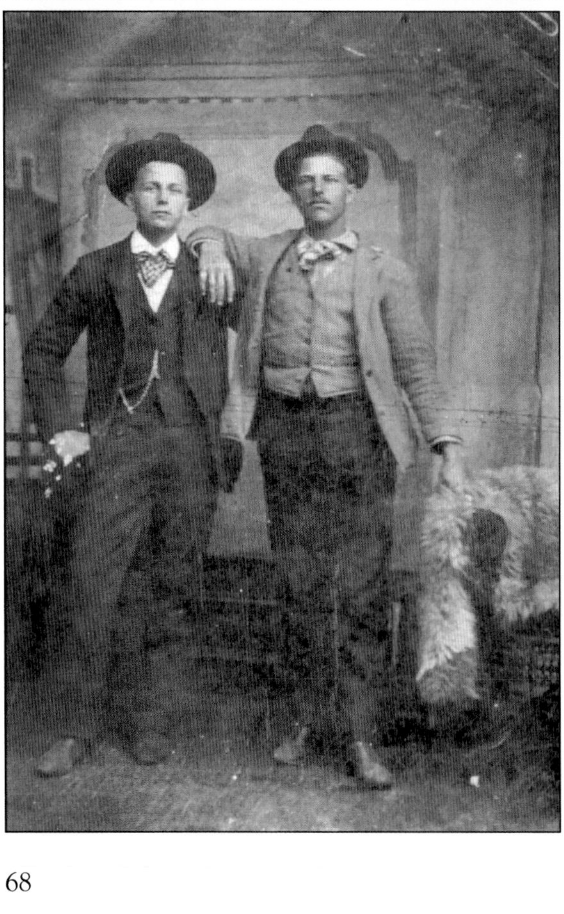

Farmers Victor Delcambre and Amadee Delcambre (left) are pictured in the late 1800s before the onset of the Great Depression, which changed the lives of farmers. Many lost their land; those who did not went into subsistence farming, growing what was needed to survive, such as cotton, sweet potatoes, corn, and okra. Most had a small pasture and a milk cow.

Pictured in 1950 is eight-year-old Iberia Parish native Kathleen Babineaux Blanco, a student at Coteau Elementary. At age 13, she worked in her father's campaign for assessor by putting flyers on car windshields during Sunday masses. Kathleen, born December 15, 1942, held four elective offices over her 24 years of outstanding service, including state representative, public service commissioner, lieutenant governor, and finally governor of Louisiana. (Courtesy of Carroll Breaux Studio.)

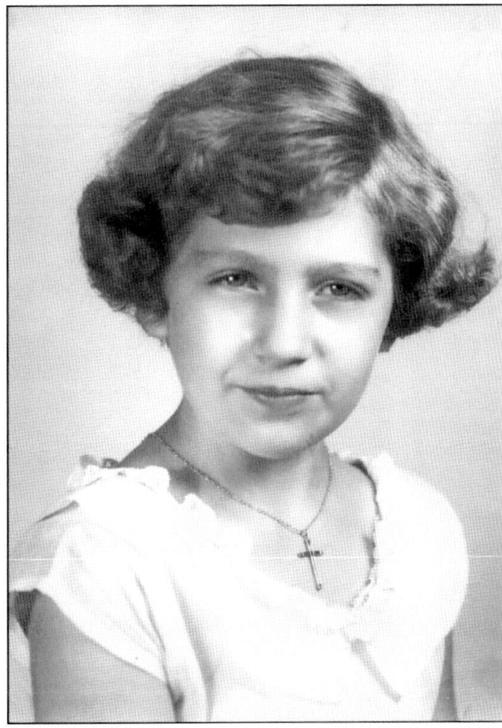

On August 8, 1964, following their wedding ceremony, Kathleen Babineaux and Raymond S. Blanco were showered with rice at the doors of Our Lady of Perpetual Help Catholic Church in New Iberia. Their marriage produced six children: Karmen, Monique, Nicole, Ray, Pilar, and Ben. In 1962, under Coach Raymond Blanco, Catholic High School won the first 11-man football state championship in Acadiana, a distinction held until 1992.

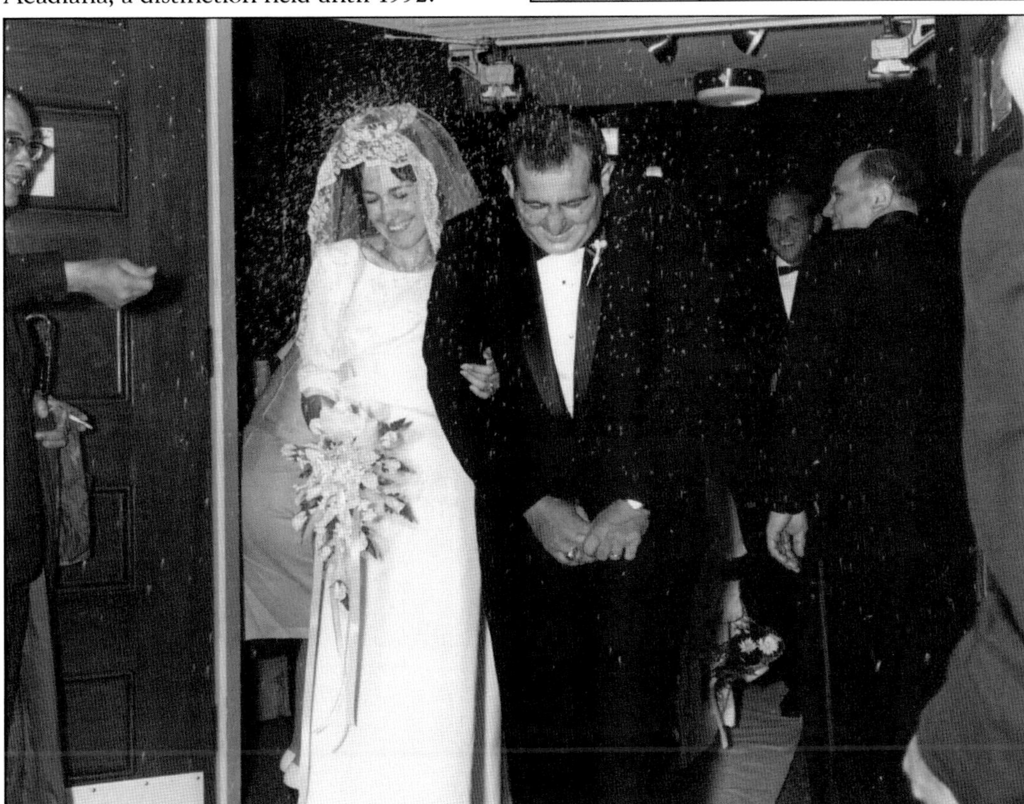

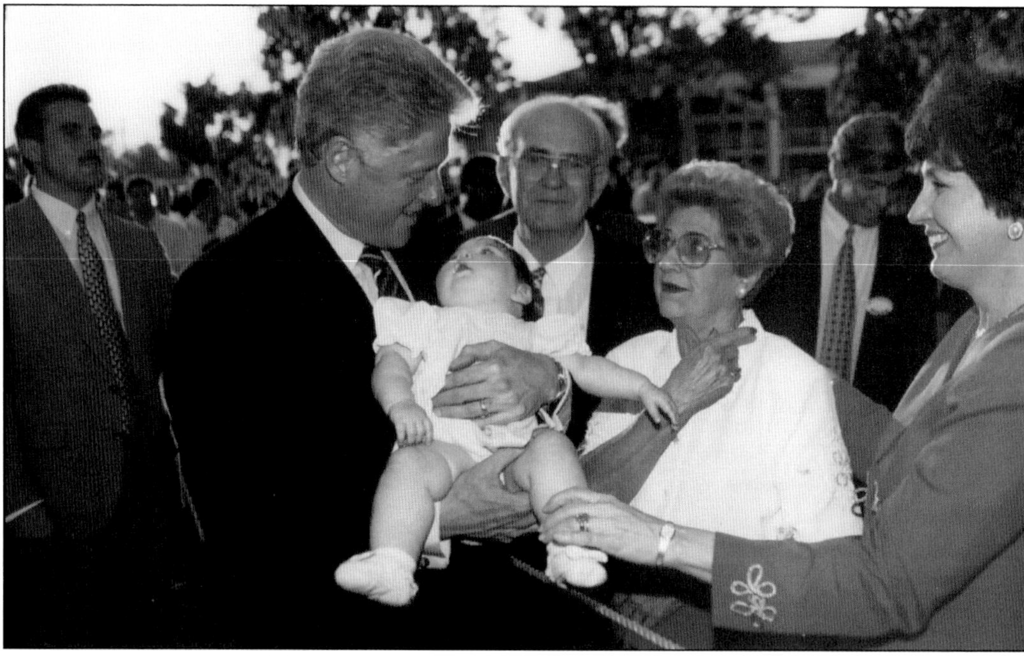

Pictured is a reception following a historic presidential address to the Louisiana Legislature on May 30, 1996. From left to right are Pres. Bill Clinton, holding seven-month-old Savannah Blanco Trumps; Louis and Lucille Fremin Babineaux, parents of Kathleen Blanco; and Lt. Gov. Kathleen Babineaux Blanco.

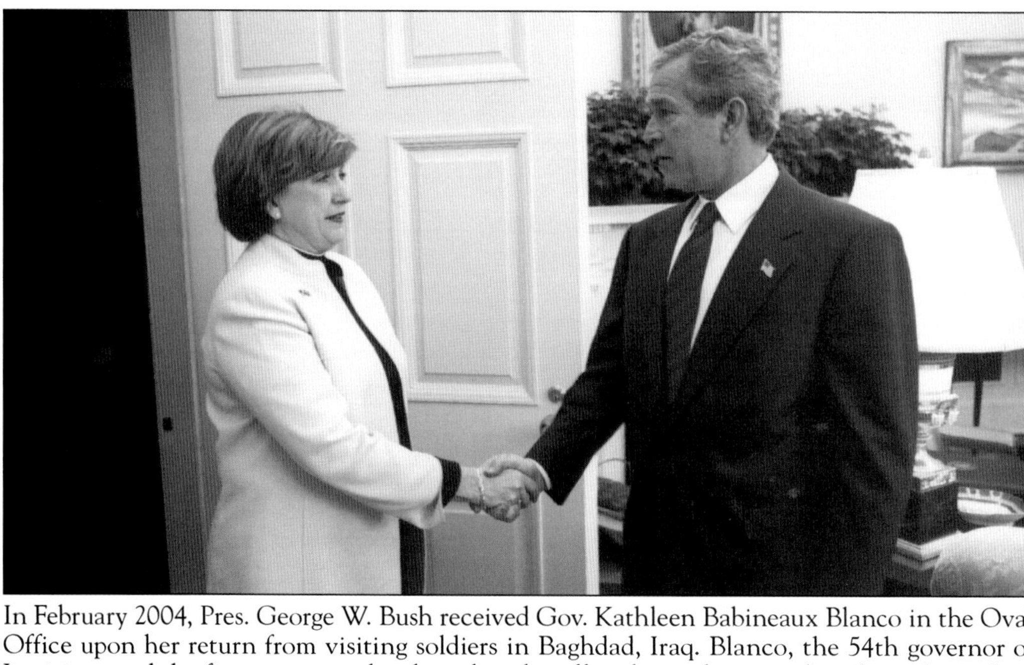

In February 2004, Pres. George W. Bush received Gov. Kathleen Babineaux Blanco in the Oval Office upon her return from visiting soldiers in Baghdad, Iraq. Blanco, the 54th governor of Louisiana and the first woman to be elected to the office, began her term by taking the oath of office in both English and French. She served from January 12, 2004, until January 2008. From 1996 to 2004, while serving two terms as lieutenant governor, she helped to expand Louisiana's relationship with the French-speaking world.

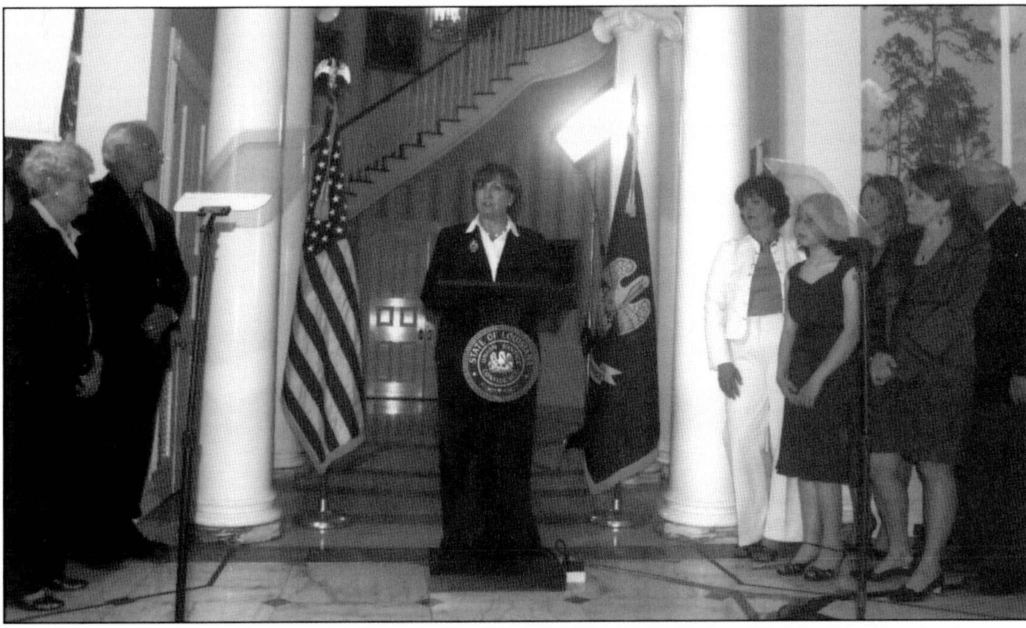

Gov. Kathleen Babineaux Blanco is pictured in March 2007 surrounded by her family during a press conference at the governor's mansion. From left to right are Lucille Babineaux, her mother; Erroll Babineaux, her brother; Governor Blanco; Karmen Blanco, her daughter; Savannah Blanco Trumps, her granddaughter; Nicole Blanco and Monique Blanco, her daughters; and First Gentleman Raymond S. Blanco.

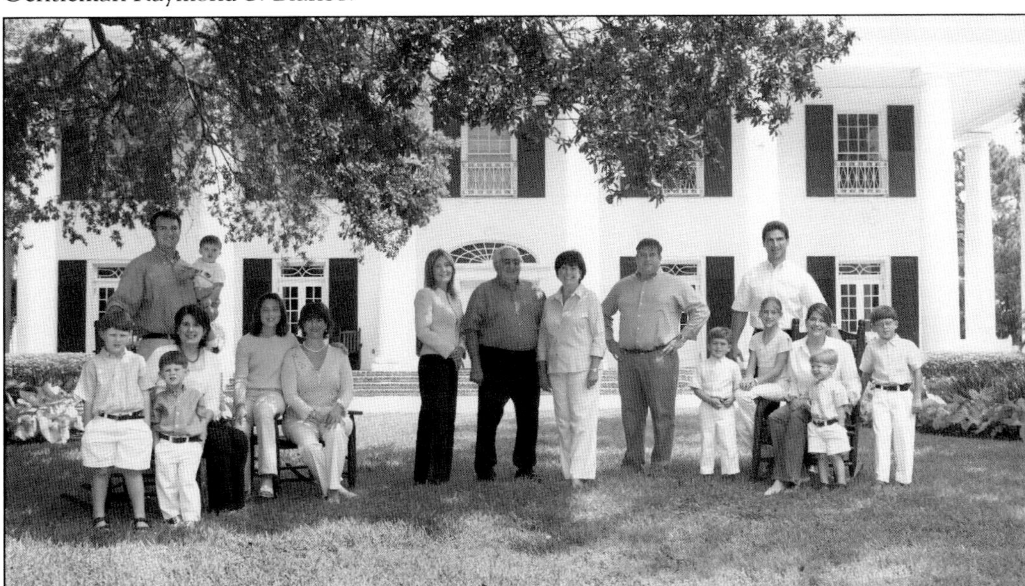

Pictured is the family of former Gov. Kathleen Babineaux Blanco in front of the governor's mansion in Baton Rouge. From left to right are Benedict Eble, Michael Eble (holding Miles Eble), Eli Eble, Pilar Blanco Eble (seated), Savannah Blanco Trumps (seated), Karmen Blanco (seated), Nicole Blanco, First Gentleman Raymond S. Blanco, Governor Blanco, Raymond Blanco Jr., Zachary Boulet, David W. Boulet (standing at rear), Kathleen Boulet (seated), Monique Blanco Boulet (seated), Samuel Boulet, and David Boulet.

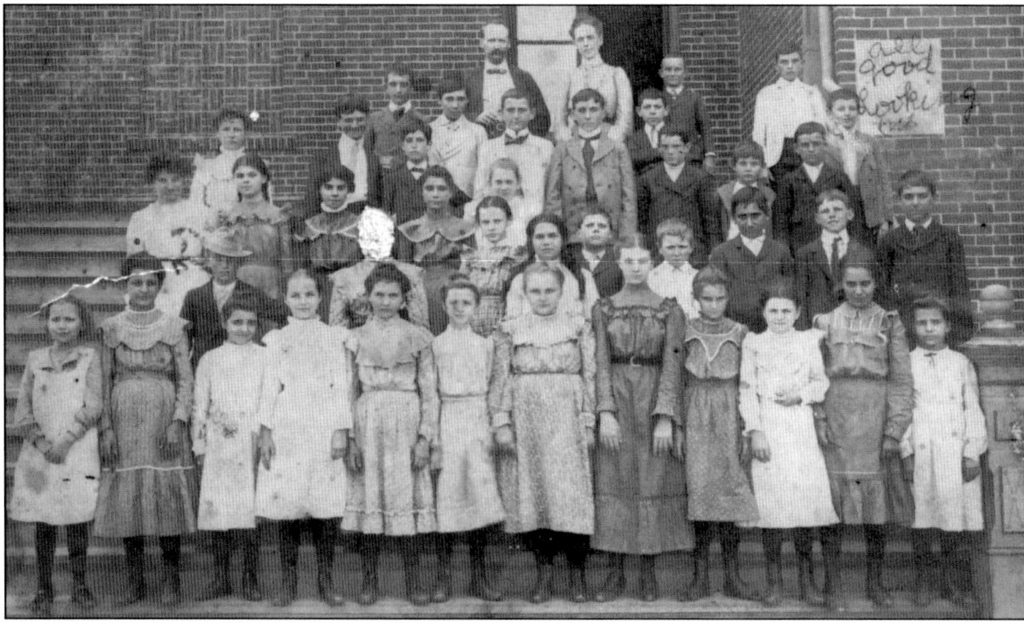

Pictured in the late 1800s are Mt. Carmel students, including Louise Darby and Camille Darby Laperouse. In 1888, the Catholic Sisters of Mercy opened two schools in Jeanerette, which were later combined into St. Joseph's Academy. In 1918, Mother Katharine Drexel, who was canonized in 2000, created St. Edward Catholic School for African American children. Other private schools in New Iberia include Epiphany Day School, which opened in the 1960s; Highland Baptist Christian School, incorporated in 1996; and Assembly Christian School.

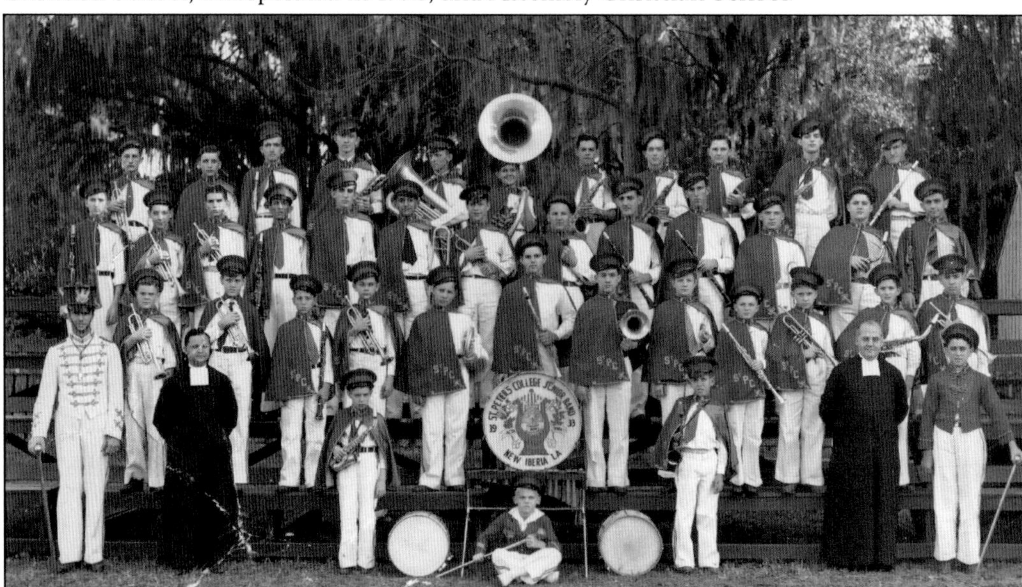

In 1918, Msgr. J.M. Langlois founded St. Peter's College, which was operated by the Christian Brothers and later renamed Catholic High School. In 1939, the school had a band that allowed adults to perform with the students. Hermann Hauser, then age 43, is pictured as the fifth person from the left in the back row. George Rader (third from the left in the back row) later became a professor at Southwestern Louisiana Institute (later USL and now University of Louisiana at Lafayette).

Eight

Interesting Characters

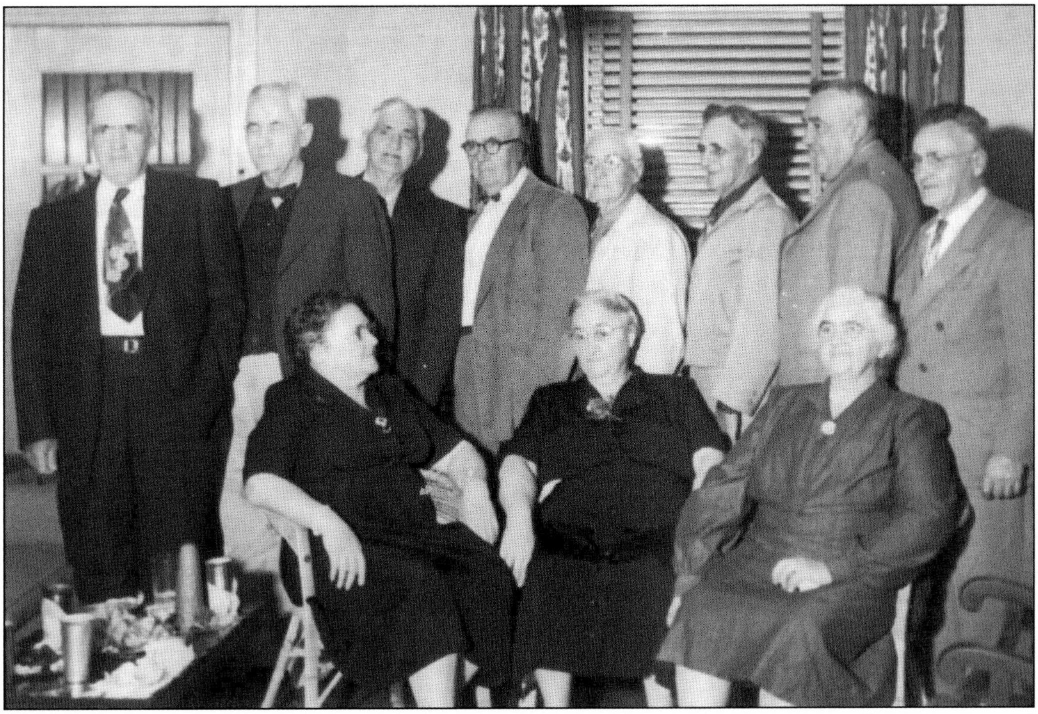

In the 1780s, Etienne de Vangine, who owned a plantation near present-day Loreauville, experimented with indigo; the crop, however, was not well suited to the climate. Pictured in 1955 are the children of Jean Edmond and Emma Patin Broussard of Loreauville, who married on March 1, 1880, and developed a large cattle and farming operation. From left to right, they are (first row) Henrietta, Felicia, and Constance; (second row) Rhule, Jean Edmond Jr., Numa, Antoine Preval, George Alfred, Gabriel George, Paul O., and Raoul. (Courtesy of Wanda Broussard Barras.)

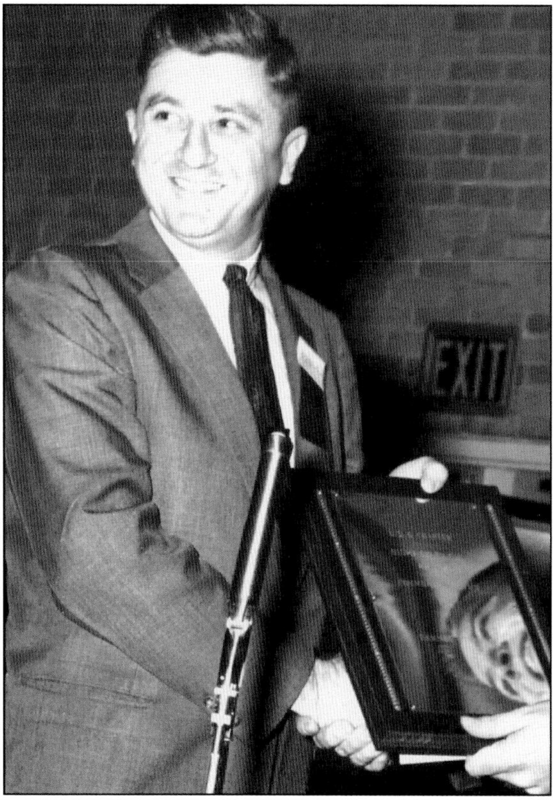

Bob Angers Jr. is pictured on January 20, 1961, accepting the 1960 Community Service Plaque awarded by Sigma Delta Chi at the Louisiana Press Association convention. Angers, one of the most honored journalists in the state, received more than 150 awards during a distinguished career. Angers was president of the Louisiana Press Association, nominated for the Pulitzer Prize in journalism, founder of *Acadiana Profile* magazine, and an avid supporter of CODOFIL.

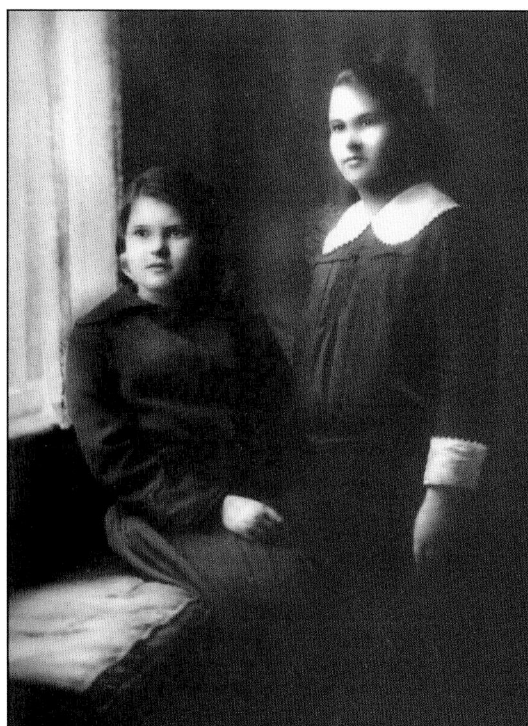

The Landrys are the third largest family in Iberia Parish and can trace their ancestry to Acadian refugees who came during the later half of the 18th century. The first Landry in the Attakapas was Firmin, a Maryland exile who settled on the upper Bayou Vermilion near Grande Pointe with his two grown sons, Joseph and Saturin. Later, he obtained a smaller tract on the Teche at Fausse Pointe near Loreauville. Pictured are Mabel Landry Lourd (left) and Clara Landry Roy, daughters of Gabriel Landry and Marie DeBlanc Landry.

Parish artists include Weeks Hall, Susan Carver, Carl Groh, Robert Gordy, Alphonse Landry, Kate Ferry, Brian Guidry, Freddie DeCourt, Pam Landry, Lou Blackwell, Jean Wattigny, Tory Dugas, Vernon Bacque, Anne Darrah, Cynthia Alleman, Melissa Bonin, Shawn Major, Kenny Greig, Scott Bailey, Lisa Osbourne, Margo Baker, Jerome Weber, Jennifer Kappel, Joyce McDaniel, Carla Hostetter, Gwen Voorhies, Darnelle Delcambre, Carrie Burke, Mary Schexnayder, Rosemary Bernard, Ella Fontenot, Chestee Harrington, Inez Rochelle, Debra Derouen, Tiny Guillotte, Joyce Crochet, Steve Seneca, Kathy Doumit, Johnny Hollbrook, Troy Leleux, April Mullen, Tricia Grubbs, Brooke Wilke, Minos DeRouen, Jacquie Delcambre, I.A. and Carroll Martin, Alphonse Hitter, Mickey Delcambre, Susan Clark, and Ernie Fournet. At their eighth grade graduation are, from left to right, Janie Bayard, Lindrea Sealy, and Mary Perrin, (granddaughter of Leonise Laperouse) who has artwork in the National Museum for Women in the Arts in Washington, DC. Pictured below in 1994, from left to right, are Kathy Baus, Opal Broussard, Melissa Bonin, and Paul Schexnayder at the Left Bank Gallery.

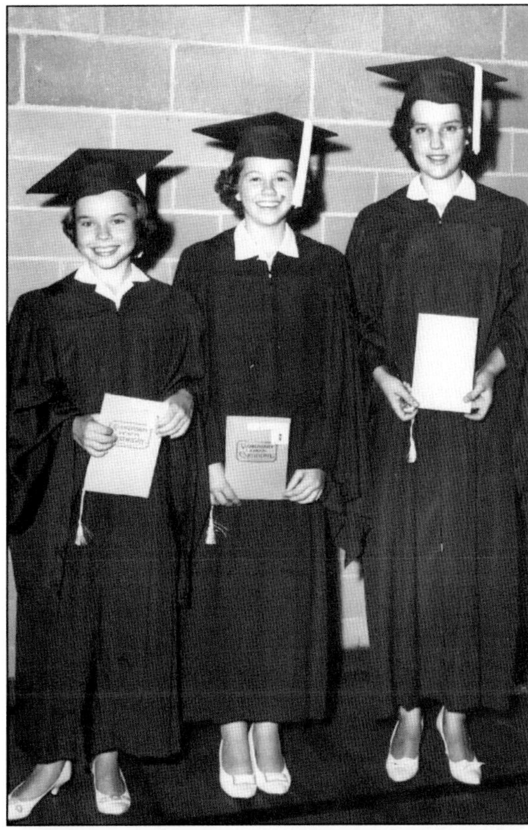

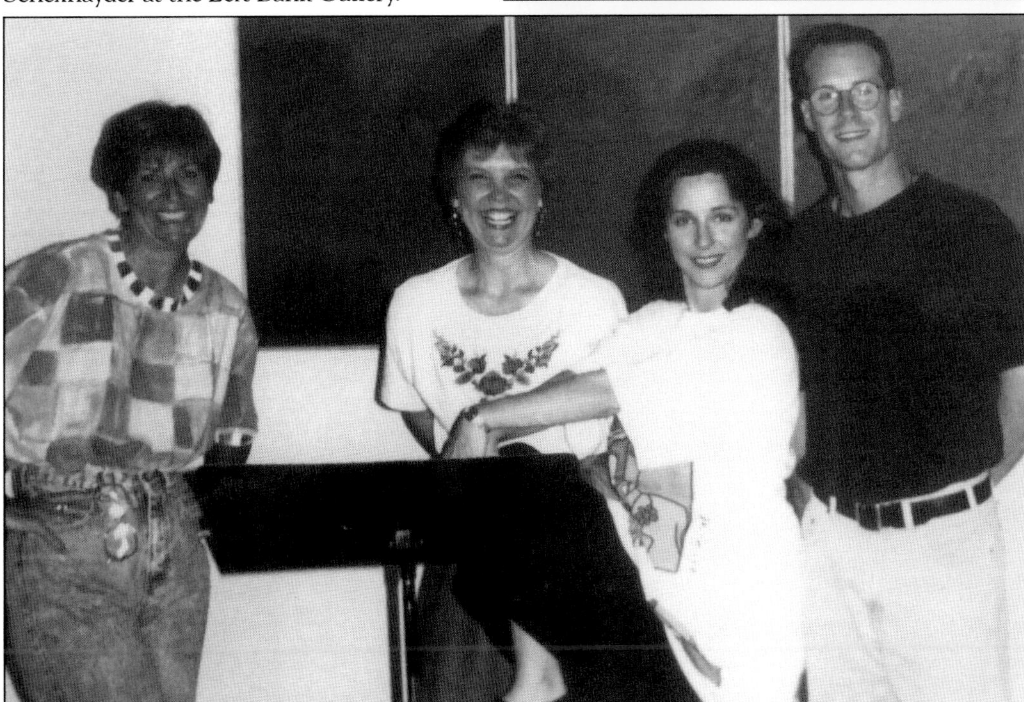

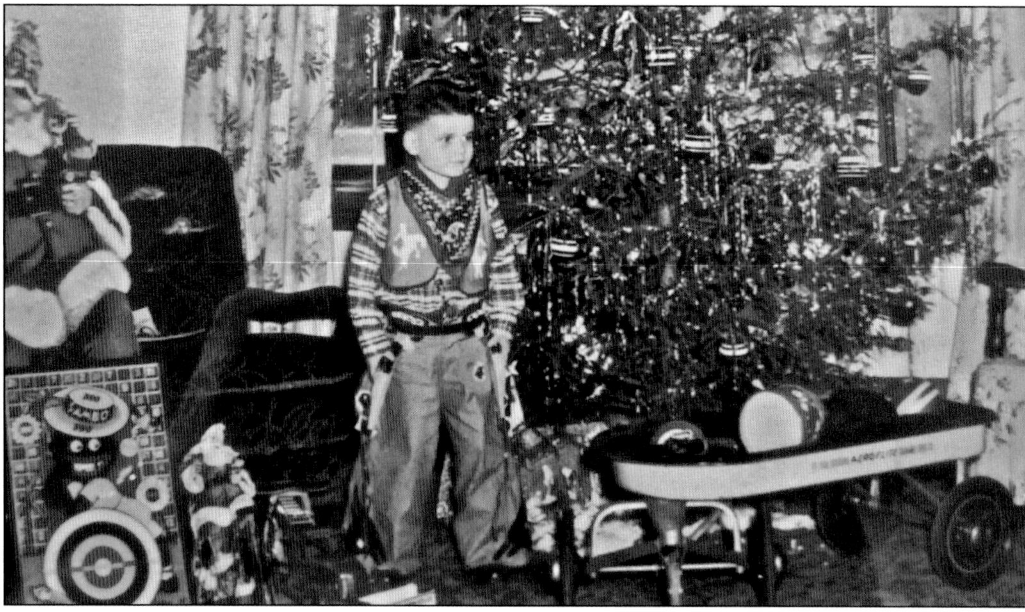

George Rodrigue is a giant of the arts. His paintings have been widely exhibited during a distinguished career as Louisiana's foremost contemporary painter. In 2008, Governor Jindal named him Artist Laureate of Louisiana. Rodrigue is pictured above on Christmas morning in his family's home in New Iberia in 1949. The photograph captures a slice of Americana, through the Radio Flyer wagon and Coca-Cola Santa Claus. Pictured in 1962 (below), Rodrigue stands with his parents, George Rodrigue Sr. and Marie Courrege Rodrigue, in front of the house that was built in 1946 by the senior Rodrigue, a bricklayer. After her husband's death in 1967, Marie continued to live in the house until 1997. She often returned to the home until her death in 2008 at the age of 103. Unable to part with this piece of family history, Rodrigue still owns the home, along with its wishing well, both built by his father. In the 1950s, the Rodrigues converted the attic into a studio for their son, the aspiring artist. The small space remains today as it did when Rodrigue left for art school in 1962.

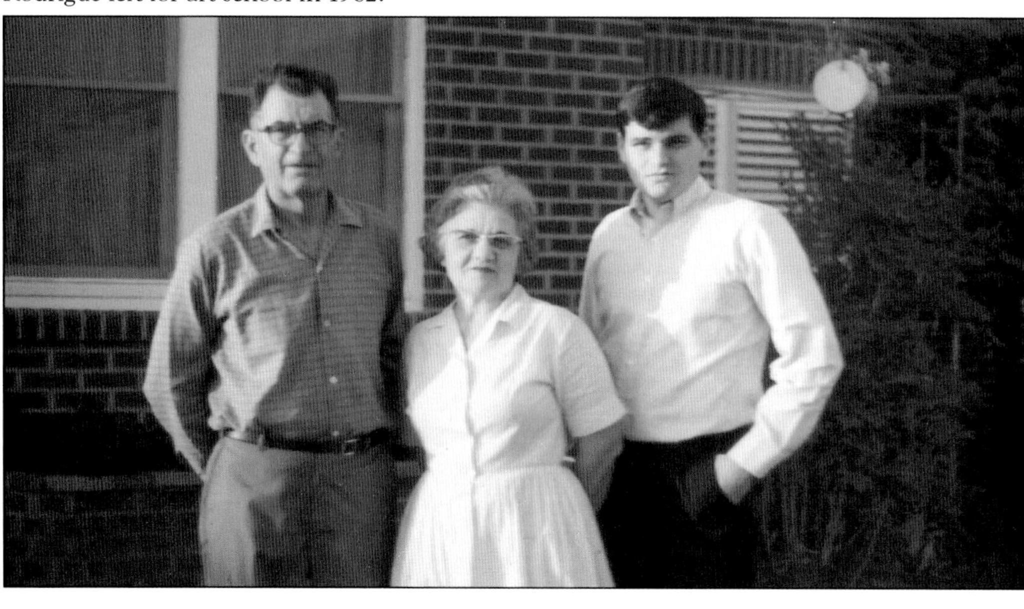

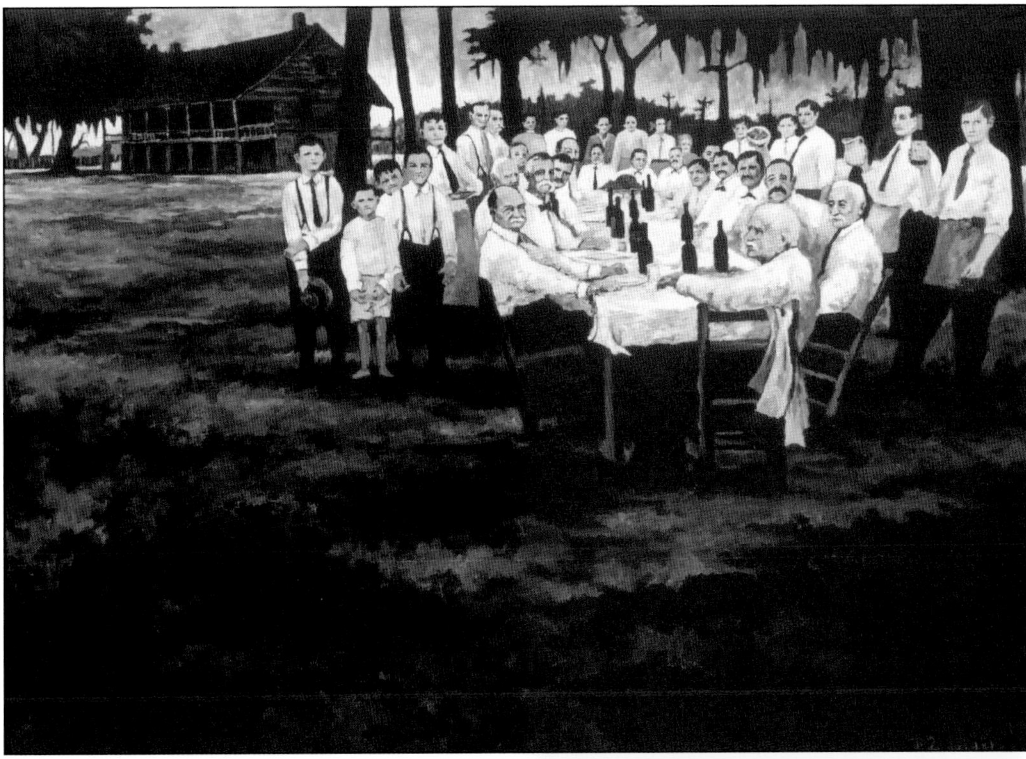

Shown is one of Rodrigue's early paintings, entitled *Aioli Dinner, 1971*, set at the historic Darby House Plantation. He designed the painting using combinations of photographs taken of the Ancient Society of Creole Gourmets, a group that met monthly on the lawn of a different plantation around New Iberia between 1890 and 1920. Traditionally, only men sat at the table, each with their own bottle of wine. The women, seen standing in the back row, cooked the food, and the young men served dinner. One of the older men made the *aioli*, a garlic-mayonnaise sauce.

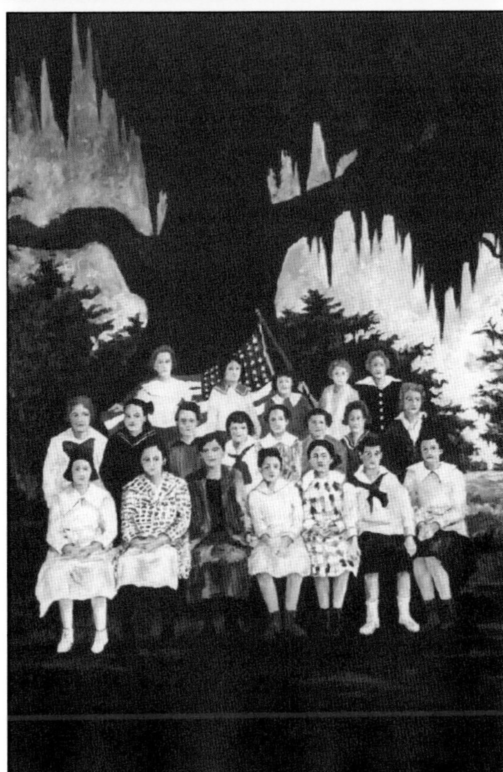

Shown is *The Class of Marie Courrege*, also by George Rodrigue. Rodrigue adapted this painting from the photograph of his mother's 1923 graduation from Mt. Carmel Academy and painted it as though the figures are cut out and pasted onto the landscape of south Louisiana. Rodrigue graphically interpreted the Cajun culture in hundreds of works, hoping to preserve his fading culture. In 1974, the painting won an Honorable Mention at *Le Salon* in Paris, the world's most prestigious art exhibition.

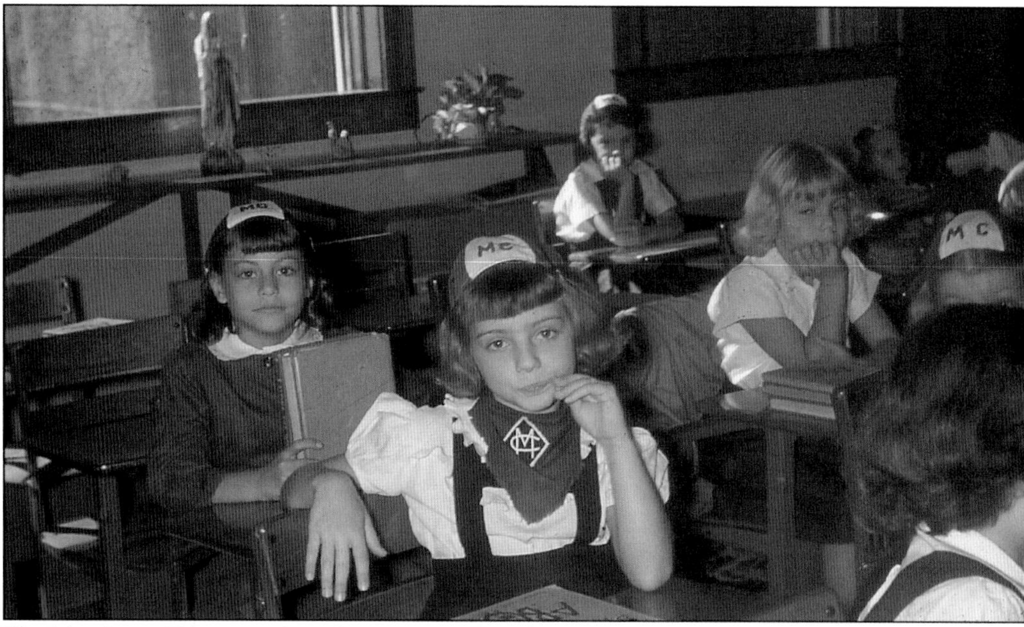

The Mandatory Education Act of 1916 required English in public schools and began Americanization. Children were punished if they spoke French on the school grounds. In 1955, the successful state-sponsored Acadian Bicentennial Celebration became the genesis for the French Renaissance in Louisiana. Pictured is Francine Schuler Garzotto (front left), owner of Poncio's Tuxedo Rentals in New Iberia, and other fourth grade students at Mt. Carmel Academy.

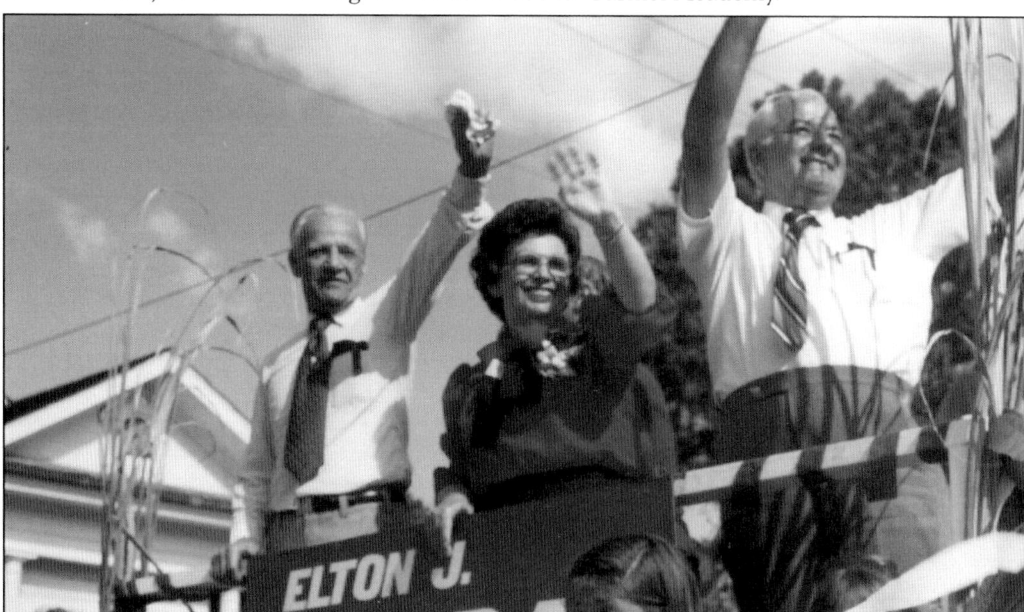

The anonymous *Breaux Manuscript*, the earliest existing local folklore commentary, noted unique systems of community support, including the *piocherie* (hoeing party) and the *couvrage* (shingling party). These activities became forerunners of modern-day festivals. In September 1983, Sugar Cane Festival parade participants were, from left to right, Iberia Parish tax assessor Elton Barras, Mazel Barras, and Clegg LaBauve.

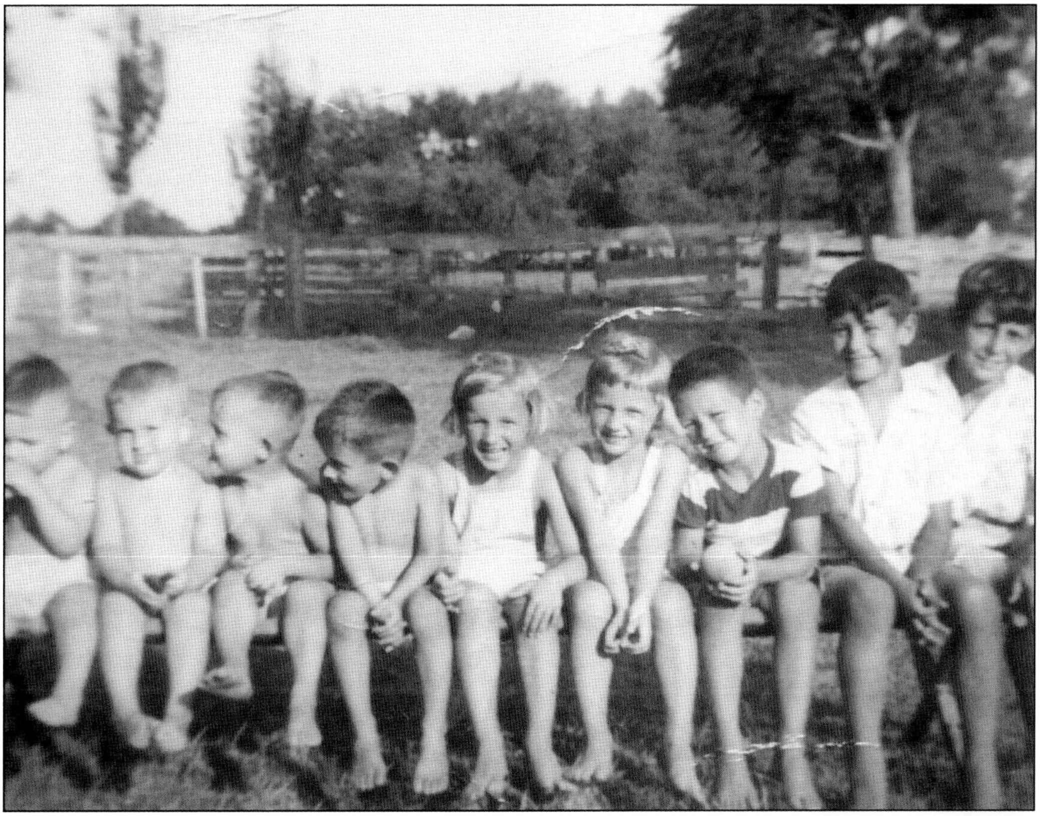

Locals have amusing *tit-noms* (nicknames) derived from a childhood event or physical characteristic, such as "Pretty Bagl," "Nu Nu," "Patate," "Bo," "T-Bud," "Moose," "Pinki," "Tu Tu," "Bootsi," "Choc," "Meosch," "Praline," "Tootsi," "Cho Cho," "Orange Dago," "Possum," "Mo-meat," "Lonk," "Foo Goo," "Butsy," "Nappy," "Su Su," "Coon," "Clabber," "Blackie," and "T-Roy." Pictured in the 1950s at Abrar and Mae Viator's house in Coteau are their grandchildren. From left to right, they are Lynn Romero, Rickey Viator, Wilson Viator Jr., Lester Viator, Catherine Alleman, Carolyn Judice, Daniel Viator, Ray Viator, and Calvin Viator.

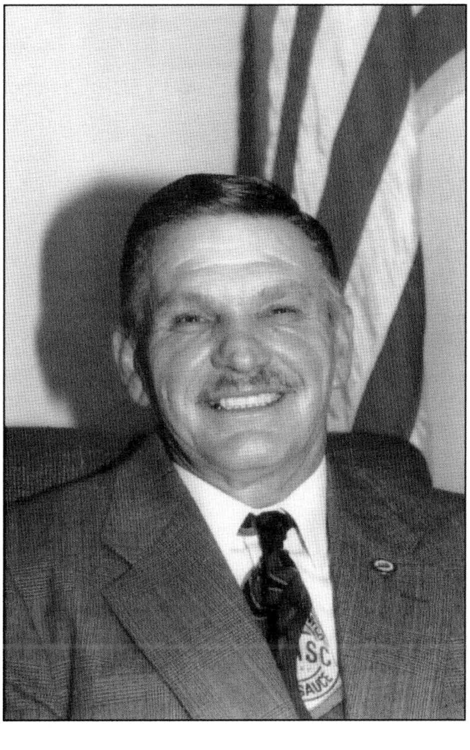

In 1990, the *Daily Iberian* selected Rep. Errol "Romo" Romero as one of the most influential individuals in Iberia Parish. In 1979, Romero was sheriff of Iberia. He was elected to the House of Representatives, succeeding Elias "Bo" Ackal Jr., and in 2002 was named a Living Legend by the Acadian Museum of Erath. In 2011, Romero was elected parish president.

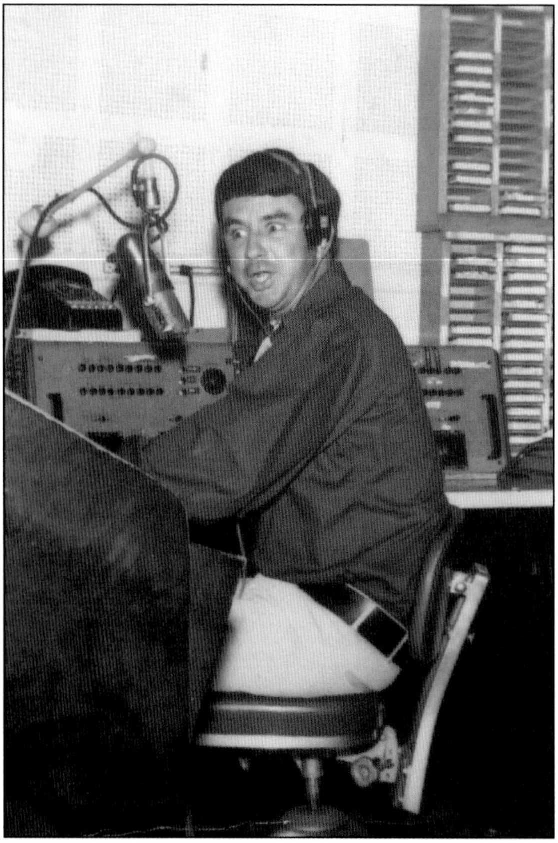

From 1960 to 1962, while a student at the University of Southwestern Louisiana, Alton "Skip" Broussard (left) was a popular disc jockey at radio station KANE in New Iberia. Don Bonin (below), the station manager, hired him. Later, while working as a disc jockey at WTIX radio in New Orleans, Broussard's on-air personality was "full-bleed" Cajun, calling himself "Skip Broussard, the Ragin' Cajun." Unfamiliar with trademark law, Broussard was stunned when he later discovered that in 1974 his alma mater had picked up on the then-popular moniker and had changed its nickname from the Bulldogs to the Ragin' Cajuns. "I'm the only DJ with a football team named after him," Broussard quipped. By the 1970s, the athletic department, the sports information director Bob Henderson, and the student body picked up on the then-popular name and the university officially changed it in 1974.

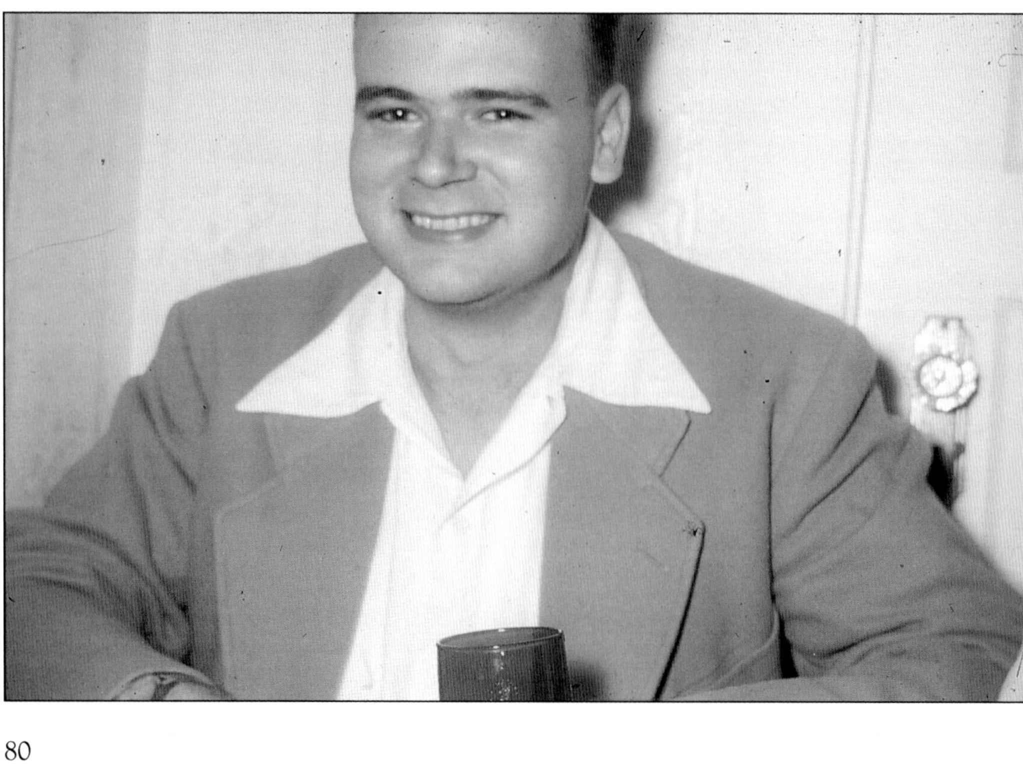

These majorettes were under the direction of Joffre Murrell, band director at New Iberia High School. From left to right are Marcelle Gremillion, Lynette Nicholson, and Dorothy Crowson. In 2008, Murrell's son Joshua "Bubba" Murrell won a Grammy award for co-producing the album *Live Worldwide: with Terrance Simien and the Zydeco Experience*, in the Best Zydeco or Cajun Album category.

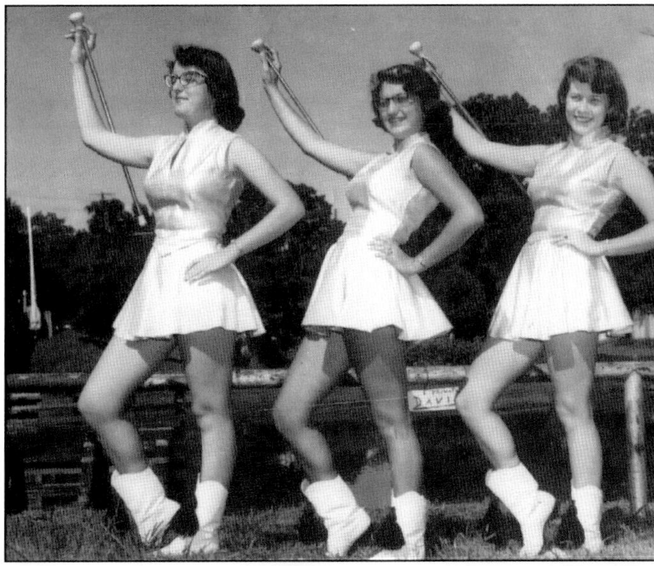

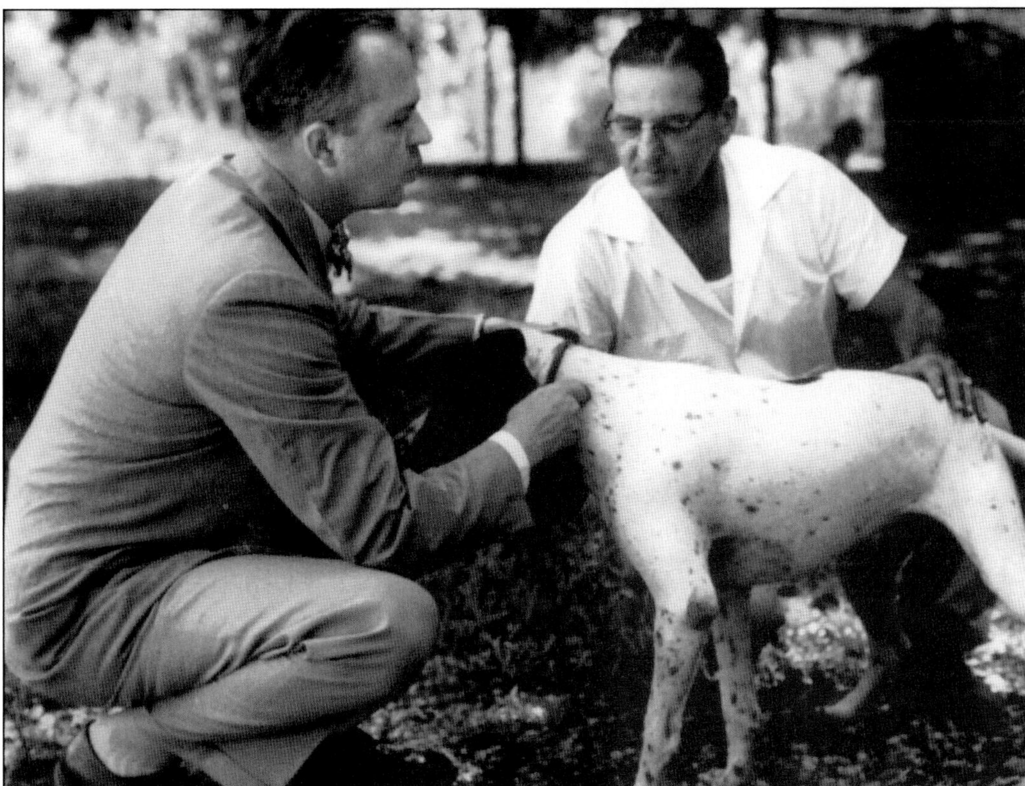

In 1891, historian William Henry Perrin visited Avery Island and wrote, "It is composed of hills, valleys, ravines, ponds, woodlands, open fields, and pastures, the whole surrounded on all sides by sea marsh, which, in the distance, has the appearance of dry, level prairie." In 1952, Walter McIlhenny (left), president of McIlhenny Company, is shown admiring one of his champion bird dogs, while Sylvester "Sylvest" Romero, company maintenance foreman, looks on. (Courtesy of Juanita Romero.)

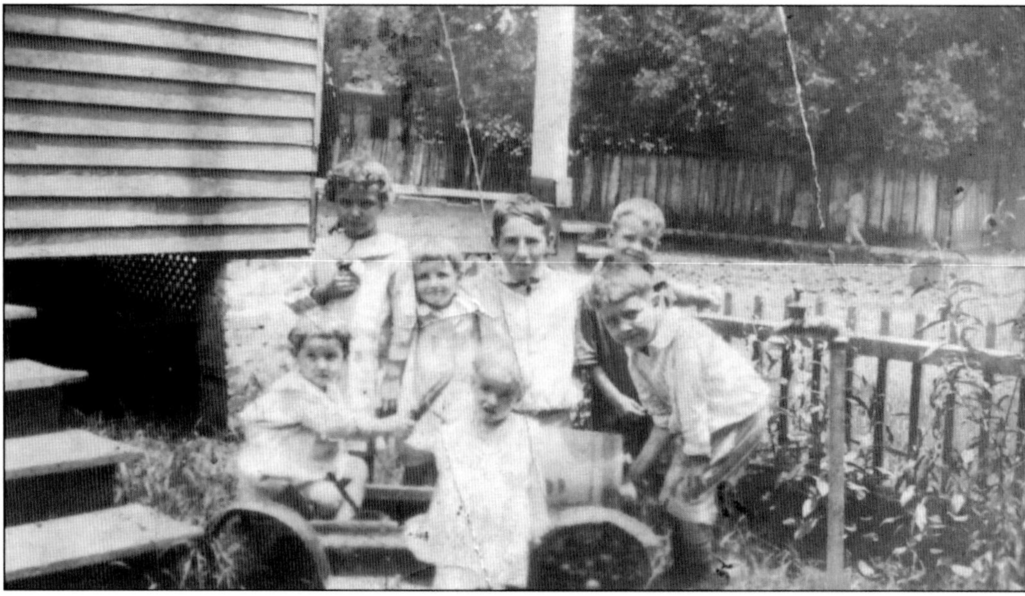

In 1891, William Henry Perrin noted, "New Iberia was laid out in 1835, and the original survey made under the supervision of Mr. Frederick H. Duperier, the father of Dr. Alfred Duperier, one of the best known citizens of the town." In 1924, young New Iberians are pictured enjoying their new motorcar on Vine Street. The driver is Willa Mae Nicholson, and Lloyd Nicholson Sr. is shown "cranking" the car.

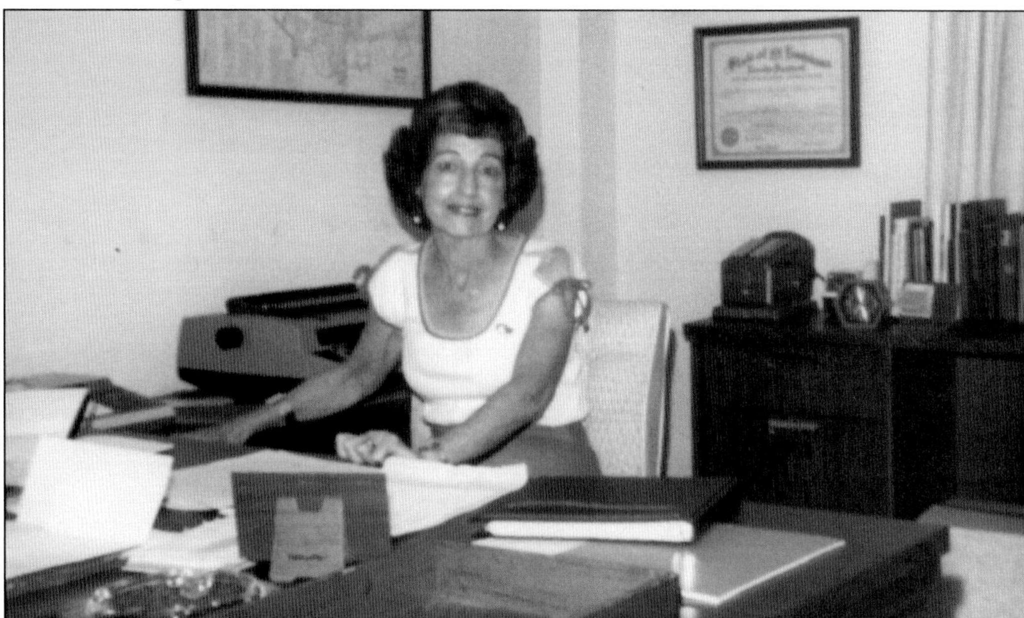

In the 19th century, New Iberia lawyers included Joseph Breaux, Robert Perry, Frederick Gates, and Walter Burke. Early doctors were Doctor Solenge (a native of France), Dr. Raphael Smith, Doctor Hacker, Dr. Jerome Mudd, Dr. Benoni Neal, Doctor Mestayer, and Doctor Blanchet. Pictured is New Iberia's treasurer and clerk Willa Mae Nicholson Ellis, who served for 33 years under mayors Armond "Kiki" Viator and J. Allen Daigre.

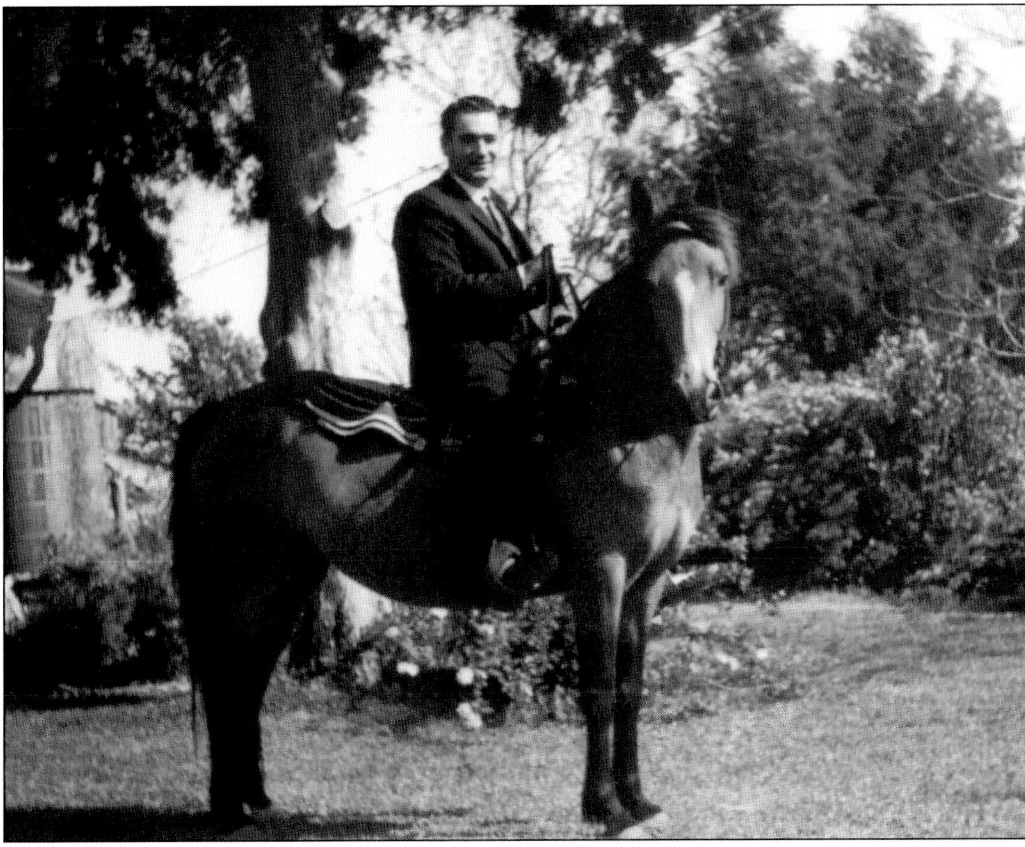

Pictured in 1958 is Elmo Rouly on his horse Betsy. Rouly, who received a Purple Heart for injuries during the Battle of the Bulge in World War II, began his public service as a member of the Iberia Parish School Board representing the Coteau area. During the administration of Sheriff J. "Nic" Derouen, from 1952 to 1956, Rouly served as a deputy. For ten years, he managed Peoples Cotton Gin of Lozes. His only child, Ross Rouly, presently operates a sugarcane farm on Norris Road.

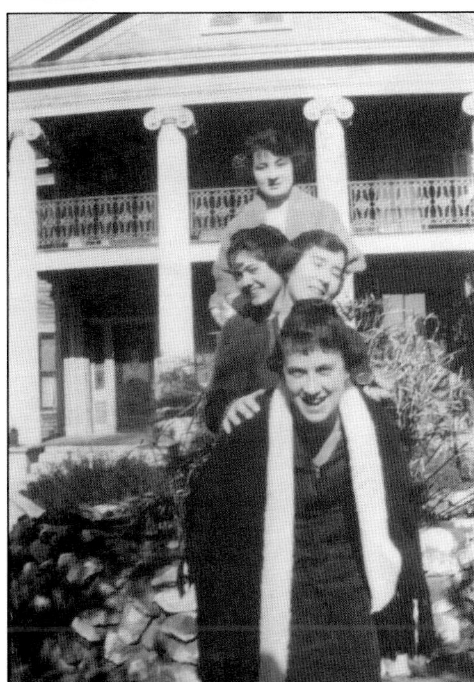

Pictured in 1930 are, from bottom to top, Eva Schexnayder, Georgine LeBourgeois, Amalita Bernard, and Adrienne Andre in front of the Moresi house on East Main Street in Jeanerette, located next to the Moresi Foundry. Eva taught at the Jeanerette and Berwick elementary schools for 47 years, and Georgine taught piano and was the organist at St. John Evangelist Church in Jeanerette.

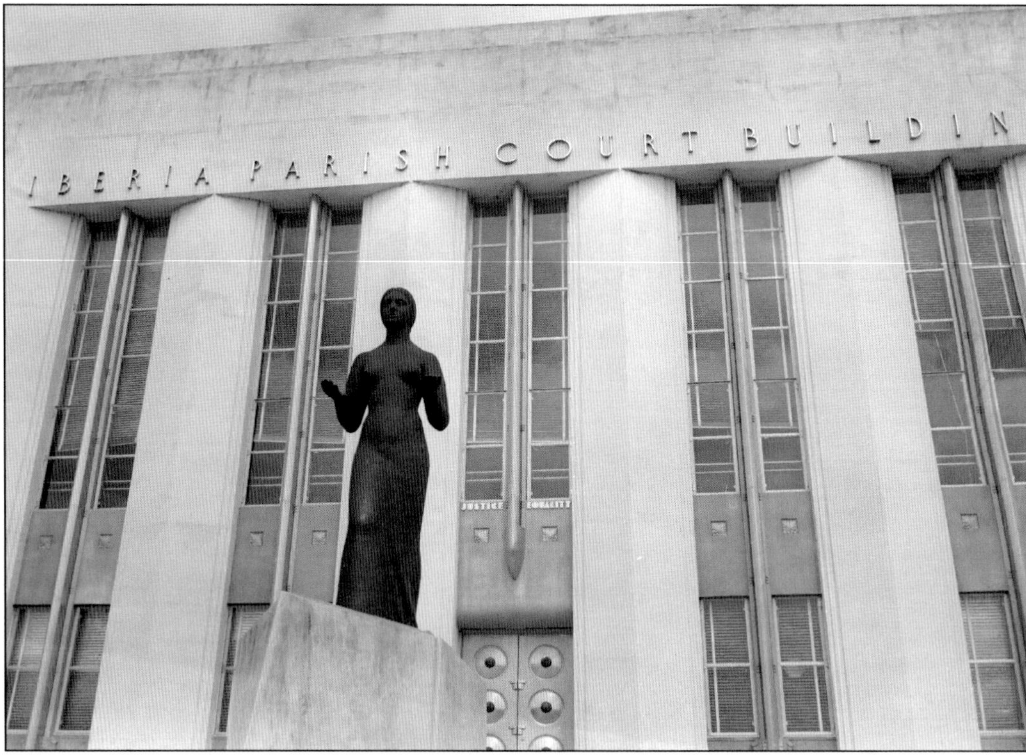

In 1939, Gravier and Haper built the Iberia Parish courthouse, which was designed by A. Hays Town in the distinctive Art Deco style. The courthouse is located on the grounds of the old Howe Institute, a school founded by the Union 6th District Baptist Association, an organization of African American Baptist churches in Iberia and St. Mary headed by Jonas Henderson. (Courtesy of Louisiana State Archives.)

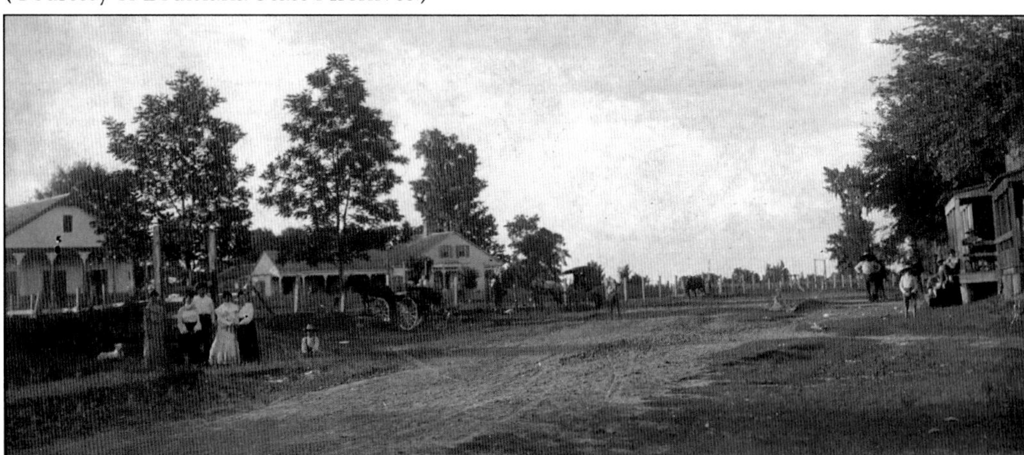

Around 1780, Joseph-François Derouen moved his family to the Attakapas and settled in the Petite Anse prairie south of present-day New Iberia. In the 1850s, bands of marauding cattle thieves roamed the countryside, thus *comités de vigilance* (vigilance committees) were organized by ranchers throughout Iberia Parish, including hamlets like Derouen, pictured here in the late 1800s. The Derouen family is the ninth largest in the parish. Most Derouens descend from French Canadian stock.

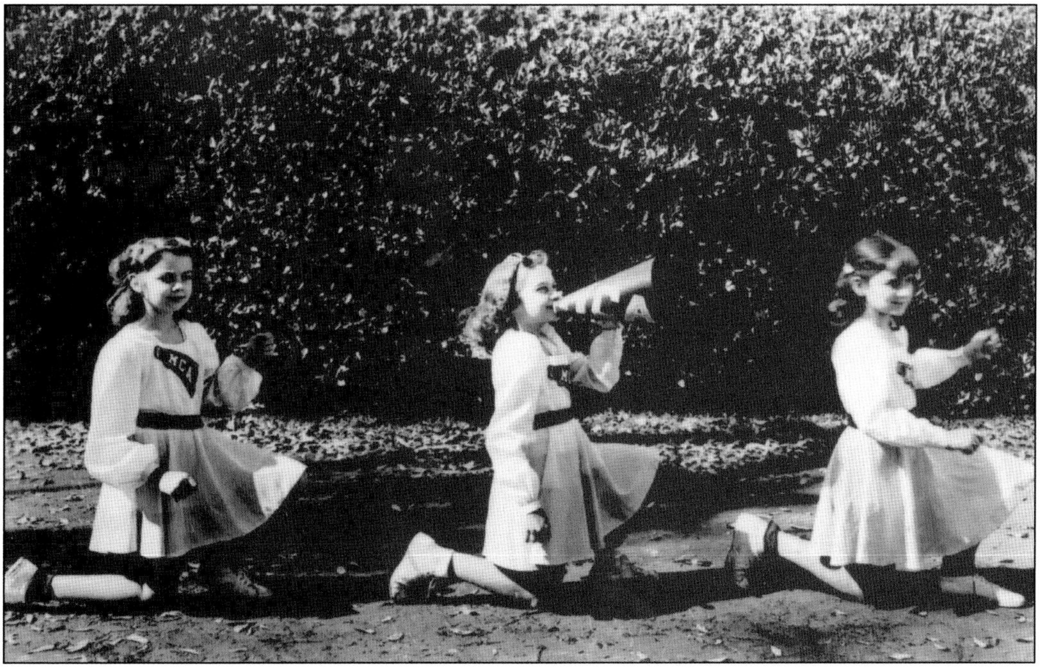

In the book *New Iberia*, edited by Glenn R. Conrad, an essay by John M. Weeks states, "Among the private schools which were established in the 1870s was Mount Carmel Convent on the east side of the Teche. This school has been splendidly supported and thousands of its graduates are among the housewives, mothers, and business women of New Iberia." In 1944, the Mt. Carmel Academy cheerleaders were, from left to right, Suzanne Delcambre Landry, Jennifer Walter Sonnier, and Clara Lourd O'Niel.

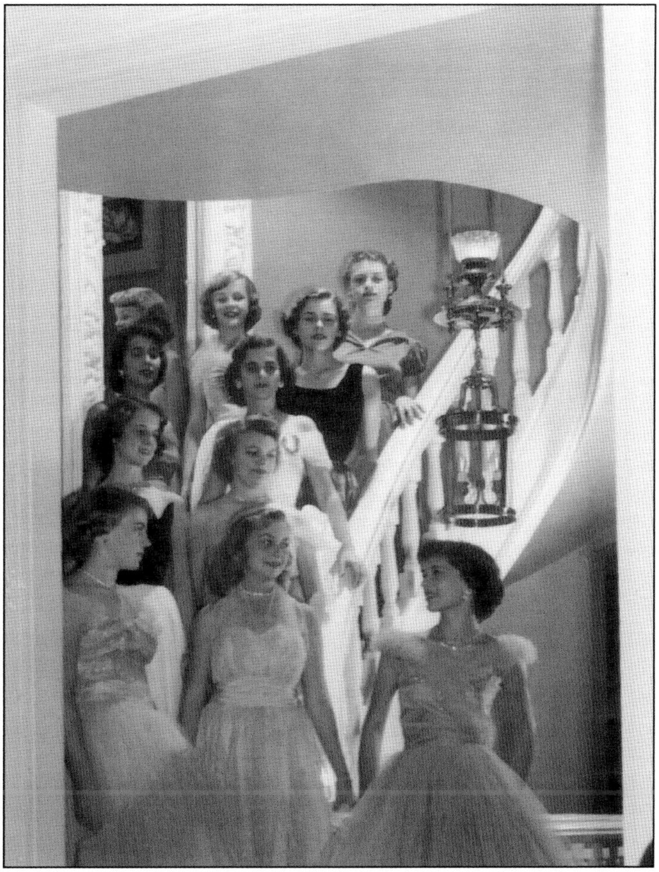

Members of the 1951 St. Peter's College Homecoming Court were photographed at the home of Yvonne Southwell. Pictured are Queen Joanna Mouhot and maids Jennifer Walter, Myrtis Mixon, Corinne Conrad, Jackie Hymel, Emma Jean Ackal, Clara Lourd, Rosemary Shipp, Sylvia Segura, and Barbara Ber.

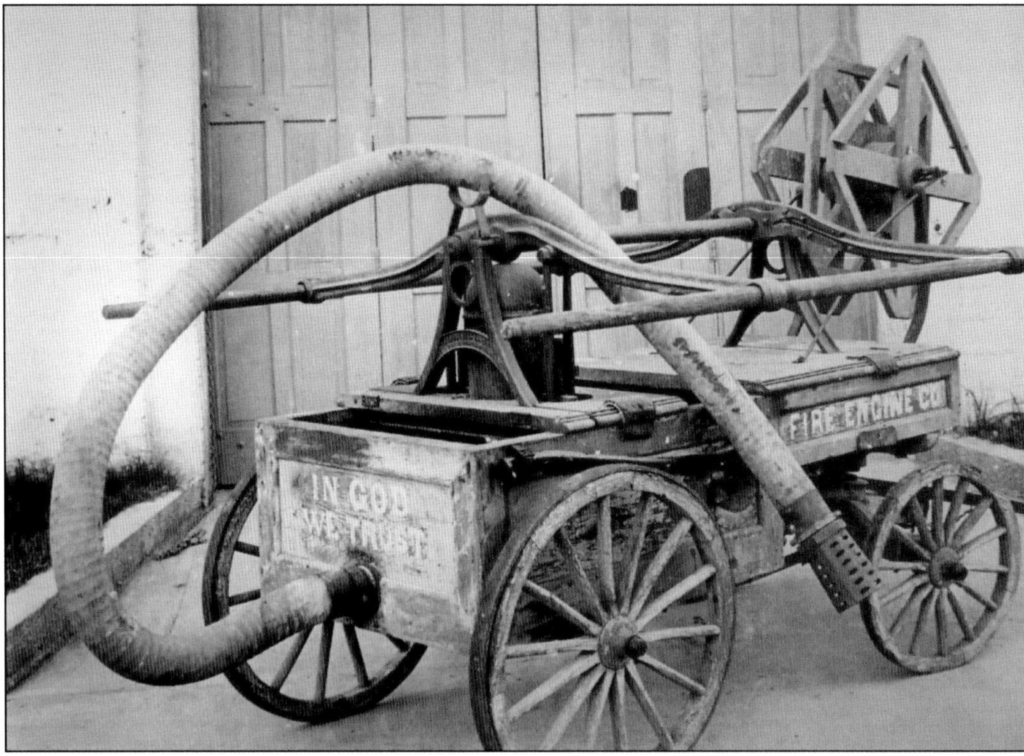

Pictured in the 1890s is New Iberia's first fire engine. On October 10, 1899, a terrible fire destroyed a large section of New Iberia's business district, including the New Iberia National Bank, Landry's saloon, LaSalle's saloon, Estorge's drugstore (where the fire began), Two Lions Hotel, Sol Adler's grocery, C.P. Moss's restaurant, Nathan Dreyfus's grocery, Decourt's barber shop, J.W. Eckart's jewelry store, State Bank of New Iberia, and James Lee's drugstore. The Segura Building was saved by the heroic efforts of a bucket brigade.

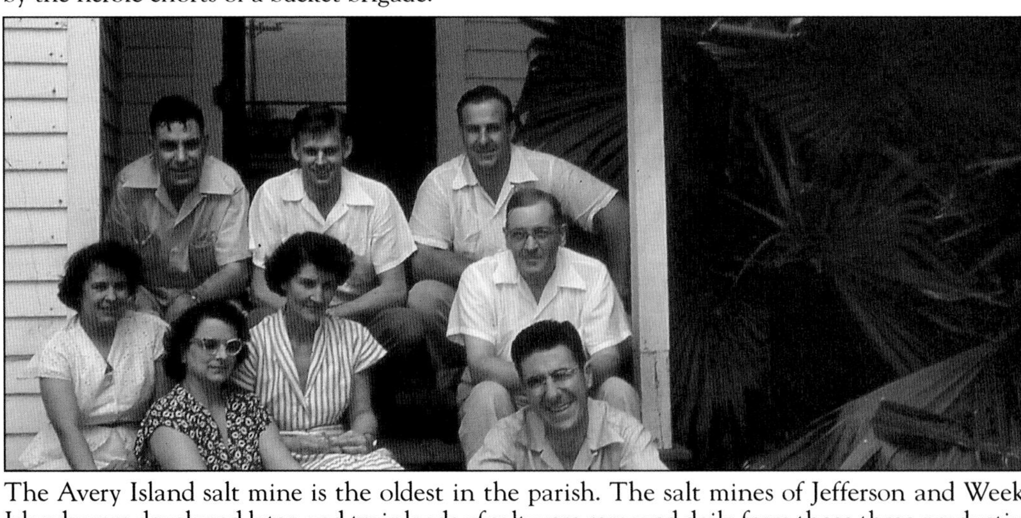

The Avery Island salt mine is the oldest in the parish. The salt mines of Jefferson and Weeks Islands were developed later, and trainloads of salt were removed daily from these three productive mines. International Salt's office staff at Avery Island are, from left to right, (first row) Raymond Reed; (second row) Claudella Delcambre, Mary Alice Dionne, Hazel Reed, and Erland Johnson; (third row) Clarence Reed, Warren Kiper, and Harold "Buster" Mosele.

The 19th-century Rip Van Winkle actor Joseph Jefferson gave name and fame to Jefferson Island and its salt dome, but the History Channel's series *Megadisasters* gave it notoriety in an episode on the 1980 disaster when Texaco inadvertently drilled into the salt mine beneath Lake Peigneur. The resulting massive whirlpool sucked barges, boats, and many acres of land into the collapsed mine. Pictured on a tour boat on Lake Peigneur prior to the disaster are, from left to right, Susan Musso, Beth and Tam Delcambre, and Katie Musso. (Courtesy of Mickey Delcambre.)

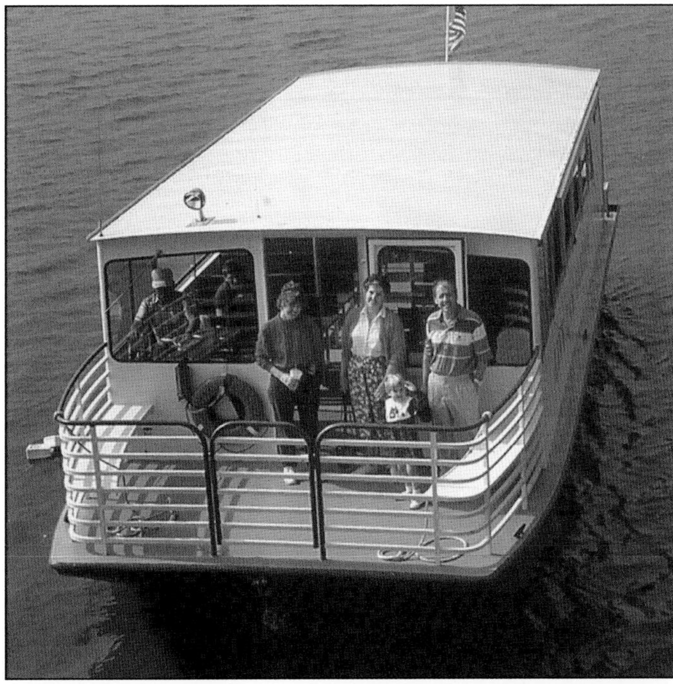

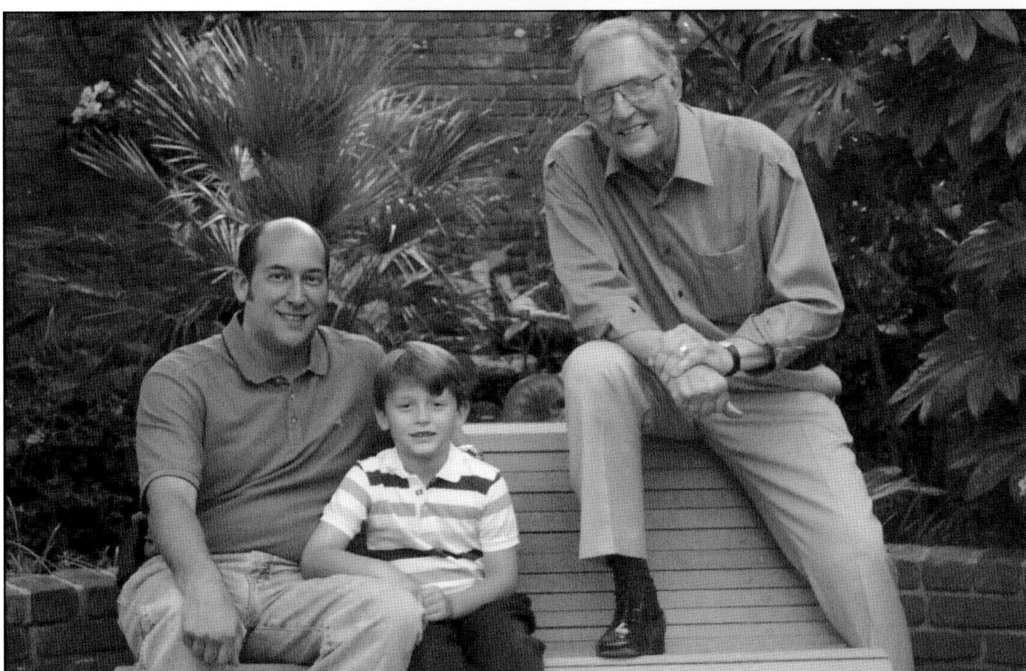

Pictured are the most recent descendants of Lt. Col. Francisco Bouligny, founder of New Iberia, from left to right: Joseph Daniel Bouligny Jr., seventh generation; Joseph Daniel Bouligny III, eighth generation; and Joseph Daniel Bouligny Sr., sixth generation. A beautiful plaza in the middle of downtown New Iberia is dedicated to Bouligny and the founding fathers, and includes a bust of Bouligny stands atop a bronze book engraved with the names of the founding fathers. (Courtesy of Camille Comeaux.)

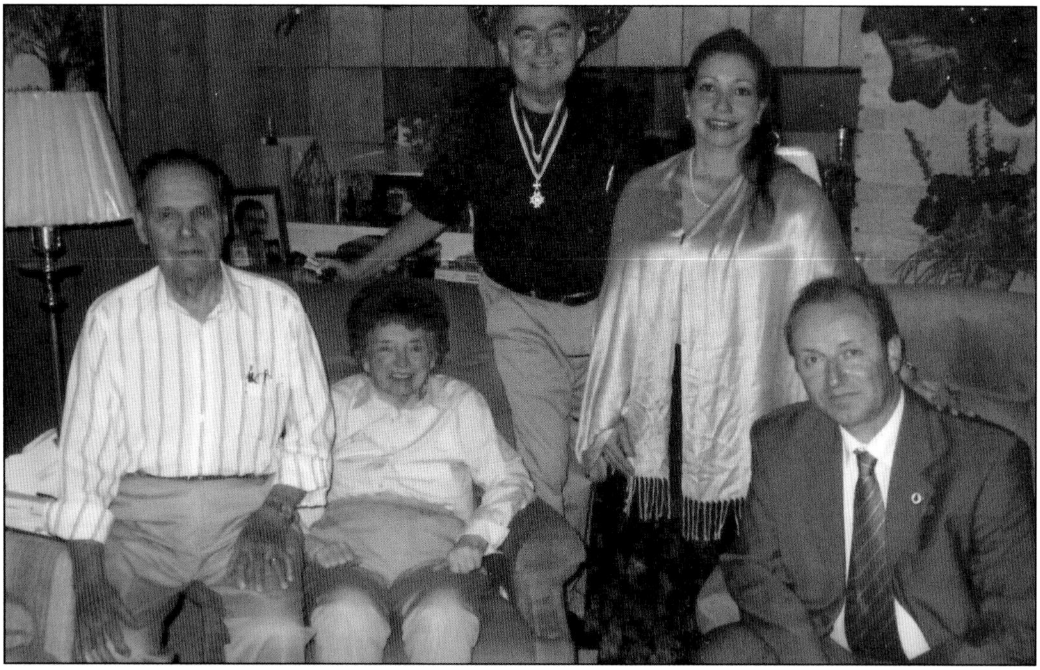

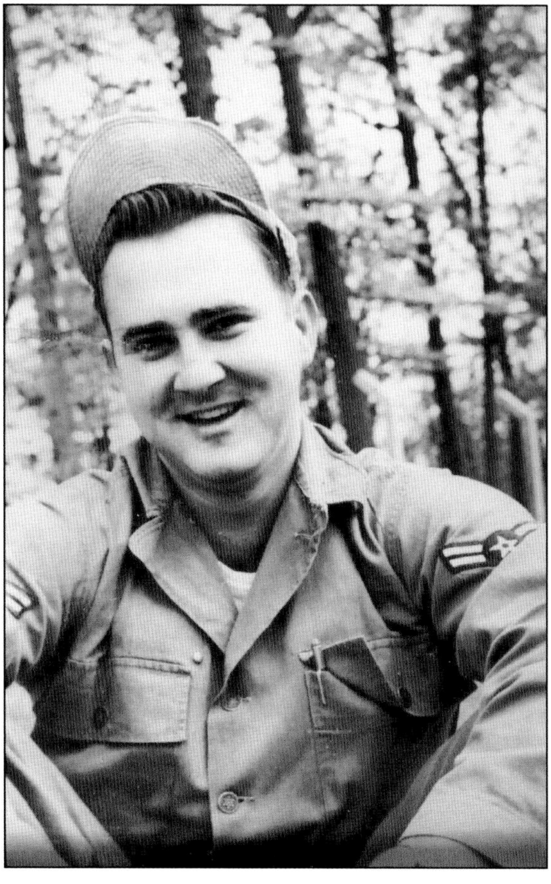

On September 8, 2007, a celebration took place commemorating the 250th birthday of the Marquis de LaFayette, hero of the American Revolution. Pictured from left to right are Leonard and Olga Breaux, hosts; Lynn Breaux, their son; Countess Irasema and Count Gilbert de Pusy LaFayette, a direct descendant of the Marquis de LaFayette. Lynn Breaux, National Society, Sons of the American Revolution's ambassador to France, accompanied the French couple to Iberia Parish. In early 2011, the countess and two of their children were killed in a tragic automobile accident in France. Count Alexandre, the eldest son, survived the crash.

In the early 1900s, local and widely grown crops were rice, sweet potatoes, sugarcane, and cotton. Initially, rice was harvested by hand with sickles. The tractor-drawn binder, and later the self-propelled combine, replaced this method. Pictured is Henry Segura, who, like many local boys, worked on a farm. In 1891, historian William Henry Perrin said of the parish, "its fields of blooming cotton and waving cane, all inspire the most pleasant emotions."

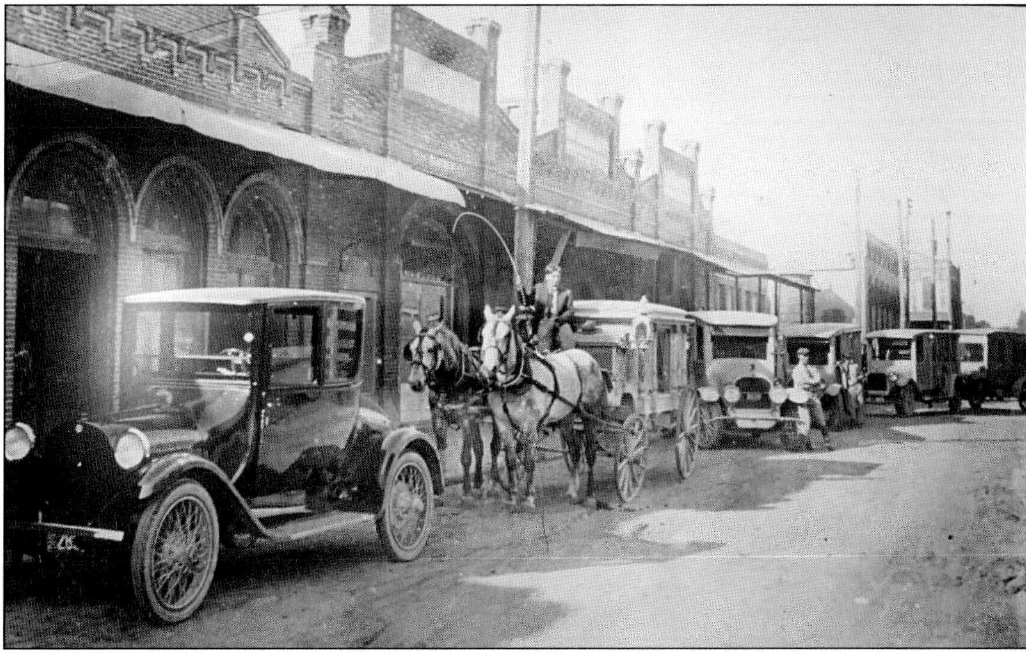

Phanat Xanamane grew up in New Iberia and went on to study at the University of Louisiana and Columbia University. He left Manhattan and came back to Louisiana to teach and help redevelop the troubled Hopkins Street neighborhood in New Iberia. He is an exponent of the necessity of innovation. This c. 1920s photograph shows a New Iberia funeral procession with a horse-drawn hearse on Hopkins Street.

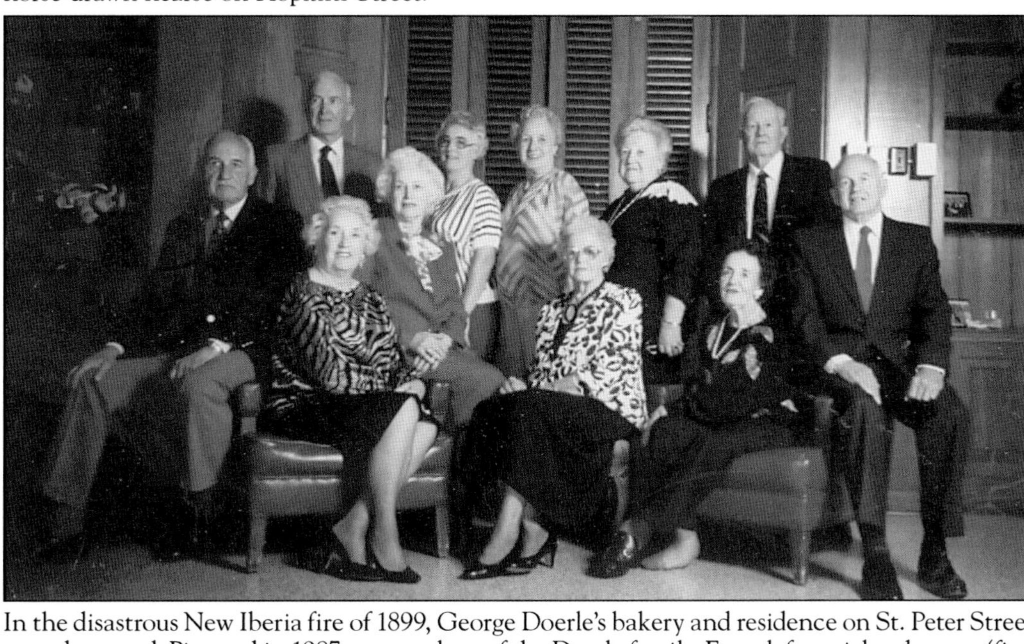

In the disastrous New Iberia fire of 1899, George Doerle's bakery and residence on St. Peter Street were destroyed. Pictured in 1987 are members of the Doerle family. From left to right, they are (first row) Robert "Bobby" Doerle, Mildred Doerle Miller, Rena Doerle Waller, Gertrude Doerle Walet, Bernice Doerle Roy, and Paul Doerle Sr.; (second row) Francis Doerle, Betty Doerle Comeaux, Thelma "Dickie" Doerle Theriot, Pauline Doerle Davant, and Harold Doerle.

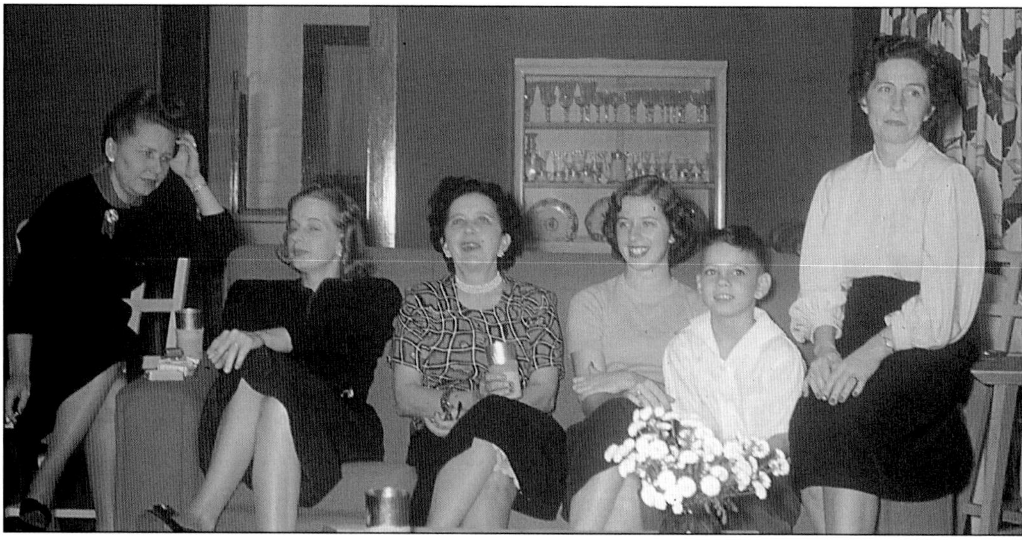

Louisiana's 1808 French Napoleonic Civil Code, which contains much Spanish law, imposed forced heirship, whereby each child inherits land equally. In other states, the law of primogeniture resulted in only the oldest son inheriting, thus encouraging out-of-staters to settle in Iberia Parish. Pictured from left to right are Miriam Emmer, Margaret Smith Denison, Adrienne Denison Derouen, Elynordel Eldridge, James Eldridge, and Ruth Denison Eldridge.

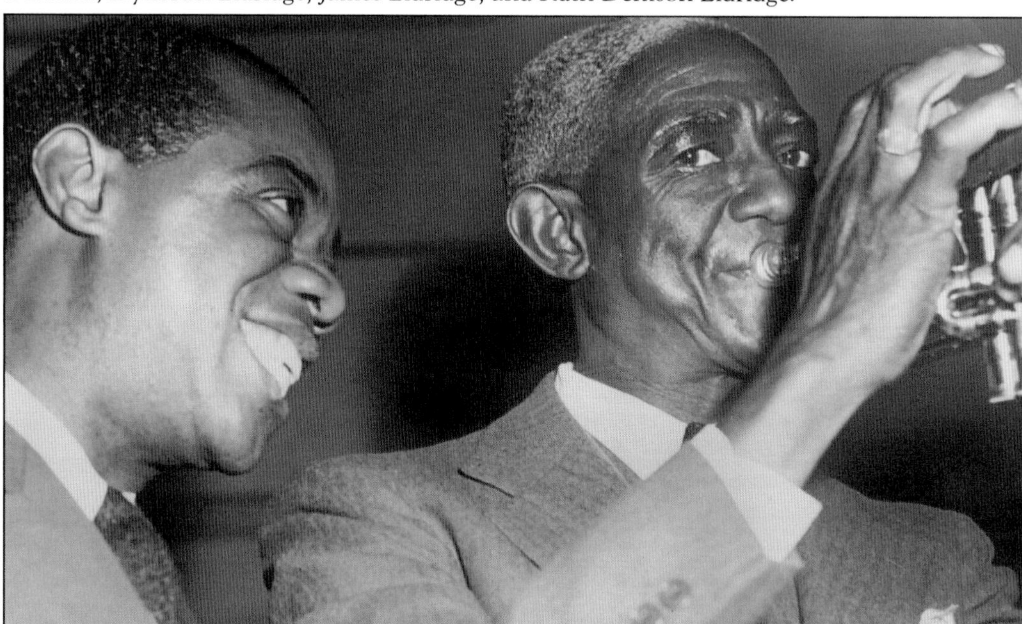

African slaves were brought to America with knowledge of tropical environments, and contributed substantially to the cultural *mélange* (mix). In 2000, Gov. Mike Foster appointed Terry Landry of New Iberia superintendent of the Louisiana State Police. In 2011, Landry was elected Iberia Parish state representative, the first African American to hold both posts. William "Bunk" Johnson (right), a prominent New Orleans jazz trumpeter who moved to New Iberia in 1915, is pictured in 1943 with Louis Armstrong in San Francisco. (Courtesy of New Orleans Jazz Club Collection of the Louisiana State Museum.)

Nine

Social and Cultural Life

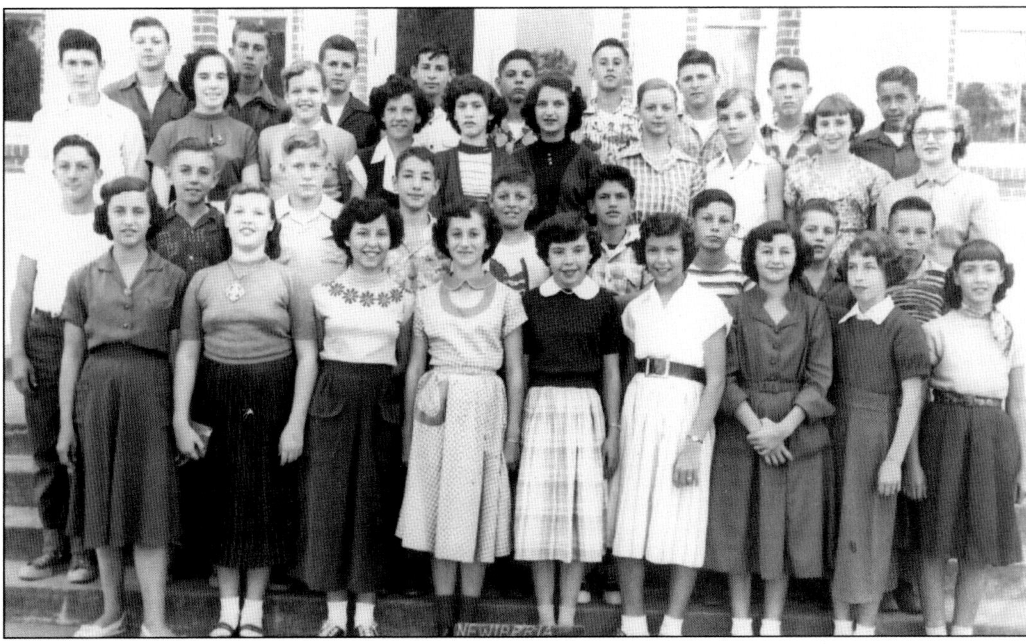

These 1953 New Iberia High School students are, from left to right, (first row) Joyce Mae Doucet, Lynnette Taylor, Gloria Miguez, Beverly Bonin, Barbara Dautreil, Janell Dooley, Joyce Hulin, Rose Mary Boudreaux, and Mary Jane Viator; (second row) Robert Arceneaux, C.J. Babineaux, Tommy Sparks, Ronald Cutrera, Glenn Derouen, George Dugas, Gerald ?, and Pierre Terrebonne; (third row) Willis Dore, Pat Krammer, Peggy Harte, Rose Lancon, Barbara Romero, Lynette Nicholson, Romona Dupuy, Catherine Anderson, Janell Landry, and Elizabeth Hickey (history teacher); (fourth row) Joe Girard, Hilton Richard, Kermit Landry, Calvin Segura, Richard Boudreaux, Ronnie Ransonnet, Alwin Romero, Leo Louviere, and Jimmy Langlinais.

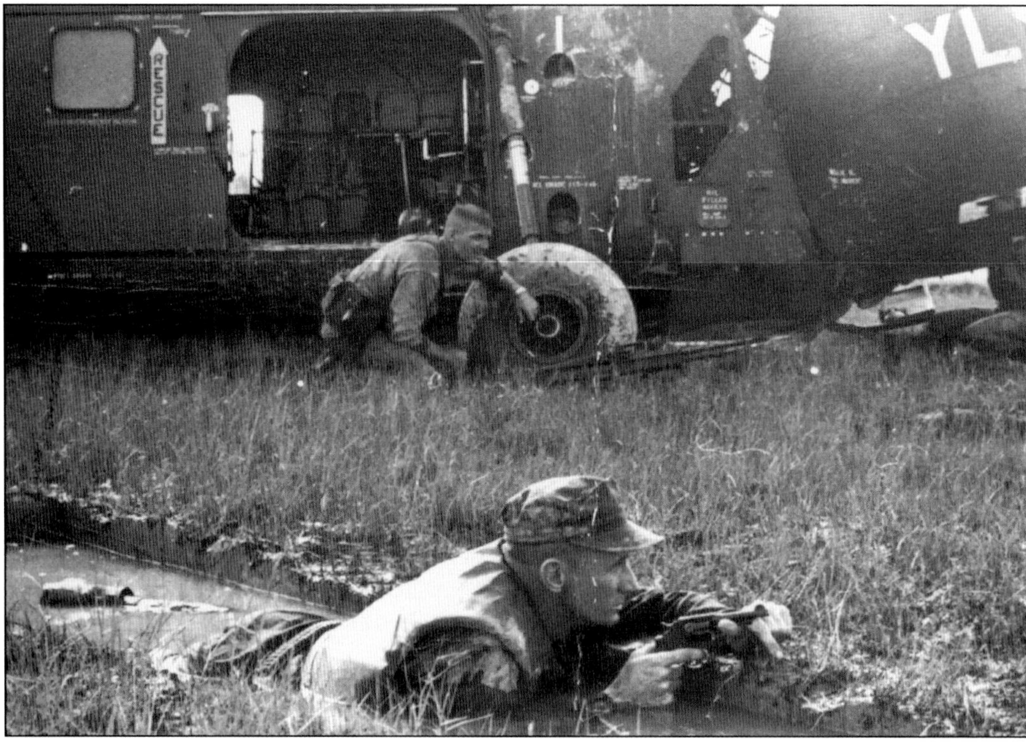

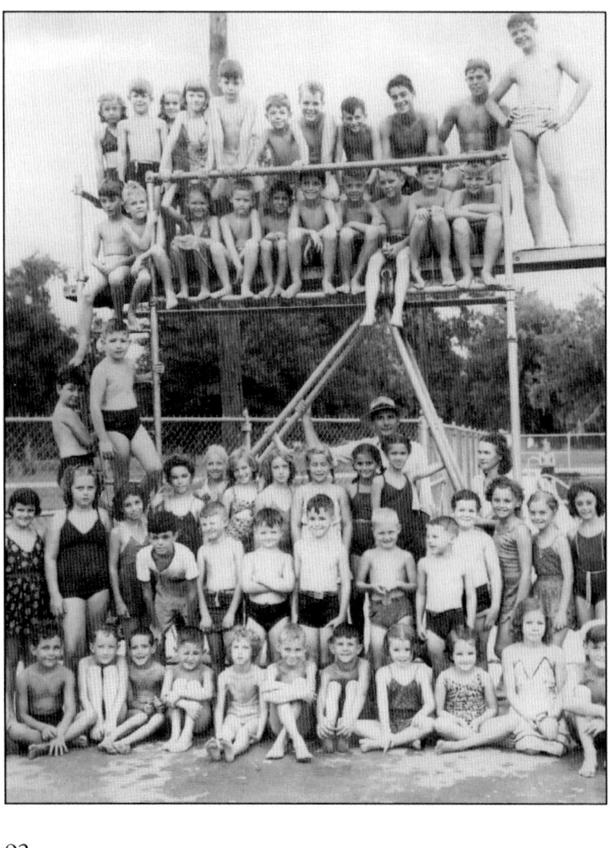

Pictured (front) in December 1965 during the Vietnam War is Iberian Lt. Col. Darcy Clasen, who, along with Sgt. Jim Fleming, his crew chief, was waiting for a maintenance team to repair their downed aircraft when a sniper's bullet struck Clasen's helmet. Fortunately, he survived unscathed and later flew the repaired aircraft back to the base camp.

Fred Broussard, pool manager (center, with hat), organized swimming lessons at the City Park Pool. Myrtle "Billie" Gates Hitter is pictured to the right of Broussard. Also in the photograph, in no particular order, are Amorette Ortie, Barbara Viator, C.L. Viator, Dickie McMahon, Owen McMahon, Puffer Lourd, Sylvia Segura, Jennifer Walters, Marie Bassin, Clara Lourd, Sally Helm, Leon Roy, Betty Hitter, Corrine Conrad, Judy Conrad, and Elise Davis.

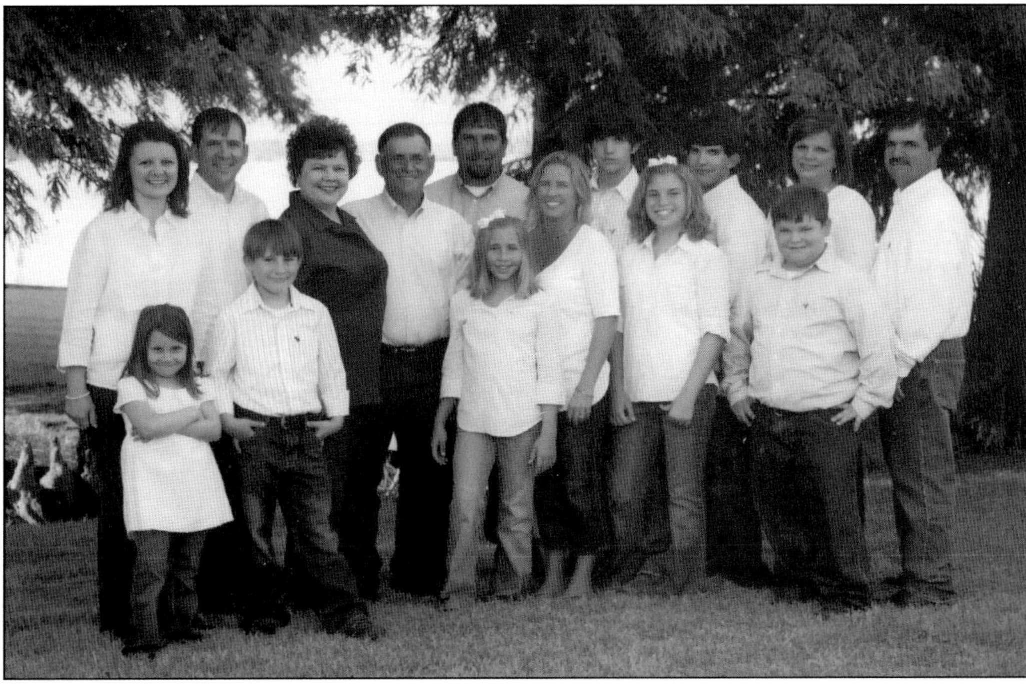

Dr. Catherine Hebert Segura, former supervisor of Iberia Parish Schools, and her husband, Donald Segura, a sugarcane farmer in New Iberia, are pictured with their family. Two sons, Juan and Jaime, have continued farming, and another son, Jarrod, is an educator. Hebert is Louisiana's most common French surname and the fourth largest family in Iberia Parish. They descend from Acadians who arrived between the 1760s and 1780s. An important line of Heberts began with Jean-Baptiste Jr., who lived near St. Martinville in 1766 and later around Fausse Pointe along the Teche.

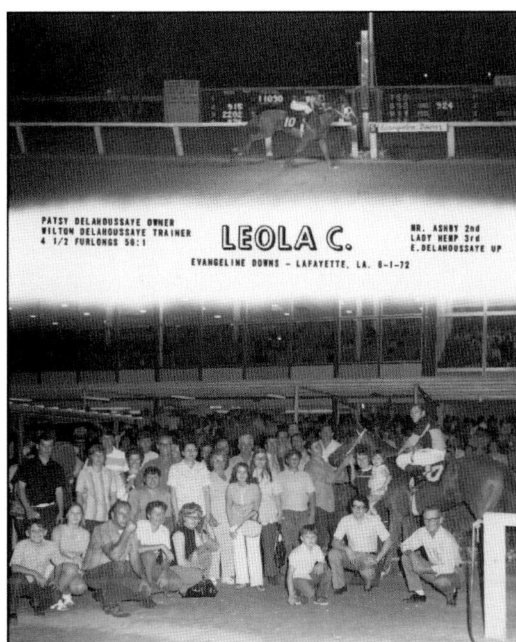

Outstanding jockey Eddie Delahoussaye, born in 1951 in New Iberia, has won 6,384 races, including the Kentucky Derby in 1982 and 1983. In 1993, he was inducted into the US Racing Hall of Fame. In 1972, Delahoussaye (pictured on horse) rode "Leola C." to a victory at Evangeline Downs. The horse was owned by Patsy Delahoussaye (holding bridle with baby Shantell Landry) and trained by his uncle Wilton Delahoussaye (kneeling). Since World War II, Cajun jockeys have won a total of 21 Triple Crown races.

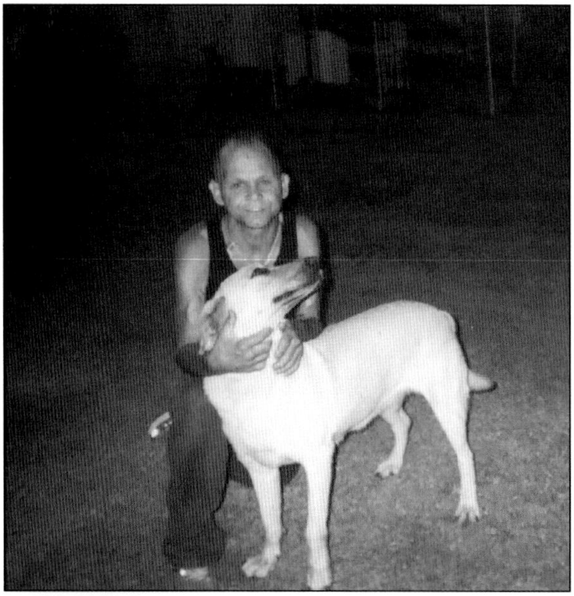

In 1979, eight-year-old Neil Aucoin of New Iberia became the first kidney transplant patient at Tulane's Southeast Louisiana Transplant Center. Prior to surgery, Neil reported to the center three times a week for dialysis. His mother, Gloria Simon, donated one of her kidneys, which was successfully transplanted by Dr. John Hussey and Dr. Frank Boineau. Neil passed away on September 17, 2011, and was survived by his father, Cornelius "Cannon" Aucoin, and his stepmother, Juliene Aucoin. Neil is pictured in June 2011 with his dog Shay.

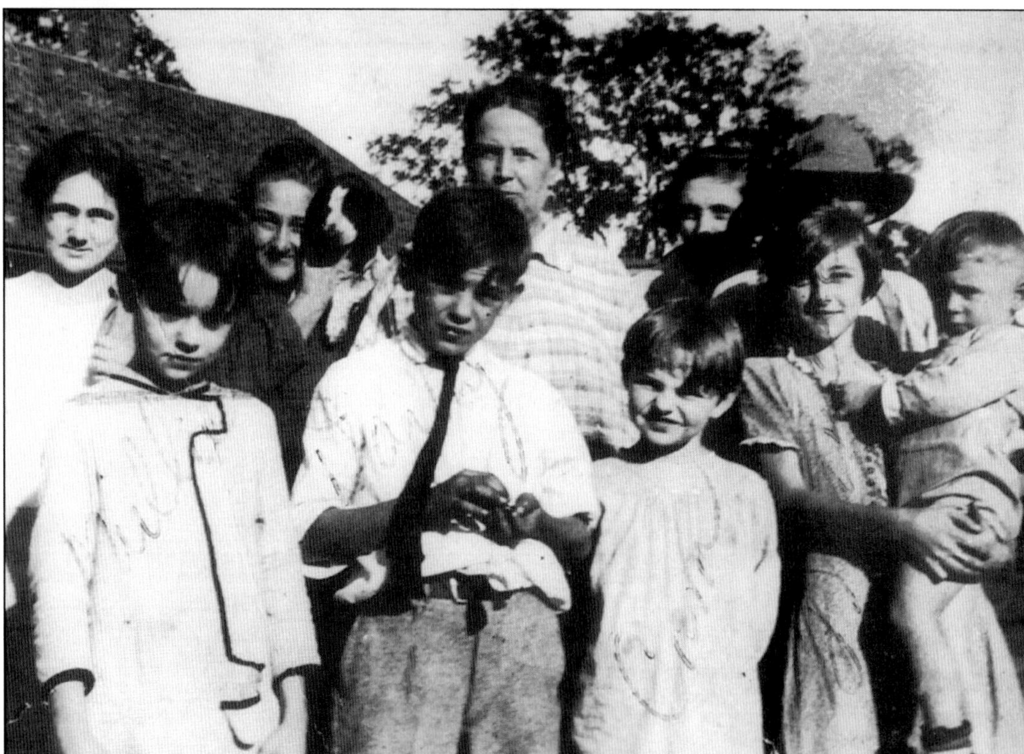

The Cesaire Darby family is pictured in the late 1920s on their land, which was originally part of a 1776 Spanish patent deeded to Jean Baptiste St. Marc Darby. From left to right are (first row) Millie Laperouse Theriot, Darby Laperouse, Camille Laperouse Thorguson, and Frances Laperouse Hebert, holding Lionel Laperouse; (second row) Louise Darby, Bertha Darby (holding dog), Cesaire Darby Jr., Camille Darby Laperouse, and Jules Darby. Darby descendants still grow sugarcane.

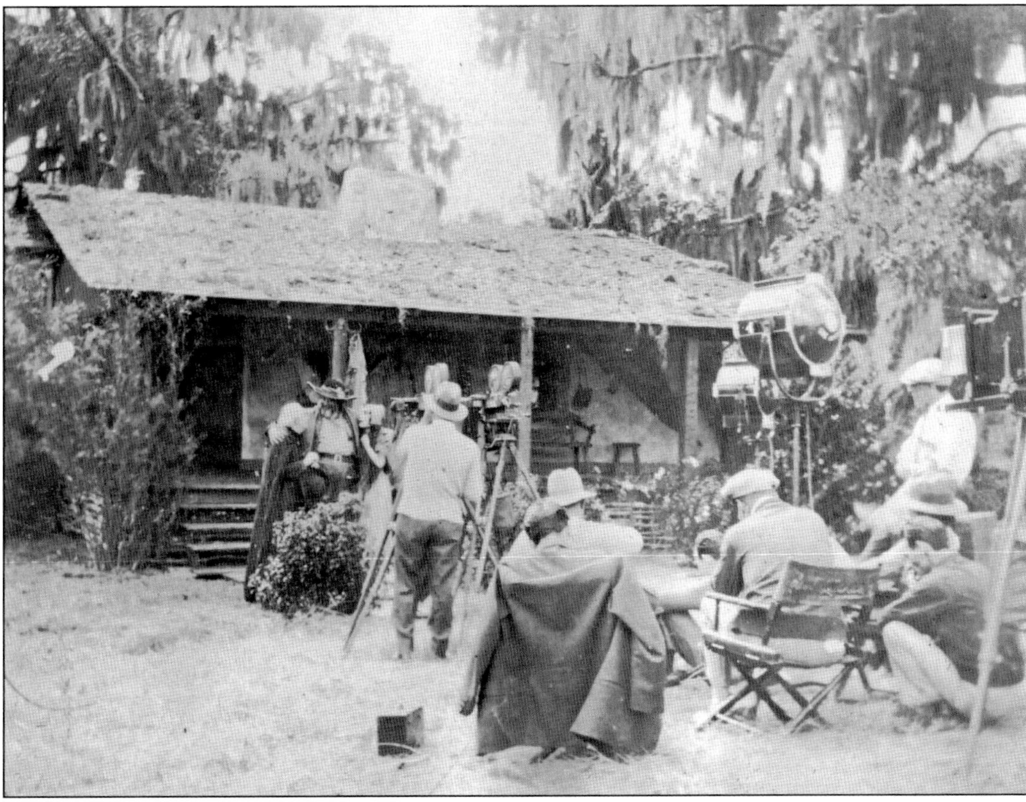

In 1929, the silent movie *Evangeline* was partially shot in Jungle Gardens on Avery Island. The movie starred Delores Del Rio and featured Ed LaSalle, Lloyd Porter, Marian Murphy, and Gertrude Plaisance. Following the filming, the departure of the movie's cast by train was a major social event in New Iberia. (Courtesy of the Avery Island, Inc. Archives.)

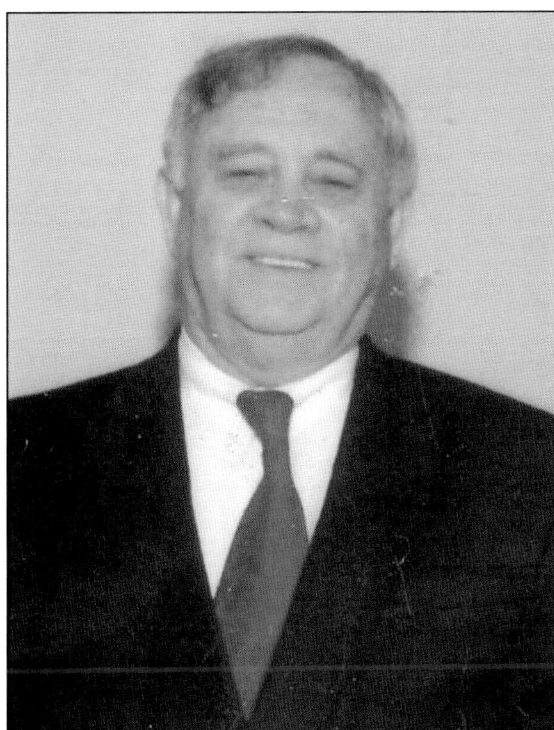

In Acadia, the Breauxs can trace ancestry to Vincent Brault, who arrived in Port Royale in the mid-17th century and married Marie Bourg. Pictured is John Richard "Dickie" Breaux, who served Iberia Parish in the House of Representatives from 1968 to 1976, was inducted as a Living Legend in 2011, and is owner of Café des Amis. Known for its "Zydeco Breakfast," the Louisiana State Art Council awarded it the Governor's Award for Promotion of the Arts in 2000. In 2011, his son Brett opened Café des Amis in New Iberia.

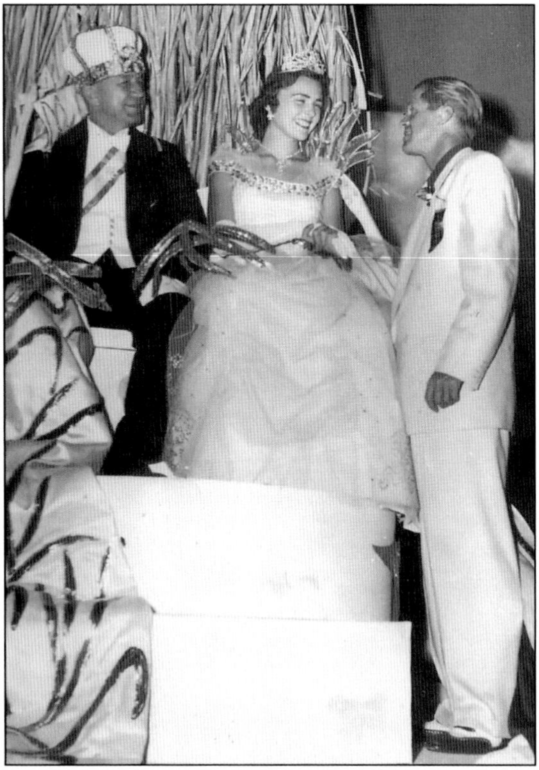

Actor Dan Duryea (right) served as one of the judges who selected Sylvia Ann Segura as Queen Sugar XI (center) on September 27, 1952, at the annual Sugar Cane Festival. Serving as King Sucrose was Murphy J. Foster Jr. Duryea was in the area filming *Thunder Bay*, a movie about the building of the first offshore oil rig and the conflicts it caused with the local shrimpers. Foster was both the son and father of Louisiana governors.

On September 28, 1952, the new Sugar Cane Festival king, queen, and judges were invited by Weeks Hall to The Shadows for a champagne toast. Pictured from left to right are Cliff Saber, George S. Healy Jr. (editor of the *Times-Picayune*), Irwin Poche (president of the Mid-Winter Sports Association), King Sucrose Murphy J. Foster Jr., Queen Sugar XI Sylvia Ann Segura, and Weeks Hall. Segura, the daughter of deputy clerk of court S.J. "Sos" and Margherite Gonsoulin Segura, represented Iberia Parish. (Courtesy of Sylvia Segura Bienvenue.)

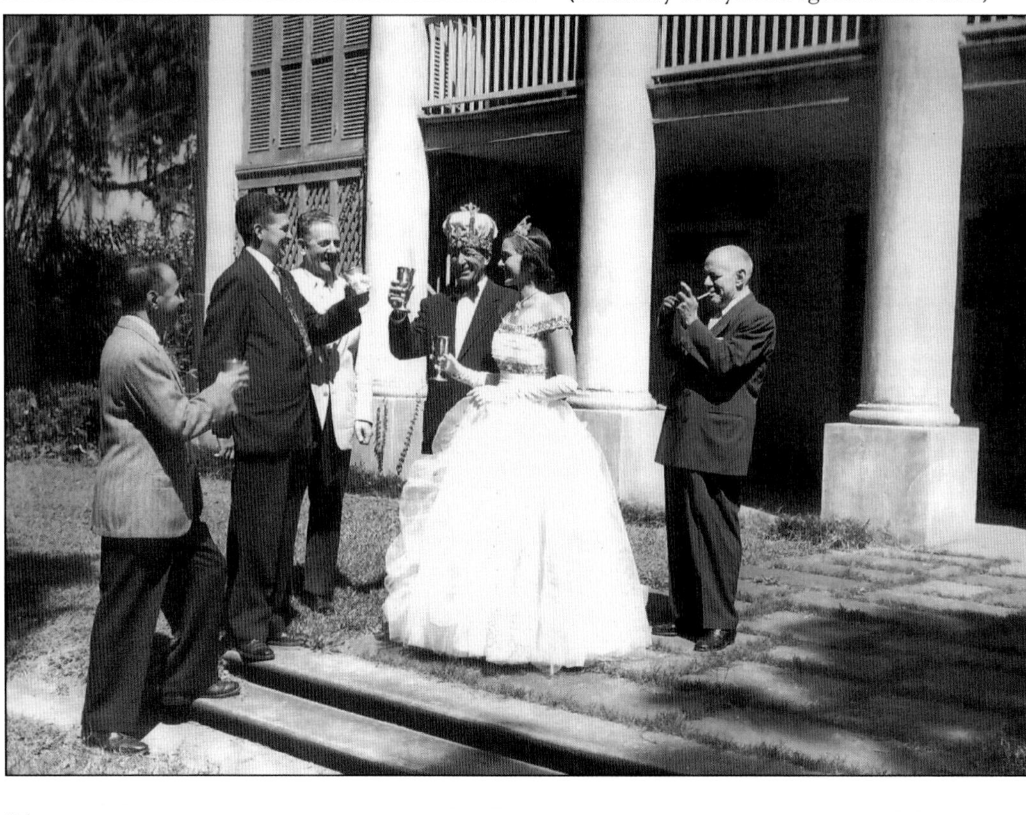

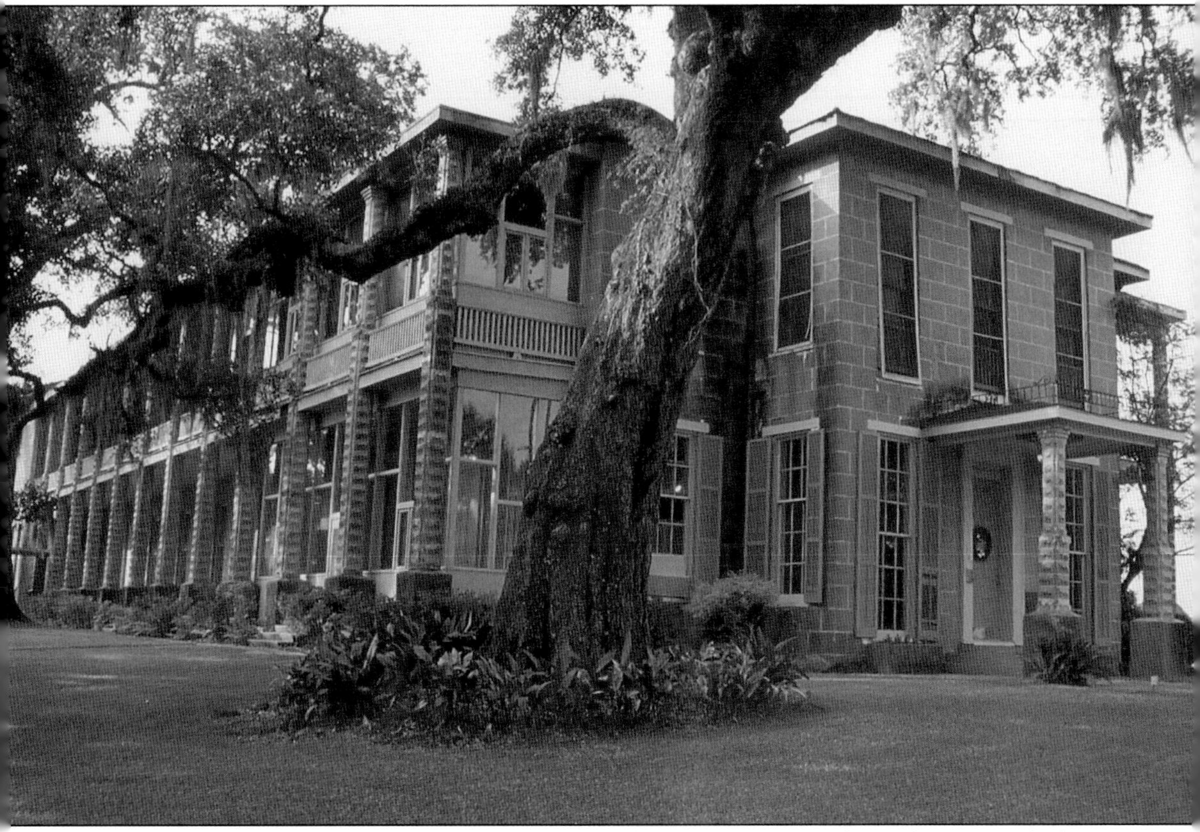

Pictured is the Frederick Duperier house, which later became Mt. Carmel Academy, a Catholic school for girls operated by the Sisters of Mt. Carmel. The school remained open until 1988, when the building was transformed into an office complex. Herman Schellstede and his wife, Eugenie Fortier Schellstede, currently own it. Legend has it that in the late 18th century, pirate Jean Lafitte dug a tunnel from the Bayou Teche to the Duperier house in order to conceal stolen treasures on the property. (Courtesy of Mickey Delcambre.)

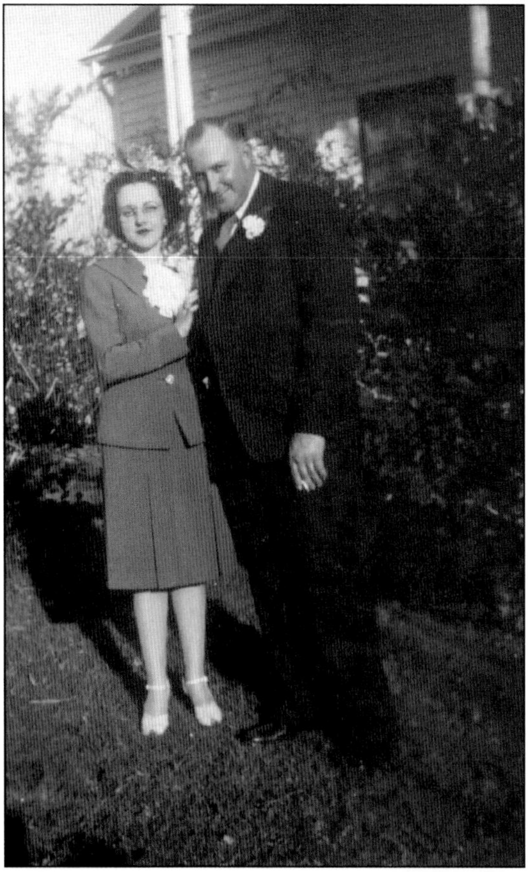

Frances Laperouse Hebert and Howard André Hebert are pictured in January 1945 at their wedding. The couple lived in Patoutville near the M.A. Patout Sugar Mill until 1955, when they moved to Peebles Plantation. In the 1970s, the town of Lydia (named after Hypolite Patout's daughter) developed after Diamond Crystal Salt Company closed the company town on Weeks Island and allowed its workers to buy the company-owned houses. Located en route to Cypremort Point, with easy access to Highway 90, the community continues to develop. Nearby is Cypremort Point State Park.

Pictured from left to right are Mary Lou Hebert Bodden, Andrea Hebert Delaune, and Nelwyn Hebert, children of Howard and Frances Laperouse Hebert. Howard's ancestor Jean Louis Hebert, son of Jean Baptiste Hebert, lived at Chicot Noir, which is now part of the LSU Experimental Farm near Jeanerette. In the 1830s, Jean Louis's son, Exhubert, bought land in the Patoutville area. Desire Hebert Jr., Exhubert's grandson, and his wife, Irma Domingues, had eight children, seven of whose descendants still maintain ownership of the land, most of which is in sugarcane.

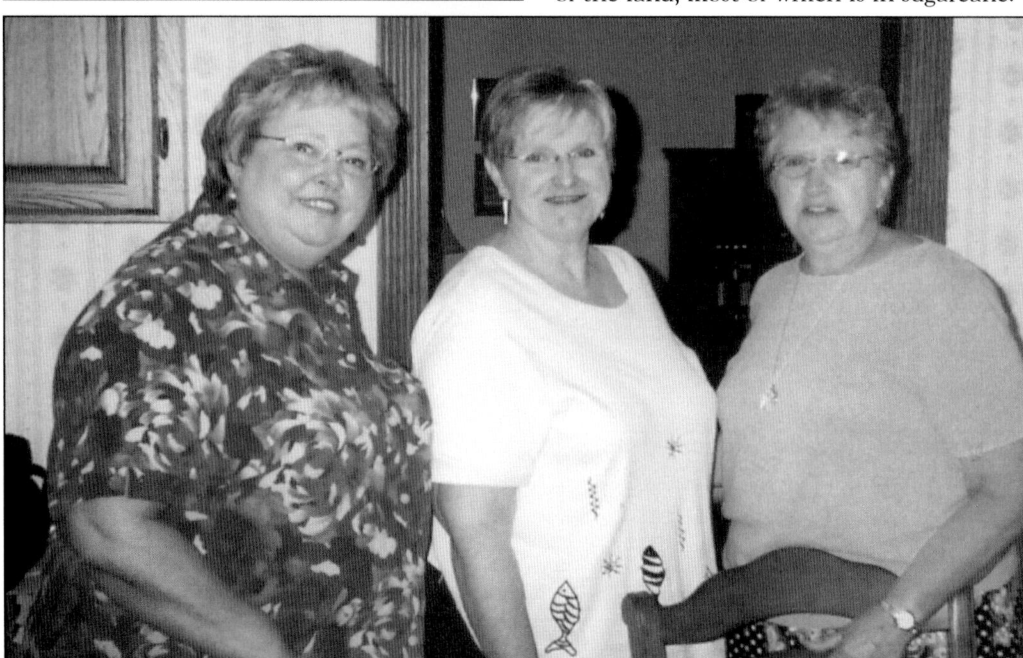

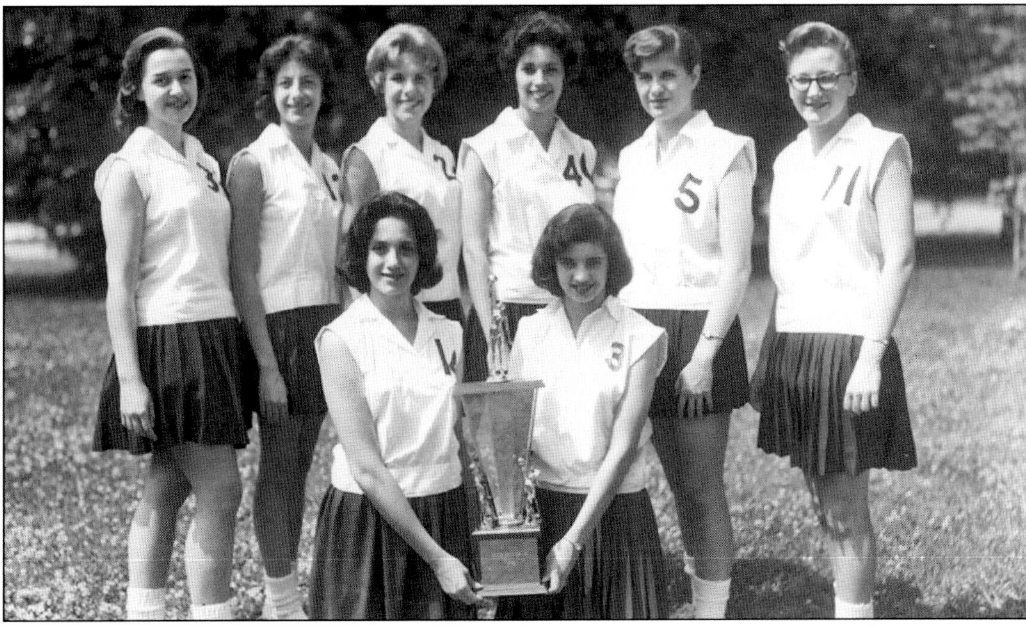

The members of the 1959 Mount Carmel basketball team are, from left to right, (first row) Mary Jo Hinton and Cynthia Theriot; (second row) Bertha Sandoz, Toni Doumit, Nancy Mixon, Susan Schwing, Elizabeth Broussard, and Wynn Murrell. Coached by Laura Belanger, Mount Carmel won the state basketball championship in 1971 and 1974. Morgan Leleux, four-time All-American pole-vaulter from Catholic High School, was named National High School Athlete of the Year in 2011 by *Track and Field*, the first Louisiana athlete to receive this honor. She was coached by her father, Shane Leleux.

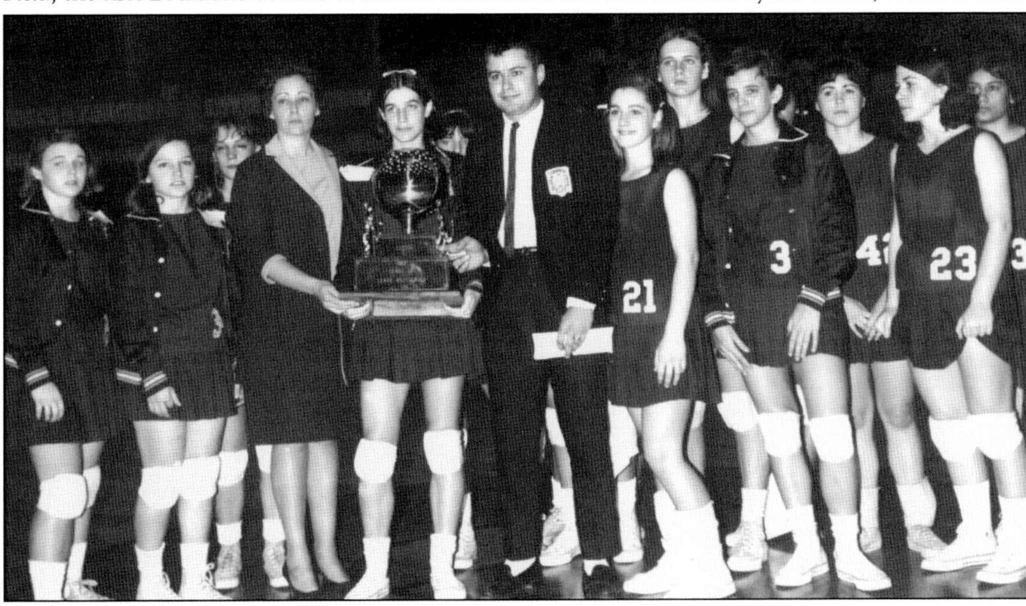

The scrappy 1967 Mt. Carmel Academy girls basketball team was state runner-up, losing to Jena by a score of 64 to 62. Coach Bernie David said, "These young women taught me more about life than I taught them about basketball." Pictured from left to right are Virginia Mixon, Regina Gonsoulin, Margery Bayard, Joan Spiller, coach David, Sandra Hebert, Carol Johnson, Mary Ann Fontenot, Carolyn Doerle, Shelia Hebert, and Pauline Ackal (behind Sheila Hebert).

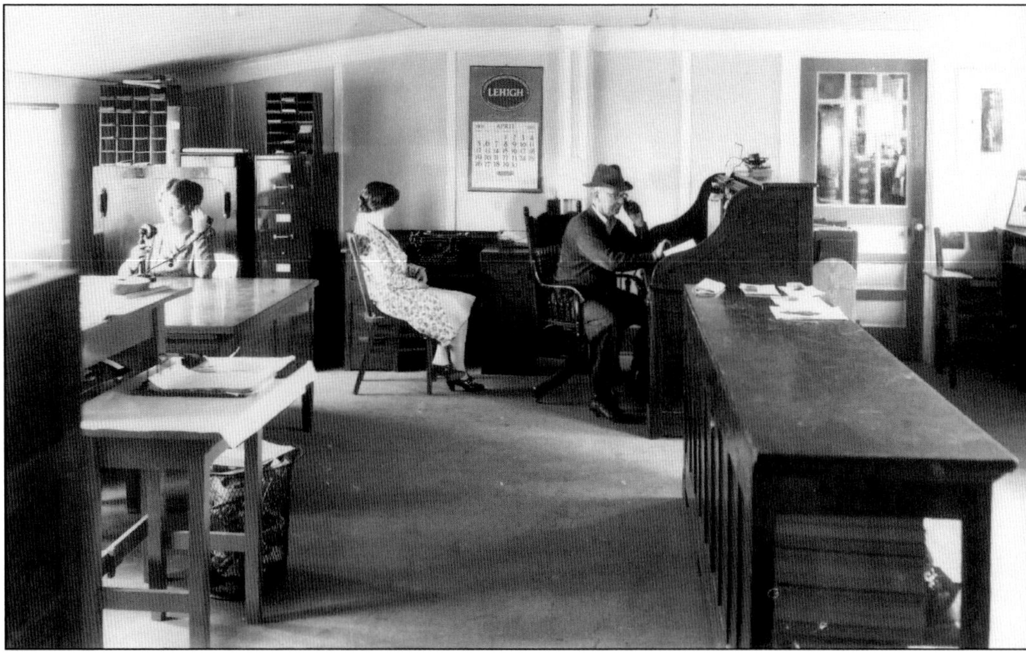

Pictured is an interior view of the office of Edgar P. Folse at the Sash, Door, Millwork Factory. The people shown are Mr. Edgar P. Folse (September 1, 1882–December 10, 1949) and daughters Ms. Julienne Folse Watermeir (Mrs. John Watermeir, December 24, 1904–February 4, 1985) and Ms. Stillman Folse Gesser (Mrs. Herman J. Gesser, Sr., May 21, 1910–April 12, 2008). (Courtesy of Center for Louisiana Studies, University of Louisiana at Lafayette.)

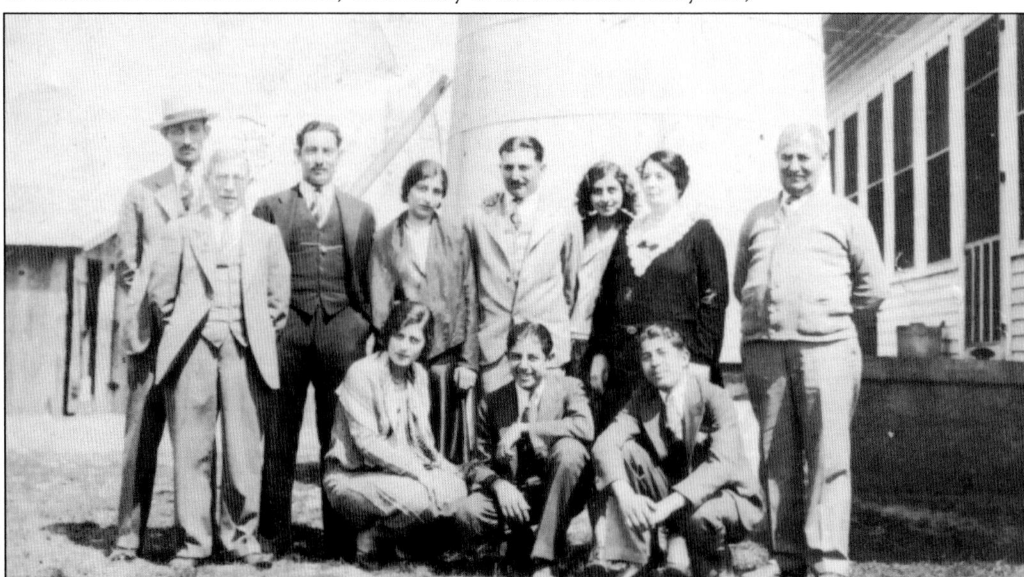

Pictured in the 1930s are members of a prominent Lebanese family. From left to right, they are (first row) Alexander Bowab, Laurence Ackal Bowab, Michael Ackal Sr., and Dr. Gabriel "Gab" Ackal (Louisiana state senator from 1956 to 1960 and president of the Sugar Cane Festival); (second row) Elias Ackal, Toffie Ackal, Loria Ackal Doumit, Mitch Doumit, Aline Ackal, Julia Betar Ackal, and Antoine Ackal.

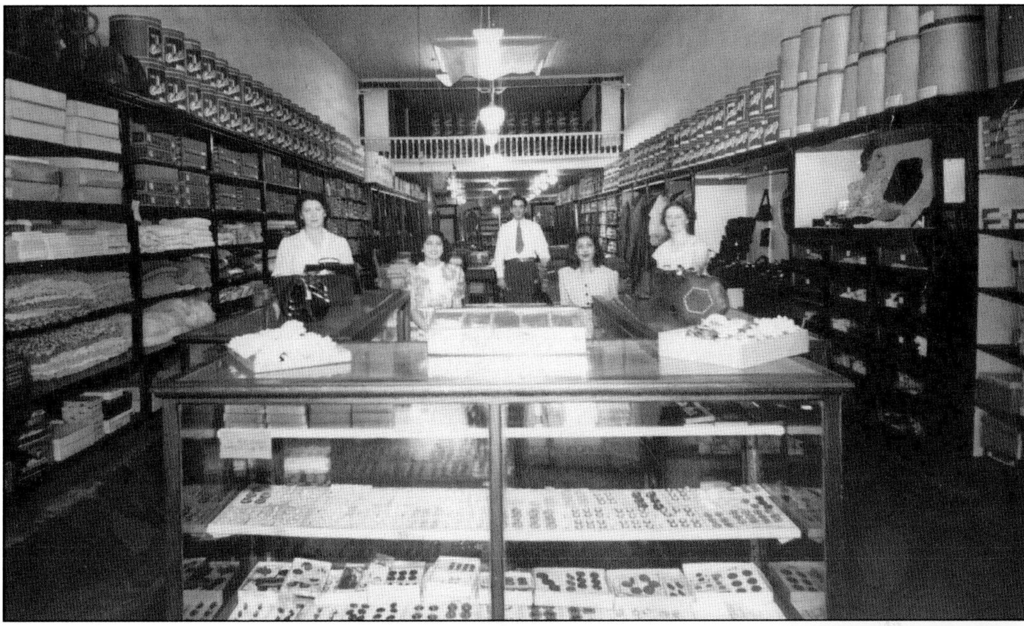

Antoine Ackal owned Ackal's Department Store, located at 110 East Main Street in downtown New Iberia, from the 1920s until his death in 1934. Thereafter, several of his children continued the business for over 60 years. Taken in 1957 after the store had just been remodeled, this photograph shows, from left to right, Helen Ackal, Aline Ackal, Non Nini, Odette Judice, and Simon LeBlanc.

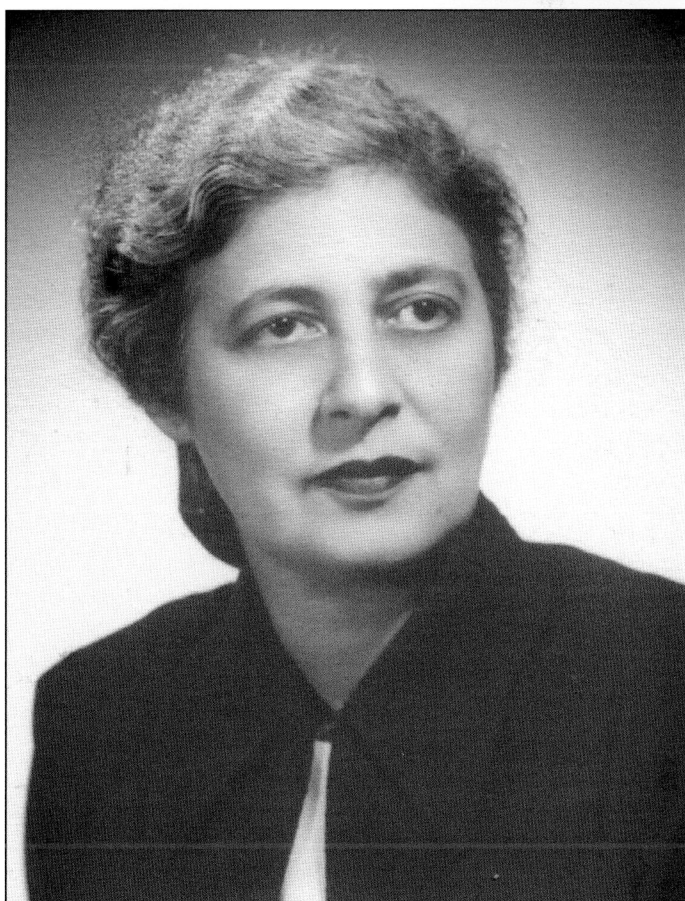

Laurence Ackal Bowab (pictured), of Lebanese descent, and her husband, A.J. Bowab, owned and operated Bowab's Store on East Main Street. The store was billed as having "New Iberia's finest footwear and ready to wear." The store was in business for over 60 years. Laurence Bowab, who lived to the age of 98, was the oldest daughter of Antoine Ackal and Julia Betar.

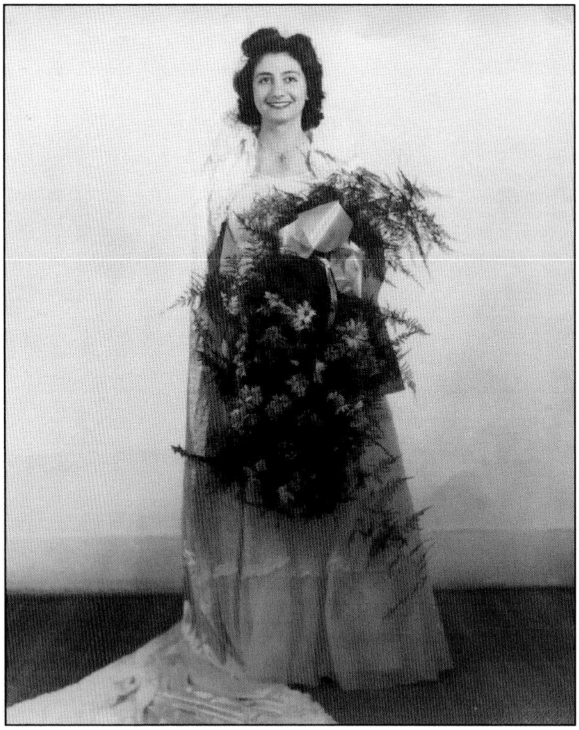

In 1943, when she was 17 years old and attending Mt. Carmel Academy, Mae Helen Elias Ackal was selected as May Queen. She crowned the statue of Our Blessed Mother as part of the school's celebration of the May Festival, which included the popular May Pole Dance.

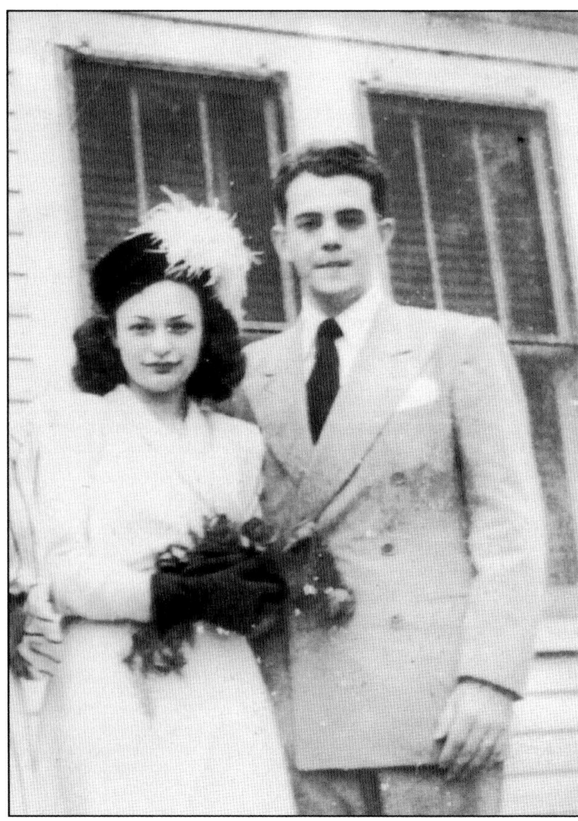

Pictured is Dr. Vernon Voohries with his World War II French bride, Jacqueline, more commonly known as "Jackie," on their wedding day. Active with CODOFIL, the Council for the Development of French in Louisiana, Jackie was instrumental in the promotion of the French language and culture in Louisiana.

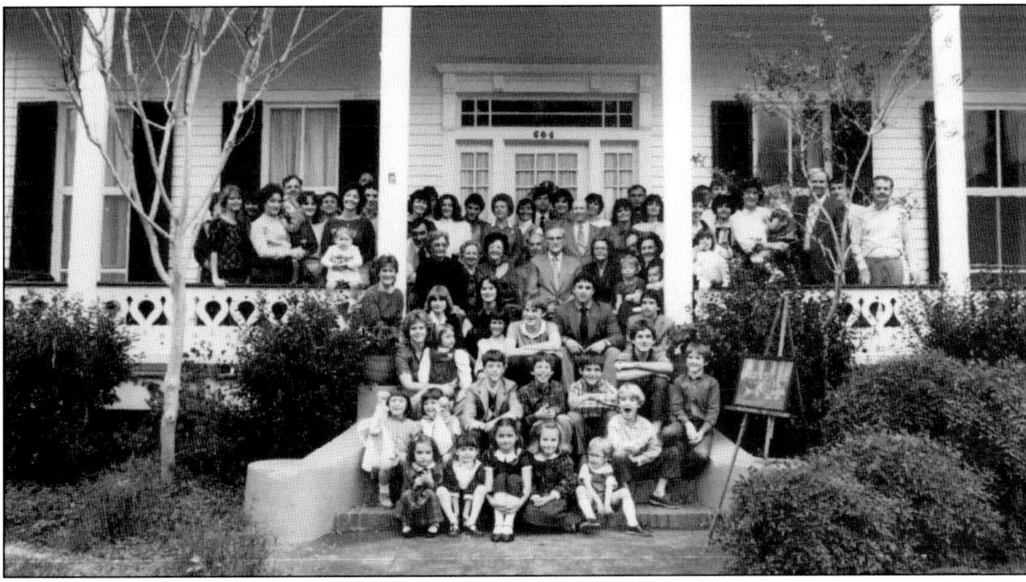

On December 23, 1988, a photograph was taken of the family of Paul Emile Voorhies, son of Judge Felix Voorhies. In 1907, Judge Voorhies published *Acadian Reminiscences*, which was made up of information gathered from his 100-year-old grandmother, an Acadian exile. The chapter titled "Acadian Manners and Customs" is important to folklorists researching folkways.

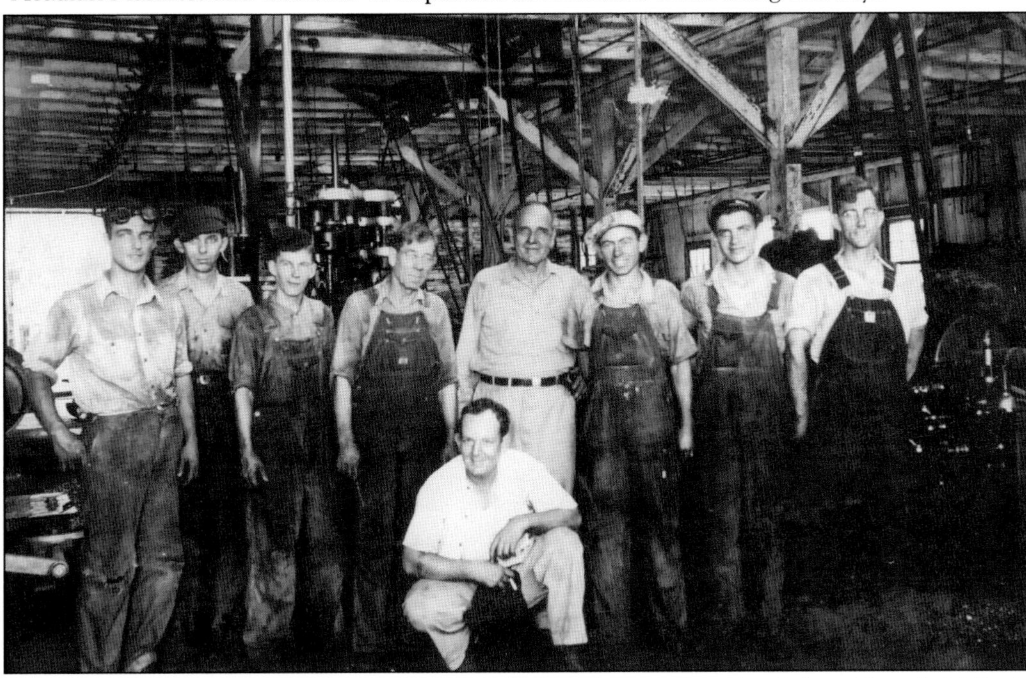

In the 1890s, many new businesses opened in the parish, including the Gebert Shingle Mill, the Joseph Russell shingle factory, the Breaux, Renoudet and Broughton sawmill, the Bagarry Ice Factory, the Broussard and Decuir sawmill, the Gall and Pharr sawmill, the Gates Seed Oil Mill, and the Lee and Brown cotton gin. The Voorhies Machine Shop employees, pictured from left to right, are Richard Voorhies, Albert Peter, unidentified, ? Sullivan (welder), Jimmy Voorhies (kneeling), Paul Emile Voorhies, unidentified, "Pretty Bug," and Cornelieus Voorhies.

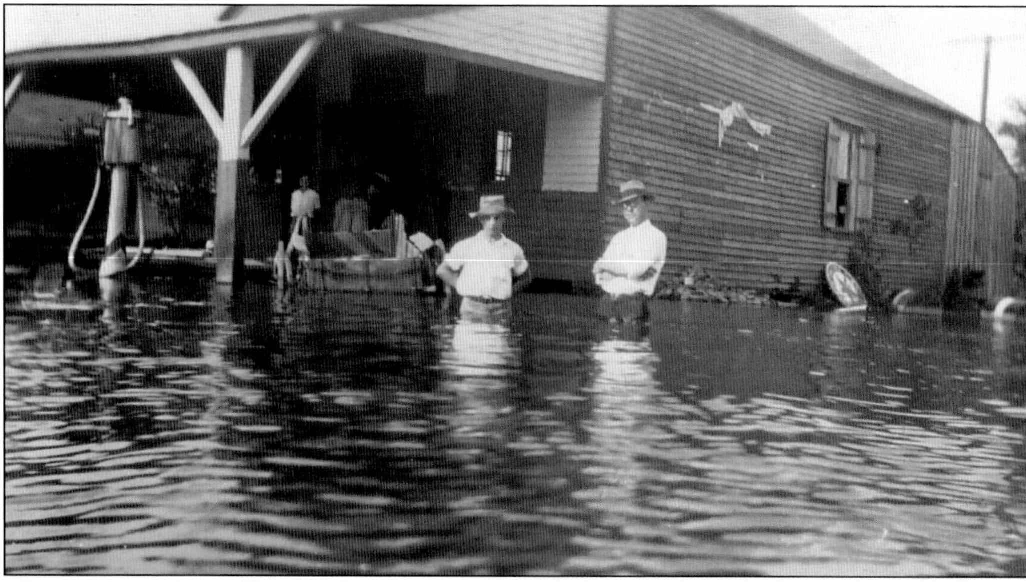

The people's indomitable spirit has helped them overcome many tragedies. One of the worst was the flood of 1927, which was one of the most powerful natural disasters of the 1900s. Pictured above are the effects of the flood at Lallande's store on Jane Street in New Iberia. Below is a photograph of the house at 713 W. Main Street in Jeanerette, where Sybil Beaullieu Sealy, who died on August 13, 2011, grew up.

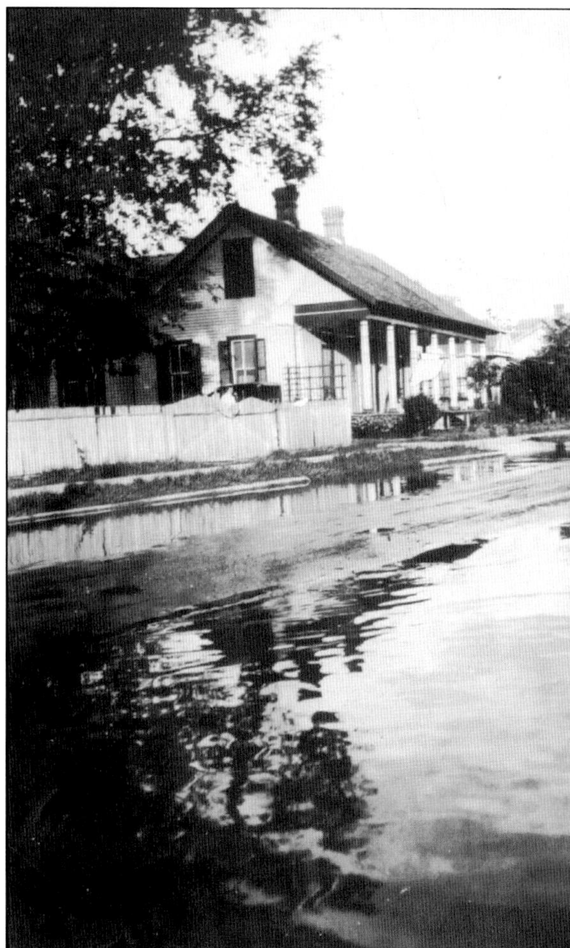

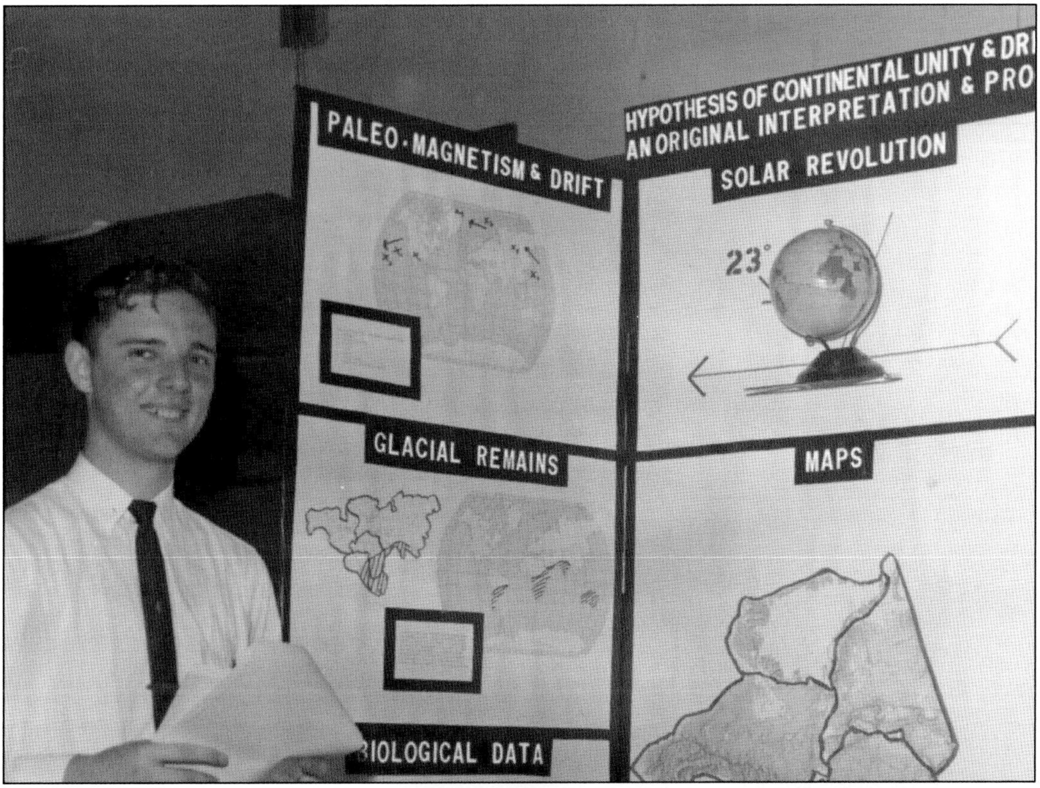

Donald J. "Doc" Voorhies taught at Catholic High School for 33 years and encouraged (i.e., required) students to participate in the school's science fair. Under his leadership, many students won district, state, and international awards. "Doc" is pictured here with his own senior year science fair project.

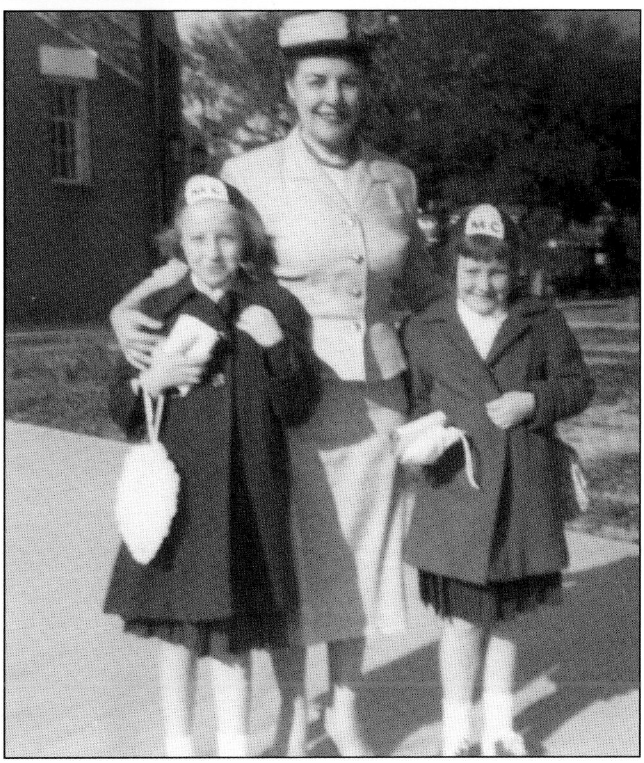

Pictured in April 1958 at St. Peter's Catholic Church are, from left to right, Nelwyn Hebert, Goldie Bujard, and Andy Hebert Delaune. The 1960s brought profound divisiveness. Many baby boomers adopted political views influenced by anti–Vietnam war protests, which often caused dissension in some families.

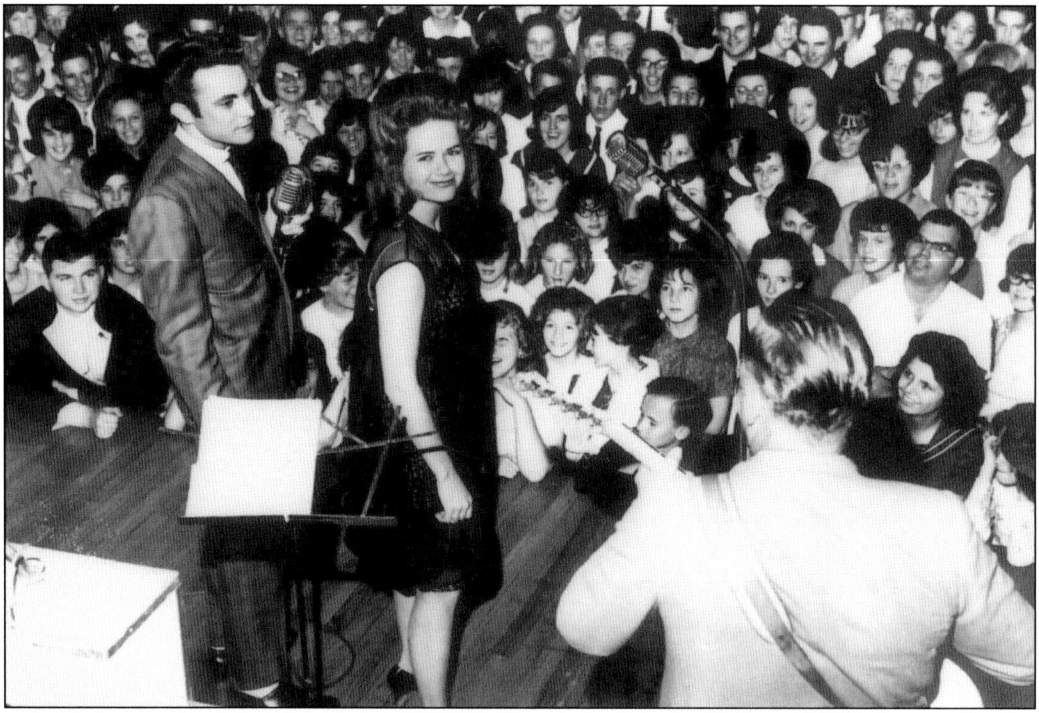

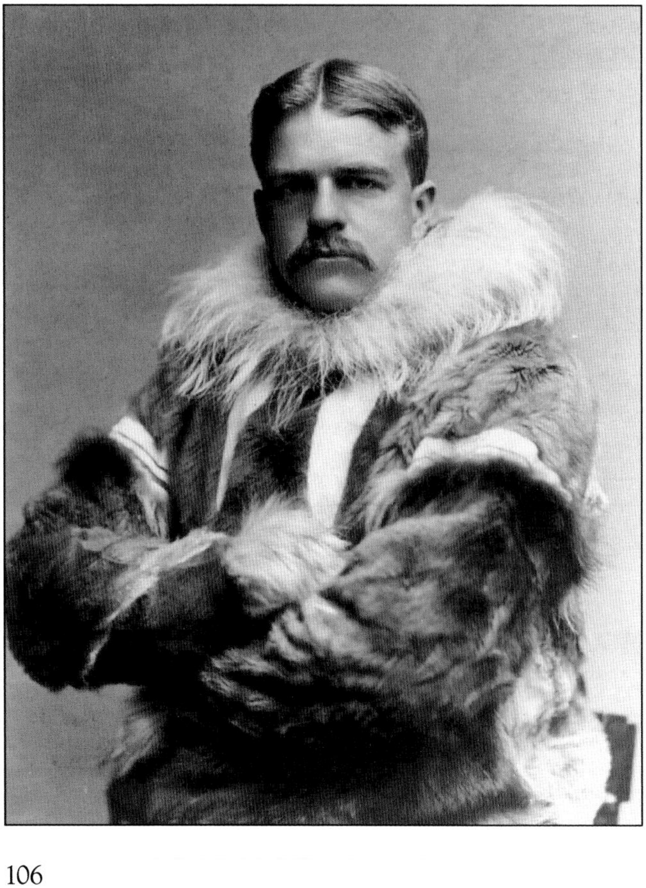

In late 1963, a crowd of teenagers watches south Louisiana swamp pop duo Dale and Grace, who had the number one song in the nation at that time, "I'm Leaving it up to You." They were performing at City Park in New Iberia backed by the band Randy and the Rockets. (Courtesy of Huey Darby/the Shane K. Bernard Collection.)

Conservationist, naturalist, and businessman Edward A. McIlhenny of Avery Island is pictured in 1898 wearing his Arctic exploration garb. Son of Tabasco sauce inventor Edmund McIlhenny and a lifelong resident of Iberia Parish, McIlhenny was fascinated with the Arctic and went on two expeditions there in the 1890s. (Courtesy of the E.A. McIlhenny Collection, Avery Island, Louisiana.)

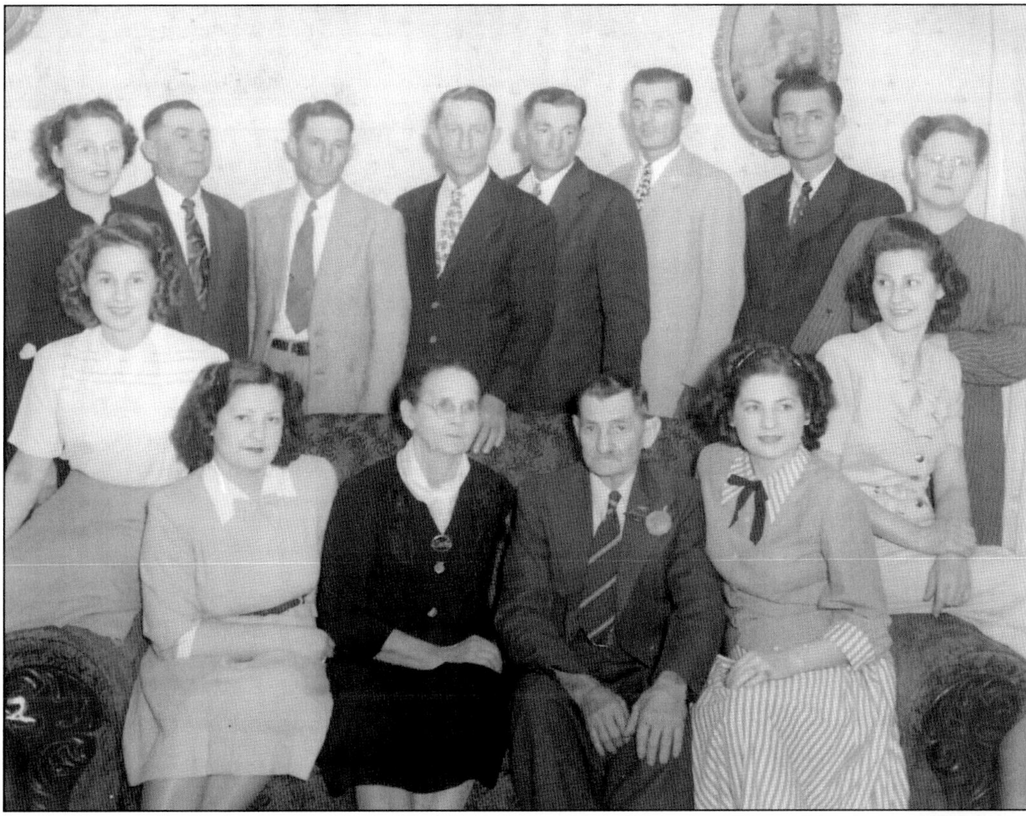

Members of the Elodie Girouard and Nicholas Landry family pictured here are, from left to right, (first row) Viola, Anne, Elodie, Nicholas, Rita, and Gert; (second row) Nola, Fauldes, Sefrien, Calvin, Oston, Lenia, Simon, and Nina.

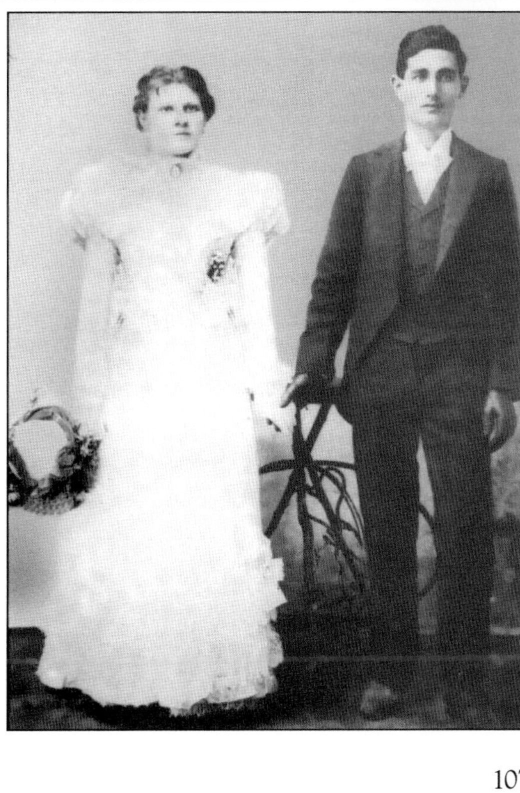

Chloe Hebert's grandparents Aristide Hulin and Elise Dronet Hulin operated a syrup mill in New Iberia before moving to eastern Vermilion Parish. Pictured in 1889 on their wedding day are Hebert's parents, Elita Marie Hulin and Clomare Hebert, a farmer and rancher.

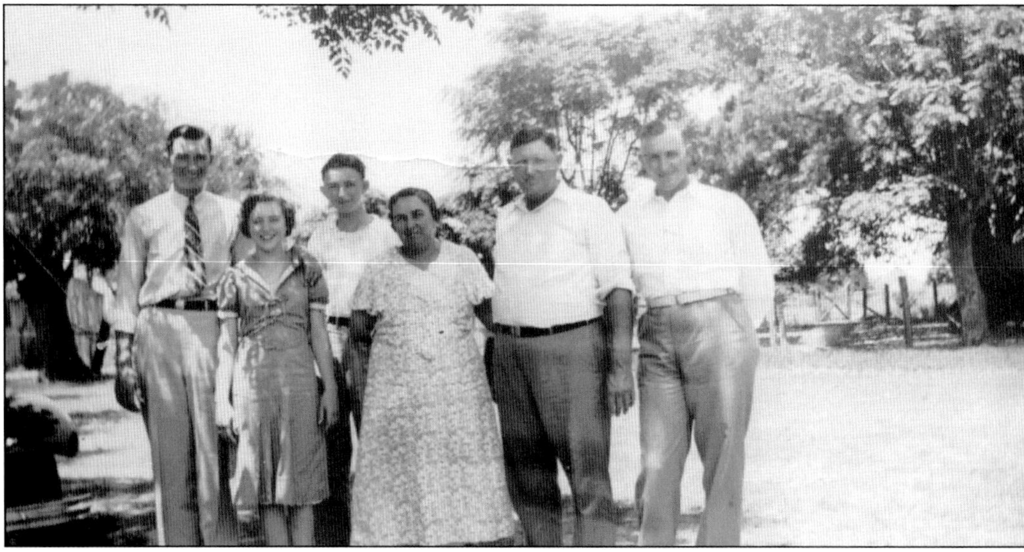

In the 1950s, schools established "canning centers" to aid locals in preserving foods and wrapping meats, eliminating the need for the communal butchering of livestock. Pictured are descendants of Desire Hebert Sr., from left to right, Leodias Hebert Jr., Olga "Pinkie" Hebert Prevost, Earl Hebert, Clothilde Hebert Hebert, Leodias Hebert Sr. (who served on the Iberia Parish Police Jury from 1928 to 1940), and Howard Hebert.

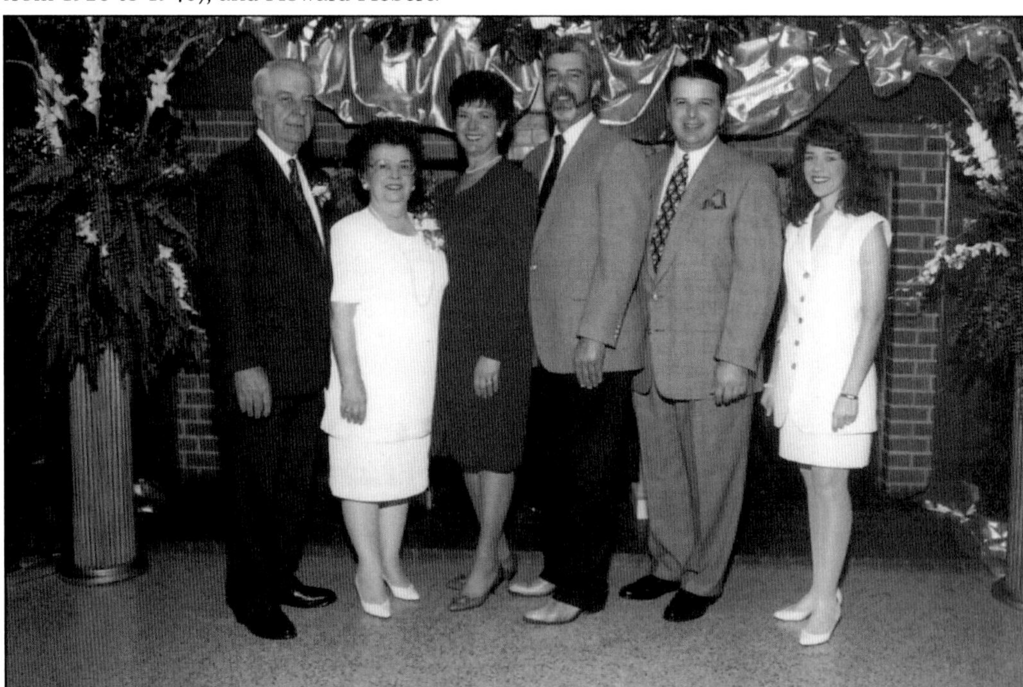

The Barras surname goes back to the Provence region of France. Joseph Barras left that region to come to Louisiana in 1757. Pictured at their 50th wedding anniversary are Elton and Mazel Barras and their children. From left to right, they are Elton, Mazel, Garneth Barras Viltz, Terry Barras, Rep. Taylor Barras (who was unopposed in 2011 for re-election to his District 48 seat), and Gina Barras Bergeron.

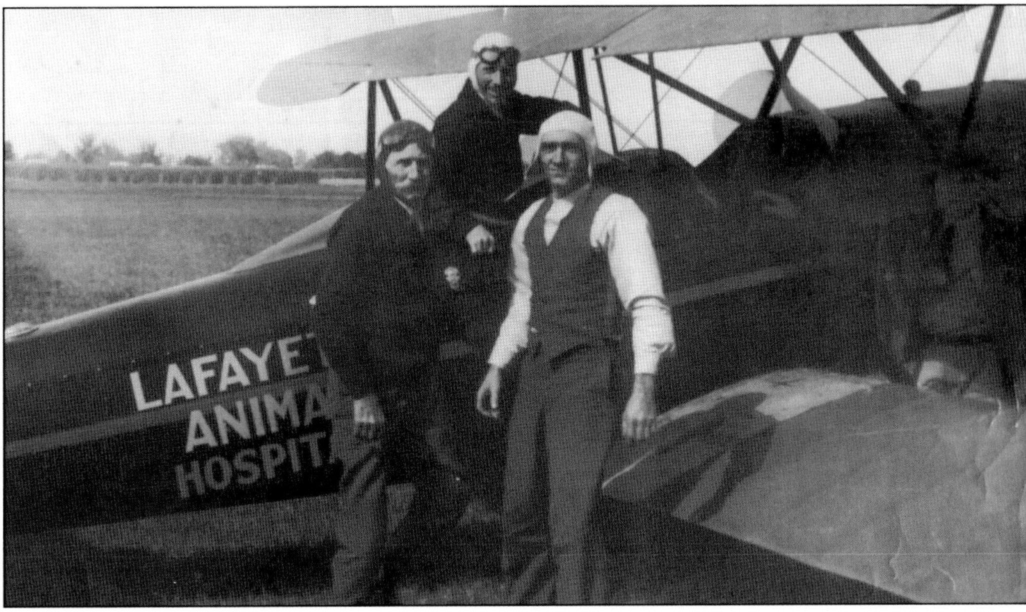

Dr. Louis Leonpacher, a veterinarian educated in Munich, Germany, was one of the first aviators in the area and was known as the "Flying Vet." In the 1920s, he began vaccinating cattle to fight diseases such as "blackleg," anthrax (*charbon*), and "red water." He often used his plane to reach remote areas, such as Marsh Island. Pictured in the 1930s are, from left to right, Leodice Hulin (whose father, Aristide Hulin, was from New Iberia), Leonpacher (in his plane), and Clairville Hulin.

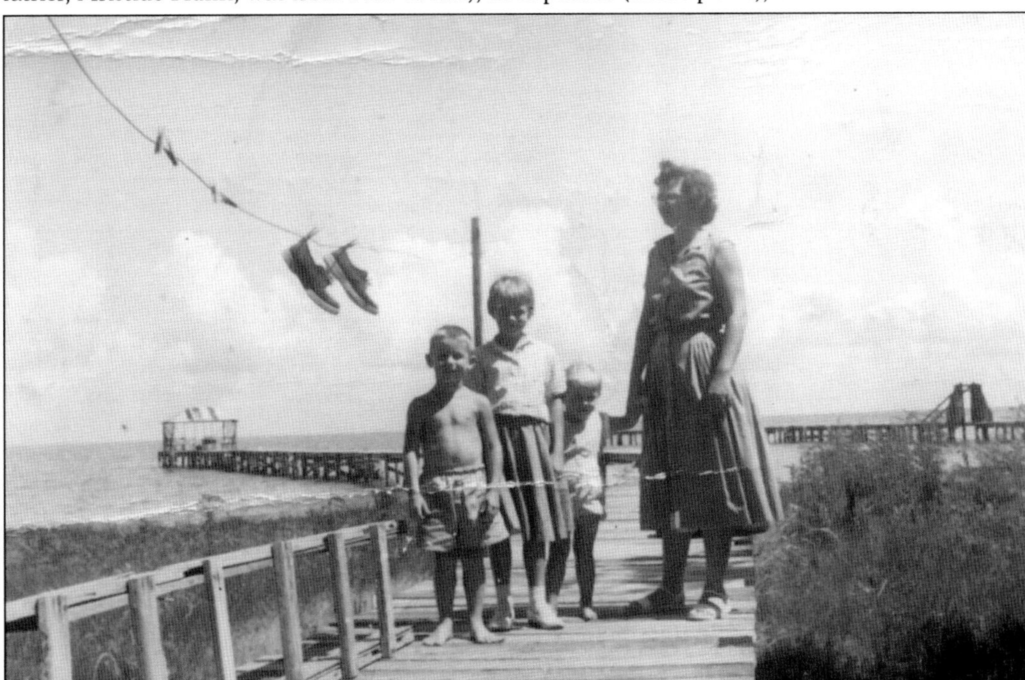

Pictured in 1954 enjoying Elton Beaullieu's Cypremort Point camp (built 1947) are members of the Richard C. Sealy Jr. family. From left to right are his children, Richard Timothy, Lindrea, and Virginia, and his wife, Sybil Beaullieu Sealy.

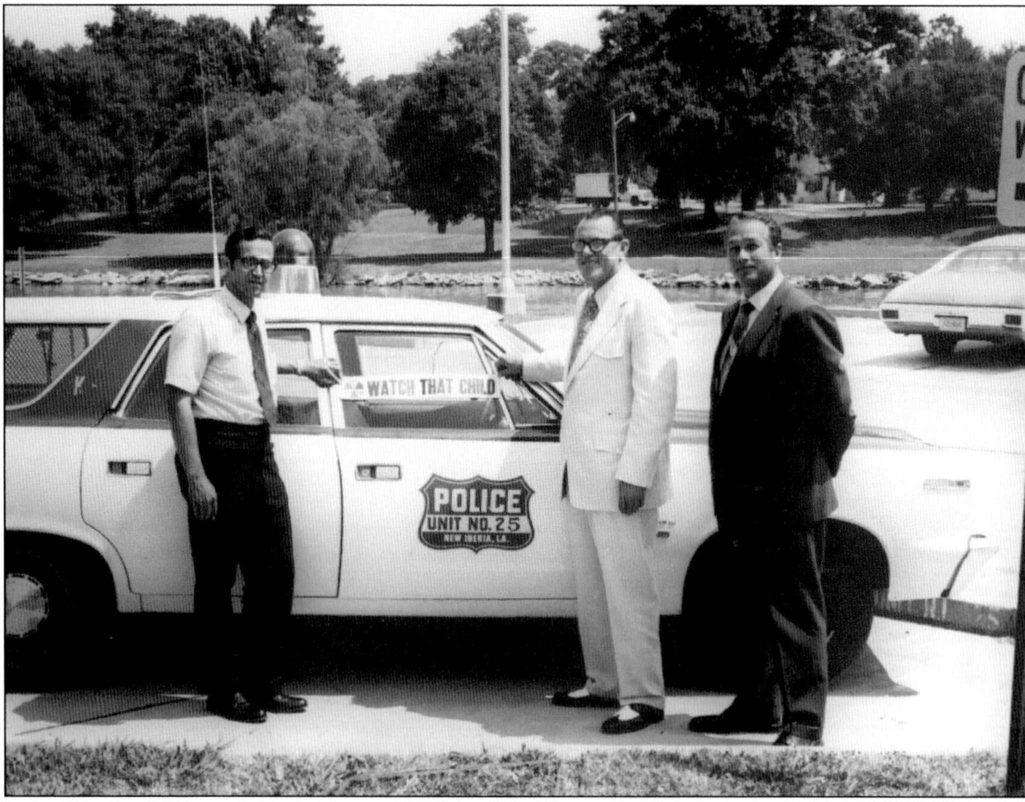

New Iberia Mayor J. Allen Daigre, Police Chief Lee Fournet, and unidentified display a bumper sticker entitled, "Watch that Child." Daigre, the second of three Daigres to serve as mayor, was in office from 1964 to 1988. His father, Joe Daigre, was mayor from 1929 to 1940.

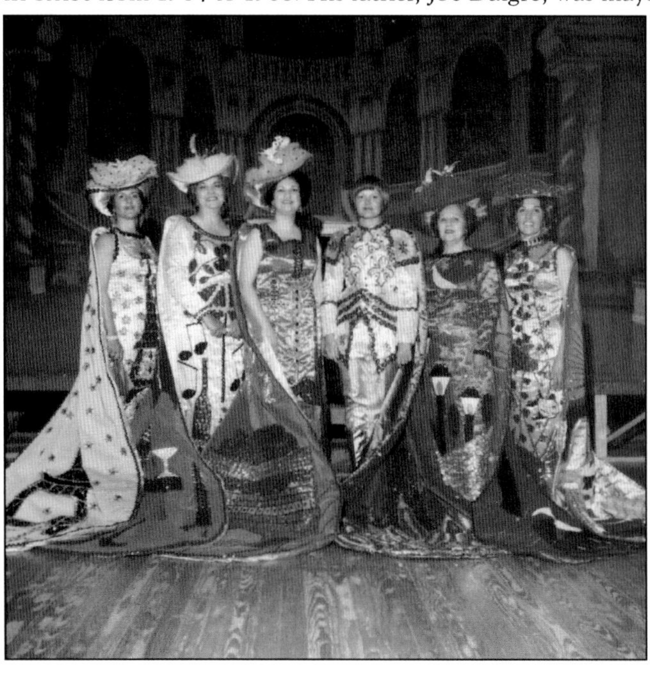

The Krewe of Andalusia was founded in 1957, and Edwin Ashey has been the captain since its founding. This 1977 photograph features the maids presented when the theme of the ball was "The Country of France." From left to right are Audrey Delahoussaye, Joyce Indest, Lynette Gosnell, Emma Fox, Josie Taylor, and Lynnette Tucker.

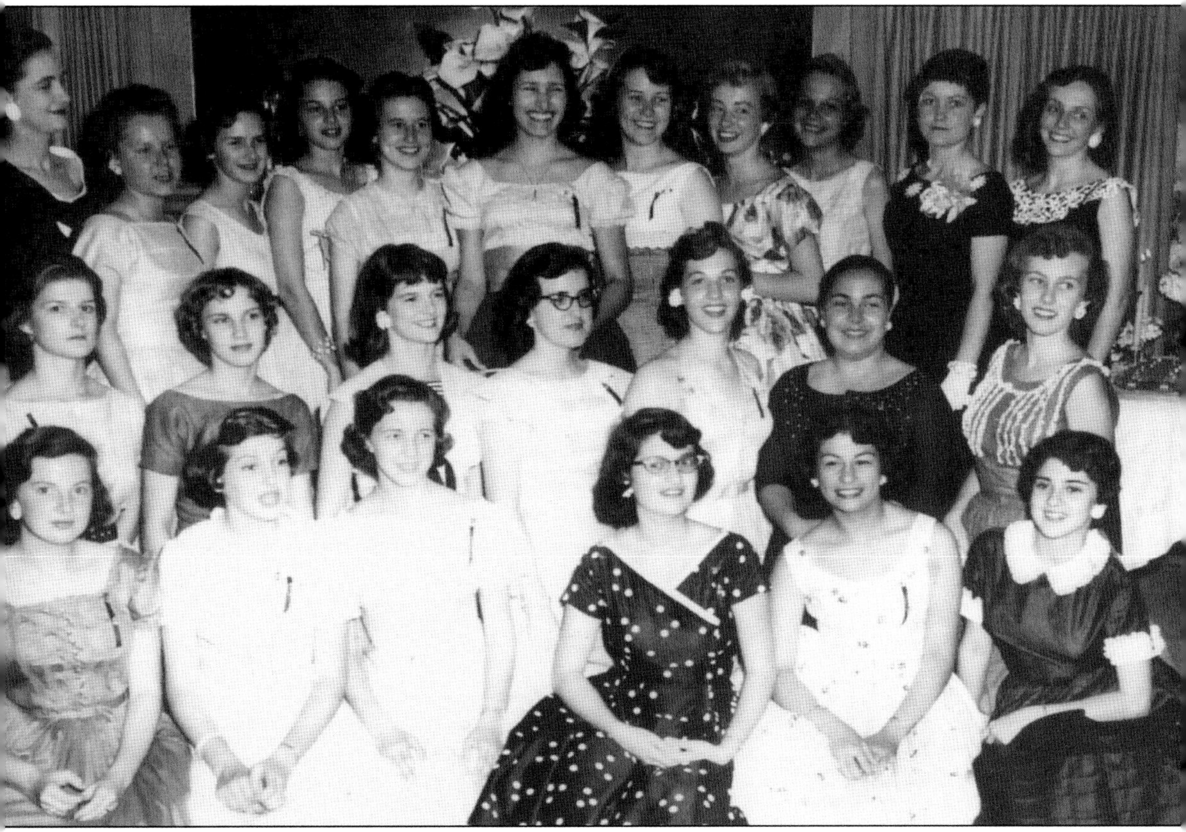

The Sub Jr. Miss Club, a Junior Federated Club, was founded in 1954 and sponsored by the Woman's Club. Members were students at New Iberia High School and Mt. Carmel Academy. Pictured in 1957 are, from left to right, (first row) Babs Bigler, Beth Amentor, Diane Laperouse, Lynette Nicholson, Fern Betar, and Lyndel Laperouse; (second row) Nancy Hoover, Betty Robinson, Janice Hoover, Lynnette Taylor, Saundra Mallory, and Joni Hayes; (third row) Mrs. O.H. Poe (advisor), Lily Emmer, Mary Lourd, Prissy Bernard, Donna Girard, Lillian Hewell, Dorothy Crowson, Janice Aldridge, Patsy West, Nancy Pontrimili, and Mildred Lourd.

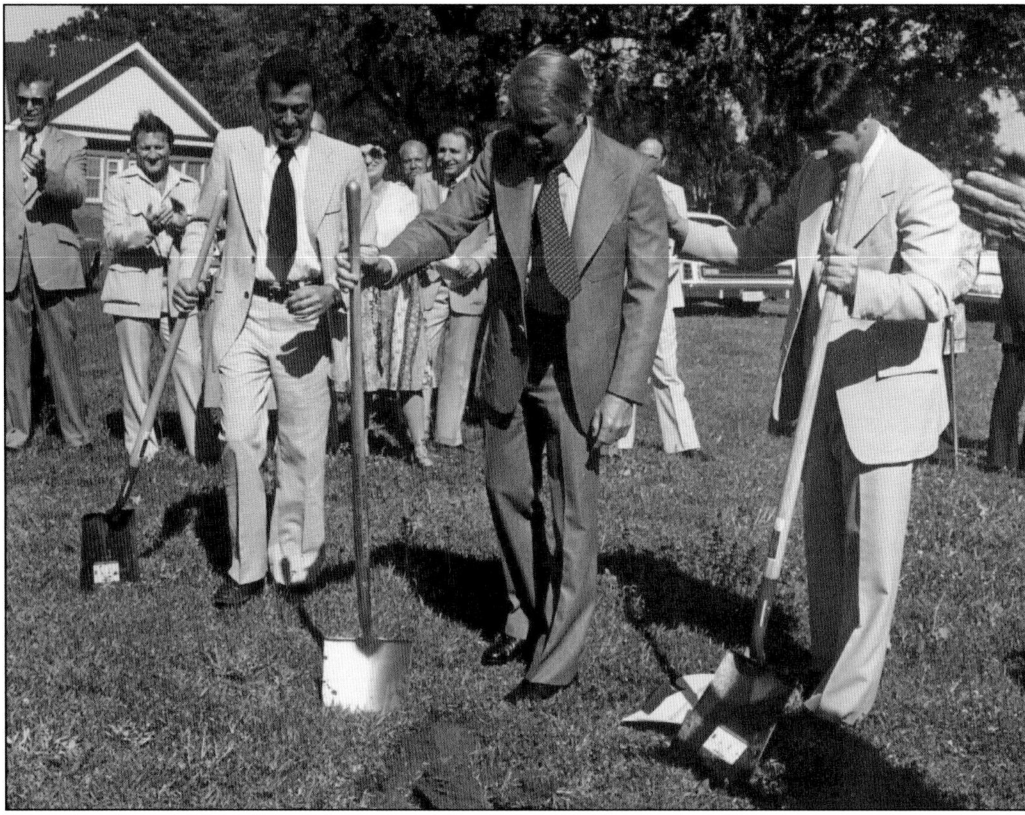

Officials attending the ground breaking ceremony for the Nelson Canal Bridge in New Iberia are, from left to right, Rep. Elias "Bo" Ackal, Gov. Edwin W. Edwards, and Sen. Oswald Decuir (later a judge on the Third Circuit Court of Appeals). Some in the background include J.P. Thibodeaux, Allen Gosnell, and Emile Plaisance.

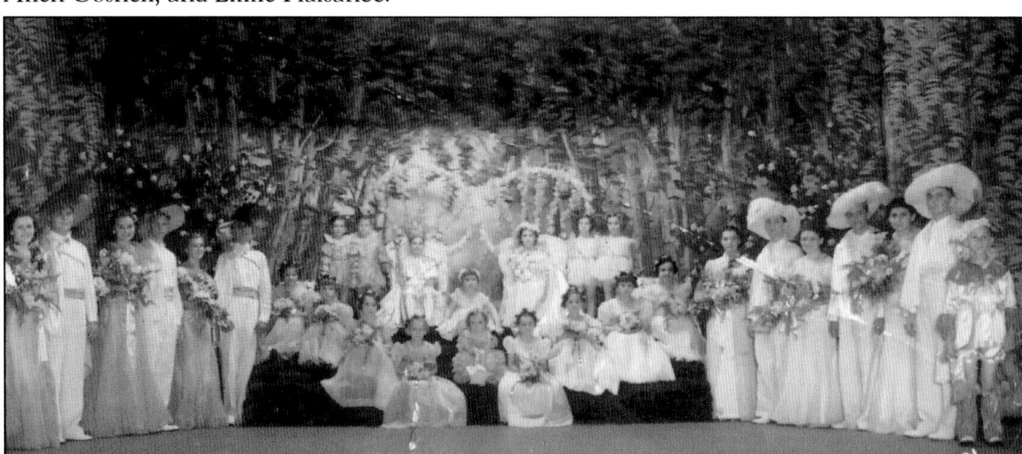

On May 25, 1936, New Iberia High School sponsored a May Festival with the theme of Carnival of Flowers. The King and his Dukes led a parade down Main Street, stopping to salute the Queen and her Duchesses. Flo Simon was Queen, and C.L. Deare was King. Dukes and Duchesses were Grace Neff, Floyd Prather, Lillian Ackal, Wilton Tilly, Lessie Babineaux, J.R. Broussard, Willie Mae Hayes, Francis Cardova, Marjorie Junca, Howard Verret, Dorothy Leleux, and Joe Davis.

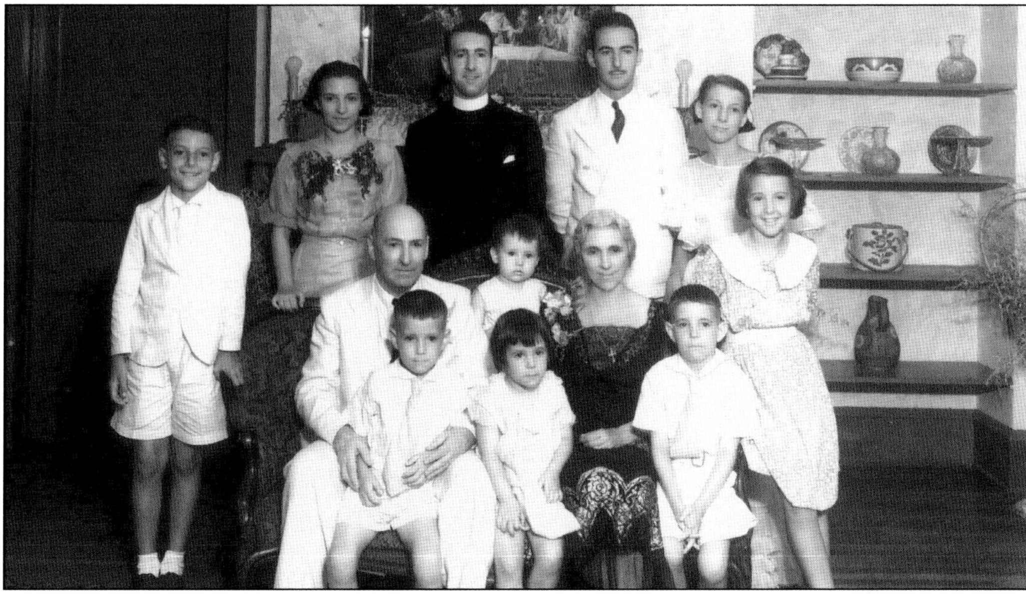

The Schwing family, from left to right, are (first row) Pierre, Henri Schwing Dougherty, and Paul; (second row) John Sr., James, Anna Blanchet Schwing, and Flora "Terry" Schwing Broussard; (second row) George, Mary Schwing Robbins, Father John Schwing, S.J., Jules, and Anna Louise "Cookie" Schwing Allain. John Schwing Sr. was executive vice president of the New Iberia National Bank. The Schwings gather every Wednesday for lunch at their parents' home. Ludie, the family cook, and Viola Villerie, her daughter, once prepared the meals. Now, Viola's daughter Audrey Francis prepares them.

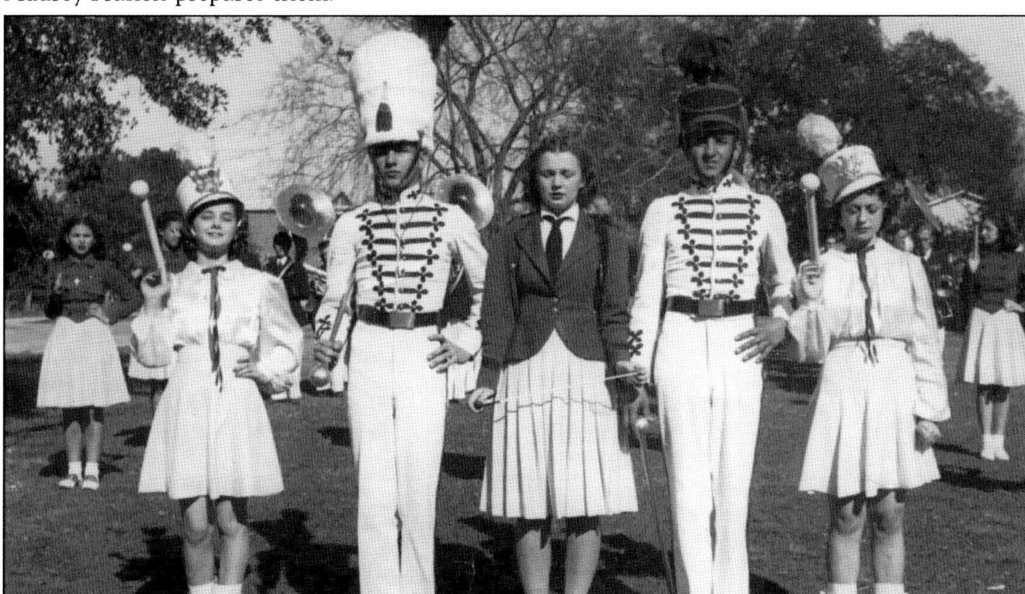

Pictured in 1940 are leaders of the New Iberia High School band. From left to right, they are Jeanette Peltier, Shirley Landry, Virginia Lomax, Vic Elias, and Rita Patout. During New Iberia's 2011 Fall Art Walk, sponsored by the Iberia Preservation Alliance as part of the Beneath the Balconies program, the New Iberia High School band performed music from *Hairspray*.

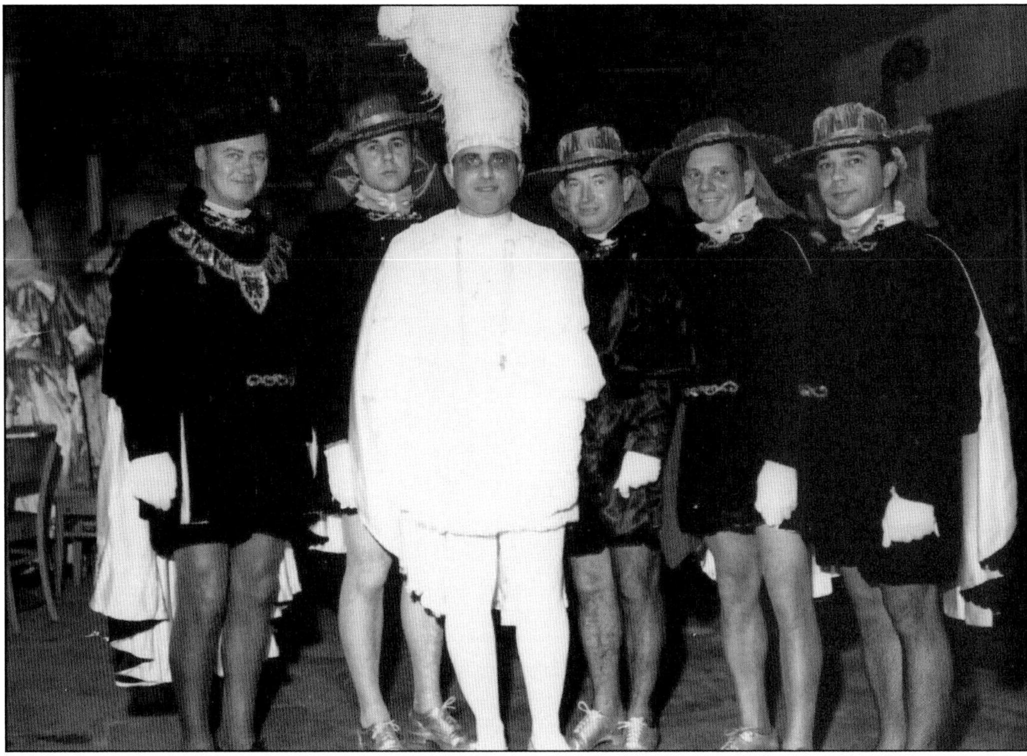

In 1877, New Iberia merchants organized the town's carnival parade for the first time, and the America Fire Company No. 2 held its annual masked ball on Mardi Gras evening. In 1957, Ed Moore, Don Delcambre, Beldon Fox, Herb LeCompte, and Ray Mestayer are pictured participating in the Andalusia Mardi Gras ball.

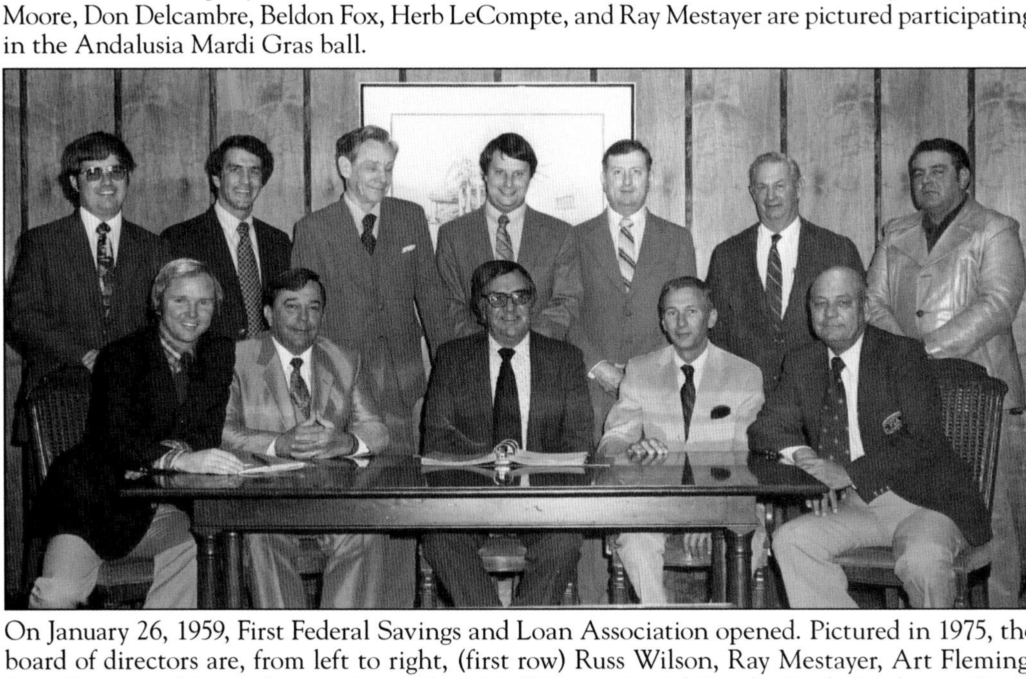

On January 26, 1959, First Federal Savings and Loan Association opened. Pictured in 1975, the board of directors are, from left to right, (first row) Russ Wilson, Ray Mestayer, Art Fleming, Jerry Simon, and Leroy Aucoin; (second row) Jeff Patout, David Doerle, Emile Duchamp, David Wormser, Dr. Jake Lahasky, Alton Lasalle, and Malcolm Viator.

William Joseph "Bill" Bayard II, who died on April 10, 2008, was the son of Dalton and Margery Bayard. He graduated from Catholic High School in 1963, where he served as student council president and was quarterback for the state championship football team under Coach Raymond Blanco. Bayard was quarterback for the USL football team and graduated in electrical engineering. (Courtesy of Janie Bayard.)

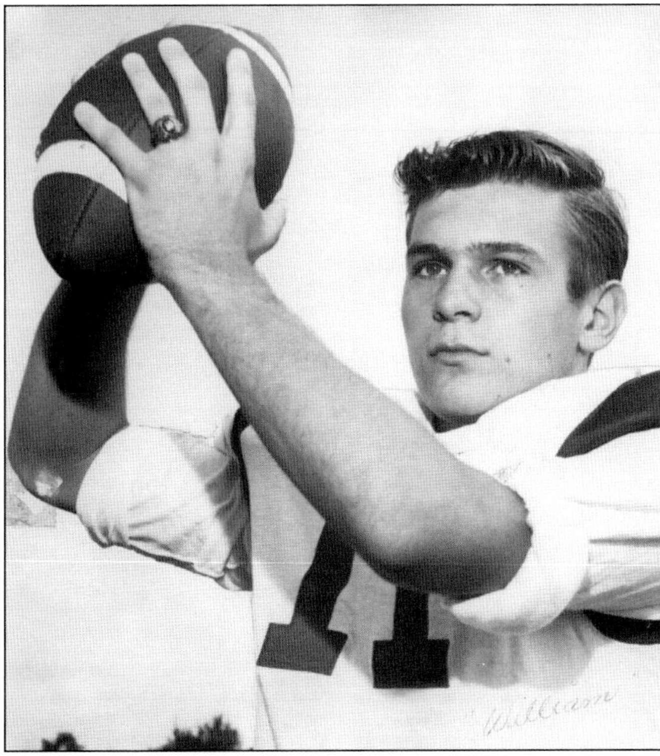

Pictured in 1953 from left to right are Iberians David Haverson, Billy Neustrom, David Neustrom, Theresa Neustrom, and Michael Neustrom, who was elected sheriff of Lafayette Parish in 2000. (Courtesy of Sheriff Michael Neustrom.)

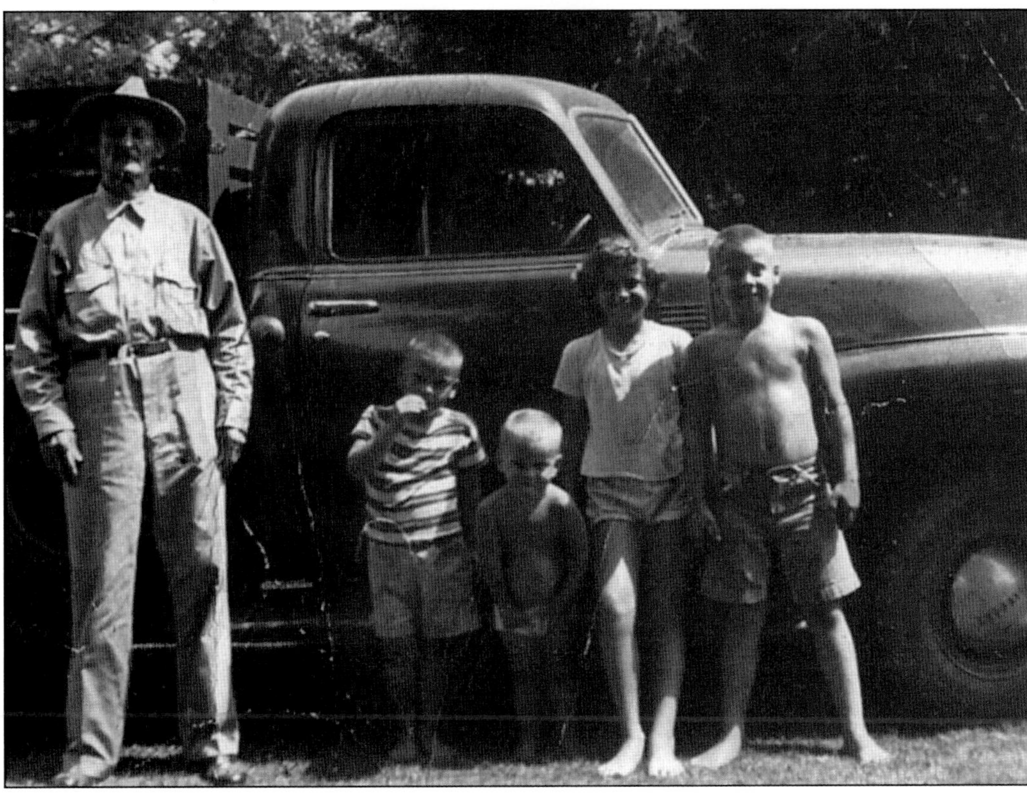

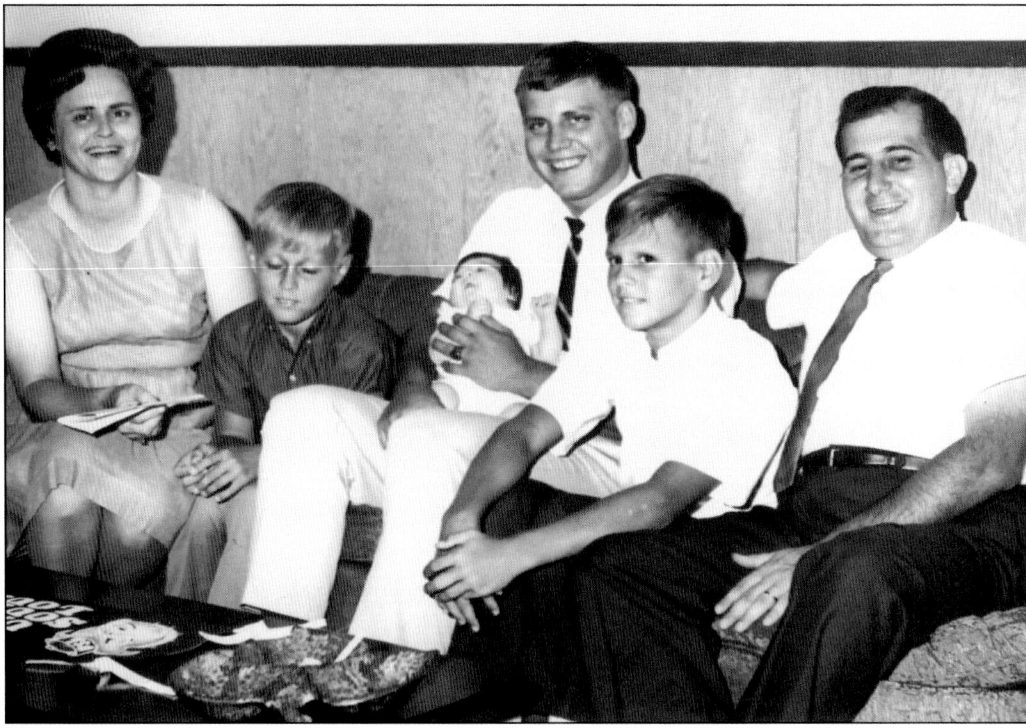

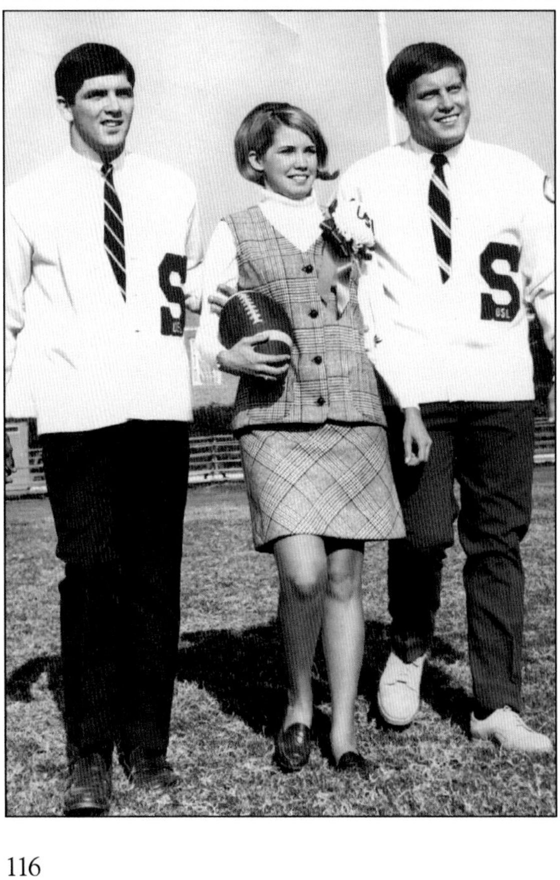

Pictured above in 1965 for the signing of a USL football scholarship by Michael Neustrom are, from left to right, Barbara Neustrom, Duane Neustrom, Michael Neustrom, (holding Karmen Blanco), David Neustrom, and Coach Raymond Blanco. Michael graduated in 1970 after winning two conference championships and serving as team captain. In 2005, he was inducted into the University of Louisiana at Lafayette Football Hall of Fame. From 1970 to 1974, he served as director of University Police. He obtained a master's degree in police science and a doctorate in criminal justice from Sam Houston State University. He was a professor of criminal justice at ULL and director of the Acadiana Law Enforcement Training Academy. Pictured at left in 1968 during the USL homecoming are, from left to right, Mickey Bergeron (who married Iberian Peggy Patout), Cecilia "Ceci" O'Keefe (homecoming queen), and Michael Neustrom (team captain). In 1969, Michael and Ceci married. They are the parents of Kimberly, Alison, Vanessa, Benjamin, Emily, and Thomas.

New Iberian private first class Houston D. Duhon (right) died in service to his country on June 6, 1944, during the invasion of Omaha Beach in Normandy, France. He was the only Cajun killed on D-Day. In 2004, the 60th anniversary of D-Day, CODOFIL sponsored a delegation to France for a memorial service at Duhon's gravesite conducted by historian Dr. Jason Theriot and Al Spoonheimer, the medic who attended Duhon. A concurrent event was held in New Iberia in Duhon's memory. Pictured below from left to right are members of the Duhon family: Ginger Thibodeau (partially shown at left); Christine Duhon Dugas, Duhon's niece; Doris Duhon Elder, Duhon's sister (holding his photo); Carrol Mestayer (now deceased), Duhon's friend who was with him for the invasion and carried his body from the surf to Omaha Beach; Warren A. Perrin, then-president of CODOFIL delivering a speech in French honoring Duhon's memory; and then-senator Craig Romero, who sponsored the concurrent resolution adopted by the Louisiana legislature honoring Duhon and all veterans.

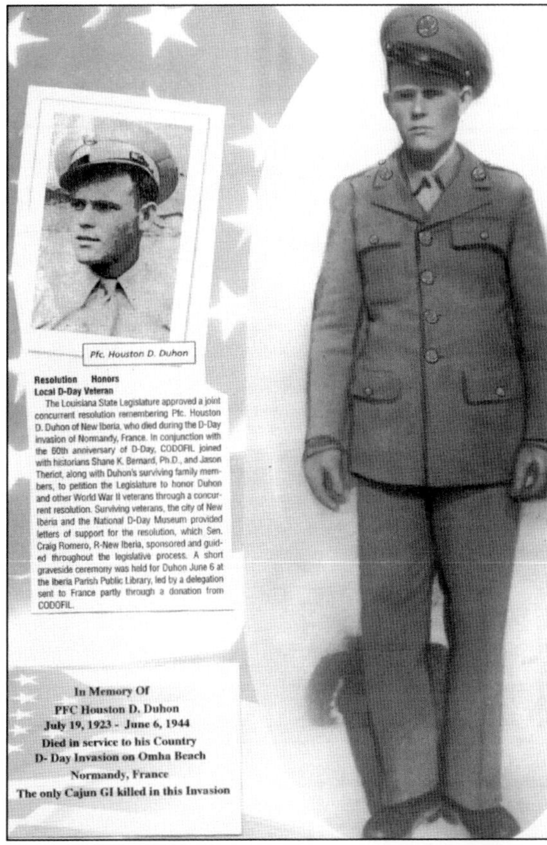

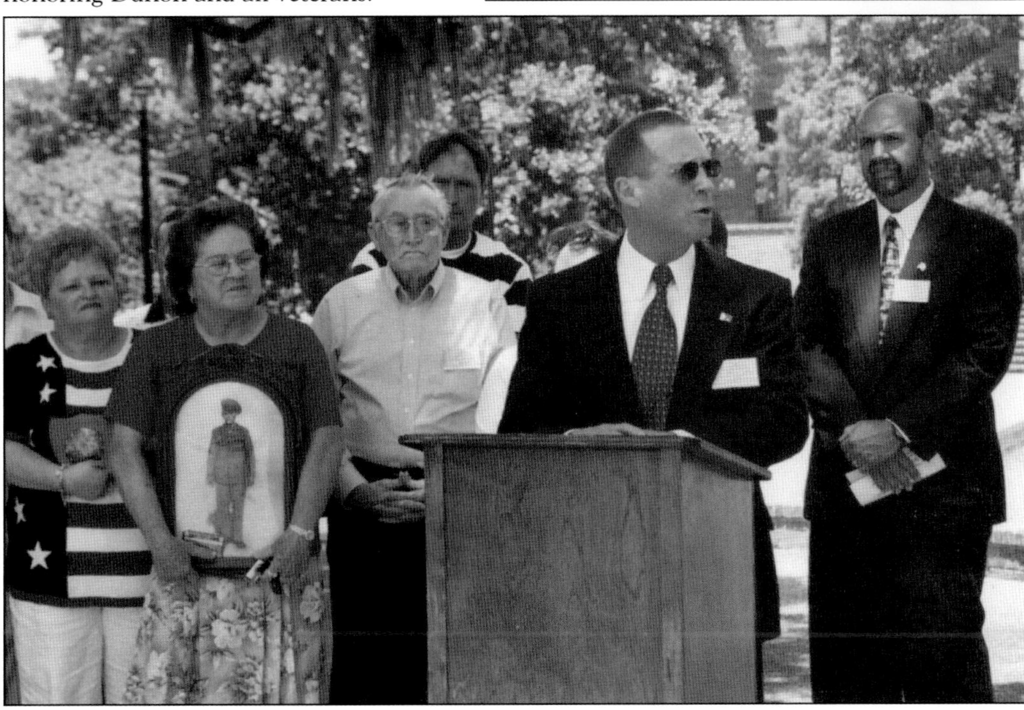

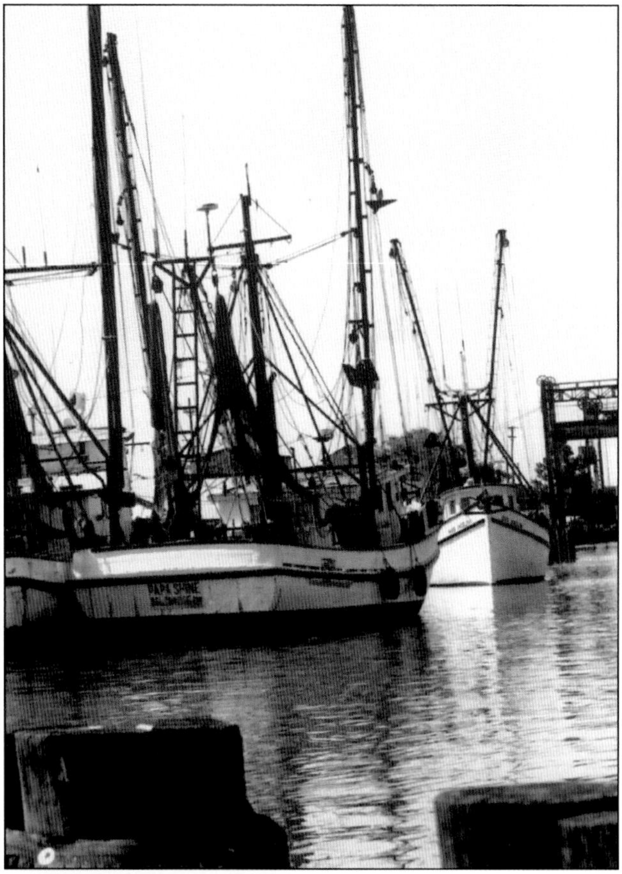

While crawfish is enjoyed throughout Louisiana, in Iberia Parish, it is celebrated. At restaurants like Boiling Point and Jane's Seafood, boiled mounds of the 10-legged crustaceans are piled in the center of the table. Fishermen seeking to haul in wealth from shellfish in coastal waters south of Iberia Parish launch their vessels from the Delcambre dock. Shrimp, crabs, and oysters are the mainstays of the industry and provide food for their table as well as income.

Since its founding, an ambiance of lively good cheer has characterized social life in Iberia Parish. Early on, Iberians enjoyed card games (*parties de cartes*) such as bourre, cockfights (*batailles de gaimes*), and horse races. Today, a spirited art and cultural community flourishes. In 2010, the Iberia Performing Arts League presented the musical *Remember When*, a look at life in New Iberia during the 1950s and 1960s.

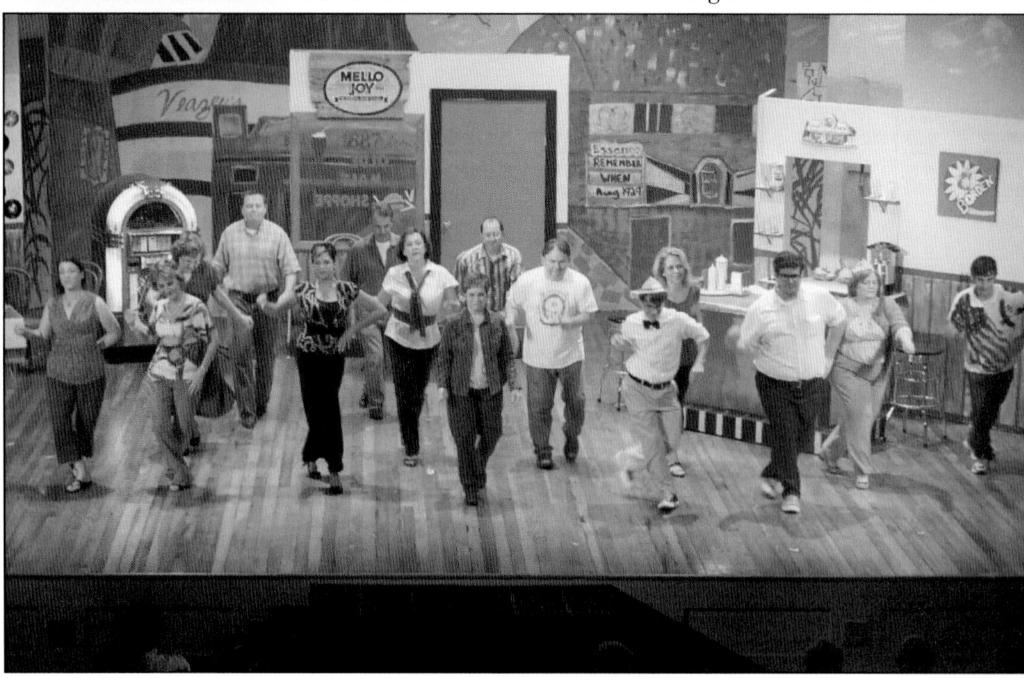

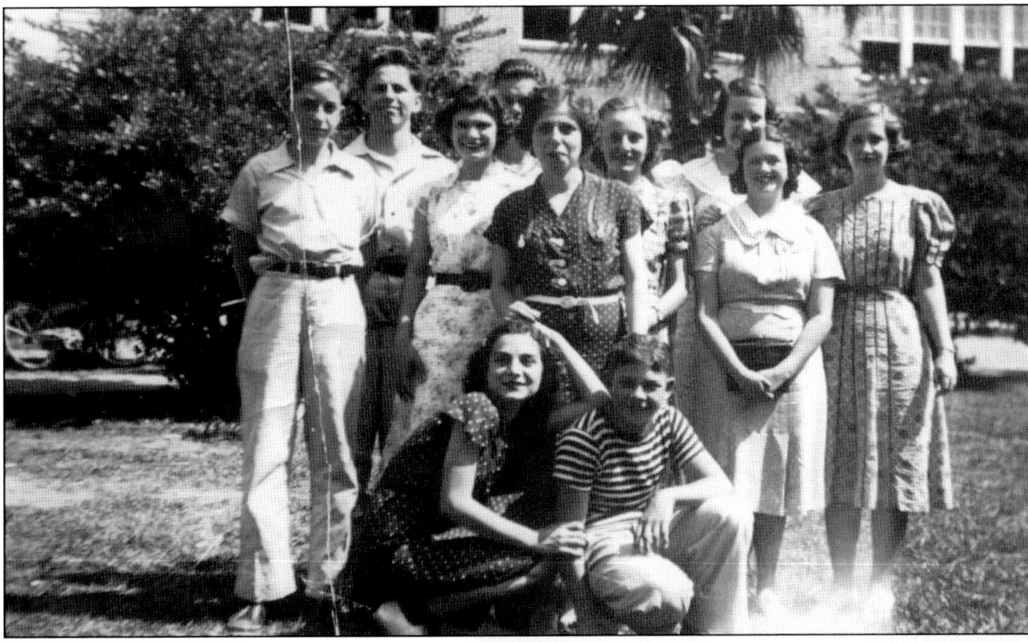

The 1939 Latin class students at New Iberia High School, from left to right, are (first row) Marie Lungaro and C.L. Deare; (second row) Richard C. Sealy Jr., Carmen Love, Louise Lewald, Doris Renodet and Flo Simon; (third row) Morgan "Bud" Falconer, Sam Caulking, Martha desGrávelles, and Mabel Hine. (Courtesy of Richard C. Sealy Jr.)

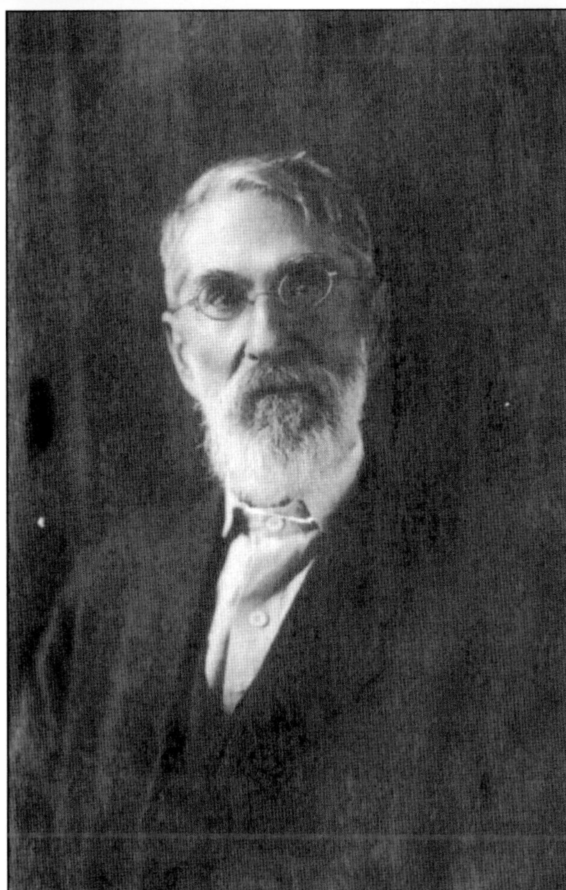

On January 26, 1861, Gov. Alexandre Mouton, the first of four Cajuns to serve as governor, presided over the state's secessionist convention. Antoine Adolph Romero (pictured), born in 1843, was a descendant of the original settlers of New Iberia and a veteran of the Civil War. He and his wife, Marie Romero, were born and raised in Iberia Parish and were the parents of Elie Adolph Romero, grandparents of Adolph Romero, and great-grandparents of Rogers Romero, a cultural preservationist.

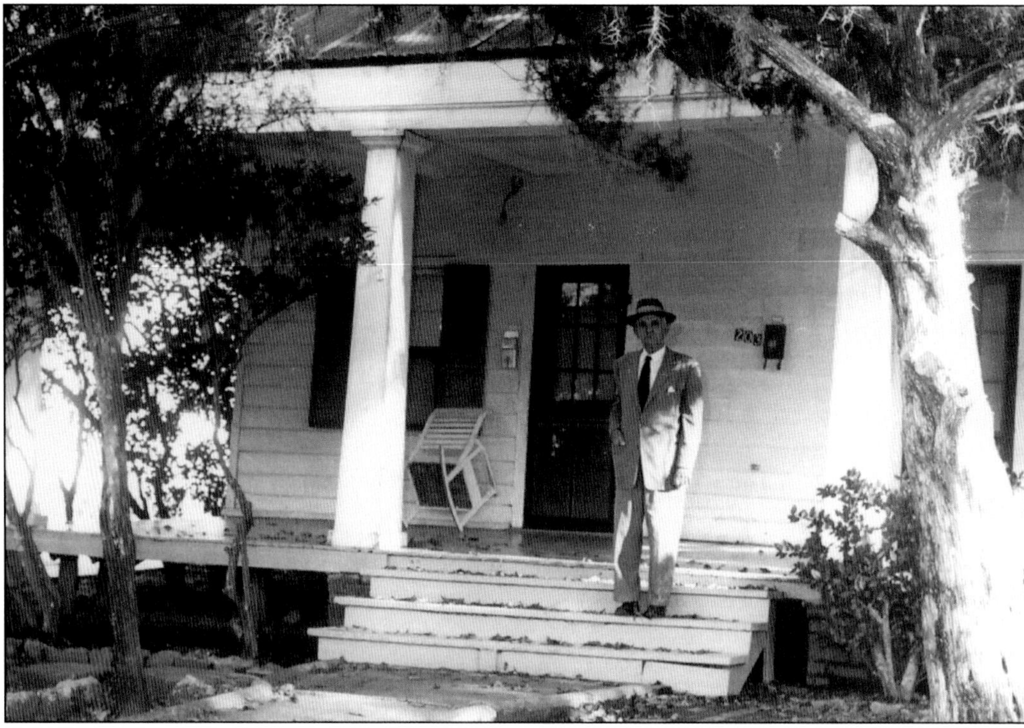

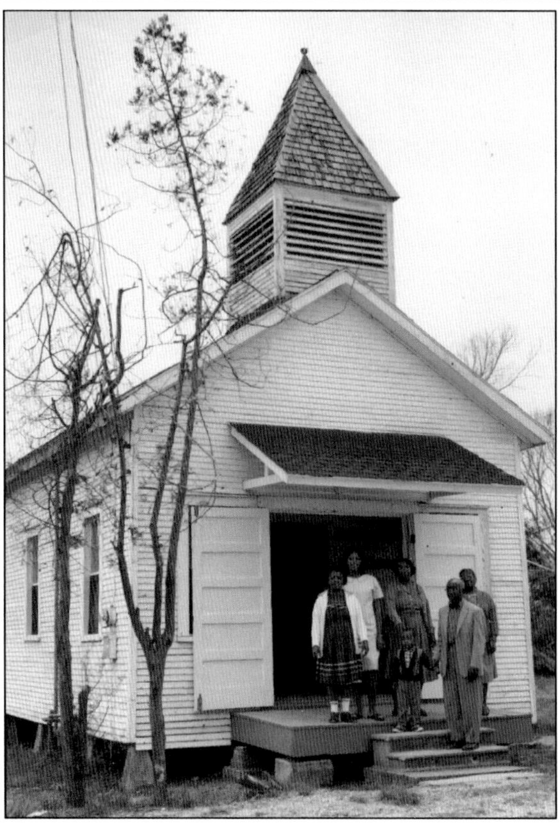

The Lamperez home, built in the 1830s, once stood at 203 Front Street in New Iberia. When destroyed by fire on April 24, 2002, it was considered the oldest frame house in the city. It was owned by four generations of the Lamperez family: Santiago and Josephine Santa Marie Lamperez, until 1881; John and Amelia Lamperez, from 1881 to 1935; Gustave Oscar Lamperez Sr. (pictured), from 1935 to 1973; and his daughter Laura Lamperez Delcambre, from 1973 to 2002. (Courtesy of Gus Lamperez Jr.)

Enmity between the races was apparent, but the prevalence of Catholicism, which spoke out against racial intolerance, buffeted relations and impeded Ku Klux Klan activity, as the Klan was both anti-Catholic as well as anti–African American. Immanuel Baptist Church on Avery Island is pictured around 1965 along with members (from left to right) Marjorie Young, Laura Sayrie, Mrs. Whitney Boseman, Ida Brown, Greggie Paul Robinson (on steps), and Joe Russell. (Courtesy of the Étié and Mosele families.)

In 1958, after a snowfall, Ermance Rouly Chastant is pictured with her collie, Shep, and her daughter Olga Chastant Breaux, mother of Lynn Breaux. From 1930 to 1945, Chastant operated the Chastant General Store in Lozes, which was used as a voting precinct and site of political speeches on Saturday afternoons. She also taught religious education to African Americans in the community.

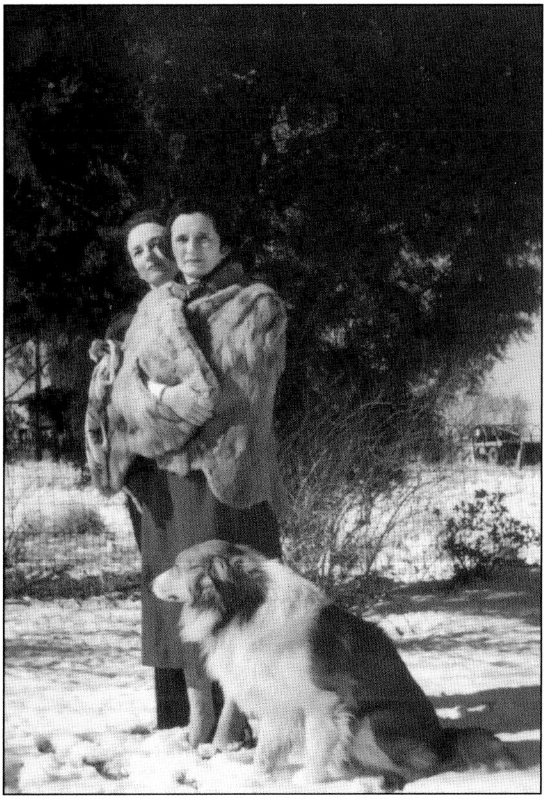

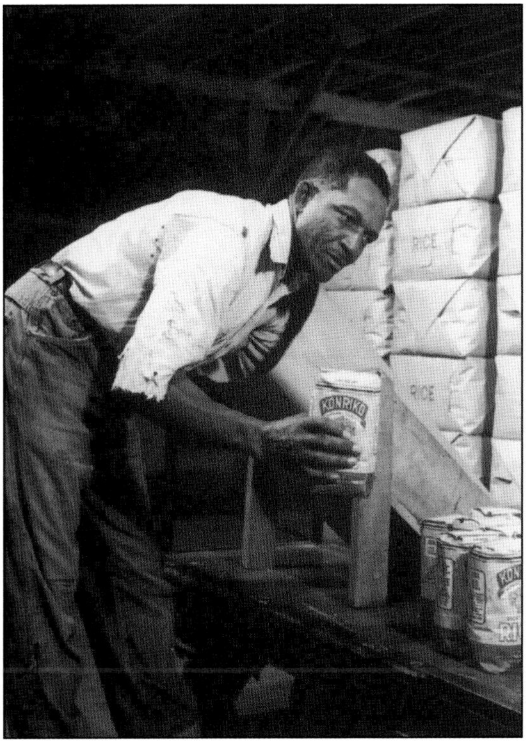

Konriko is the trade name for the Conrad Rice Company, which was founded by P.A. Conrad in 1912. In February 2012, the company celebrated 100 years of continuous operation. In 1975, Mike and Sandy Davis purchased the mill from the Conrad family. In addition to Konriko rice, the Davises have developed products like Wild Pecan Brown Rice, seasonings, and a wide variety of gluten-free items. Pictured in 1953 is a worker at the Conrad Rice Mill. (Courtesy of Konriko.)

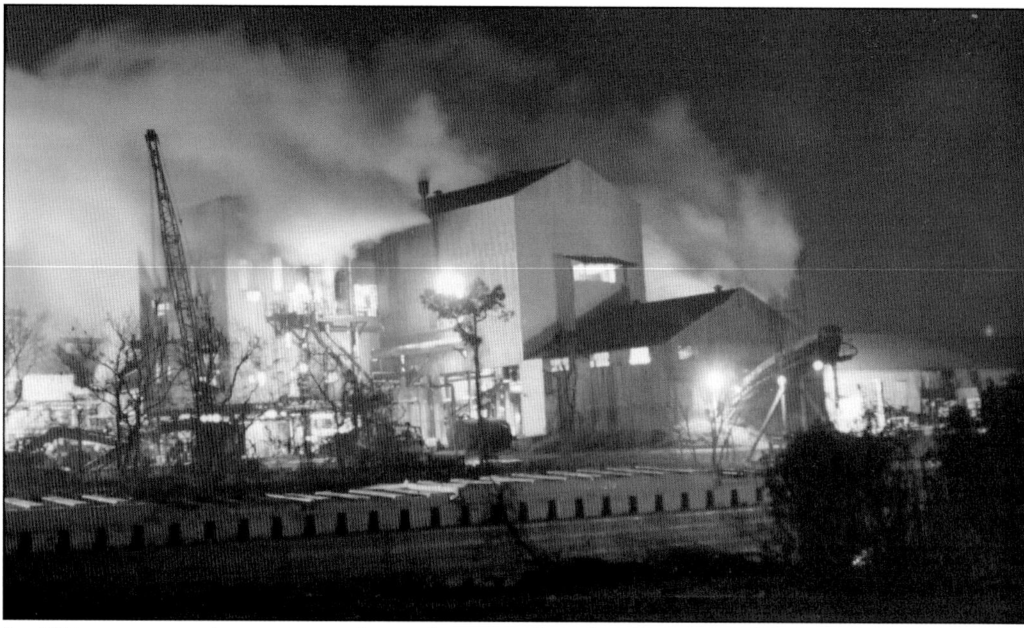

In 1751, sugarcane (*canne à sucre*) was first introduced in Louisiana from Santo Domingo and grown on the plantation of the Jesuit Order in New Orleans. *La cuite* is the juice of the sugarcane boiled down to near-sugar. This striking 2000 photograph of the New Iberia Sugar Co-Op was taken during the grinding season. (Courtesy of Mickey Delcambre.)

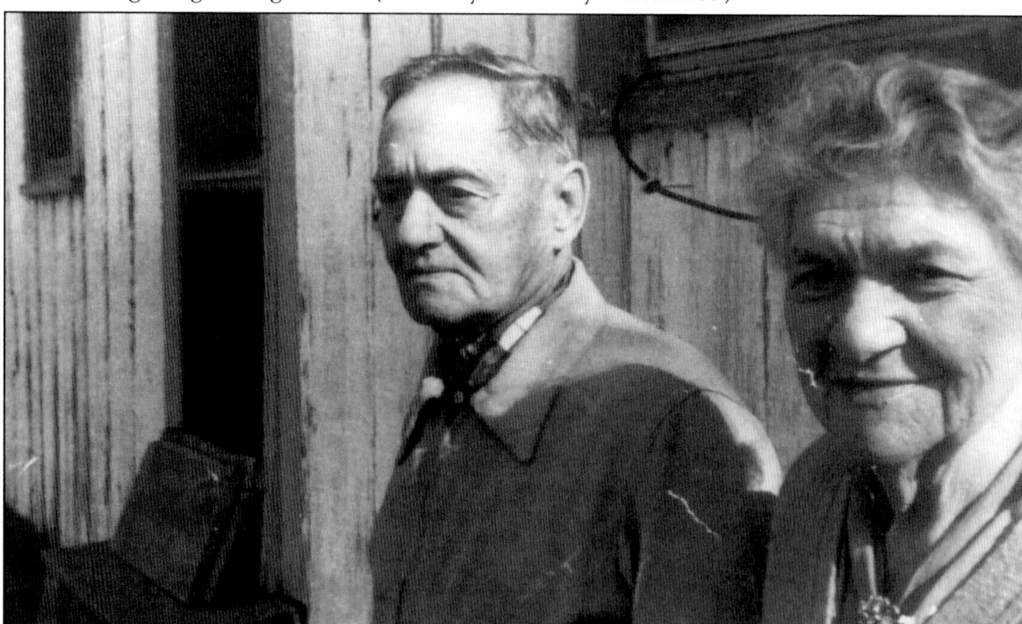

Arthur Barras, a fur trapper and blacksmith, and his wife, Ida LeBlanc Barras, were married in 1903 and lived all of their lives south of Delcambre, where they raised four sons: Simon, Jackson, Paul, and Harry. For many years, Louisiana led the nation in wild fur production. In the early part of the 20th century, the parish's mink, muskrat, raccoon, and nutria pelts were in great demand worldwide.

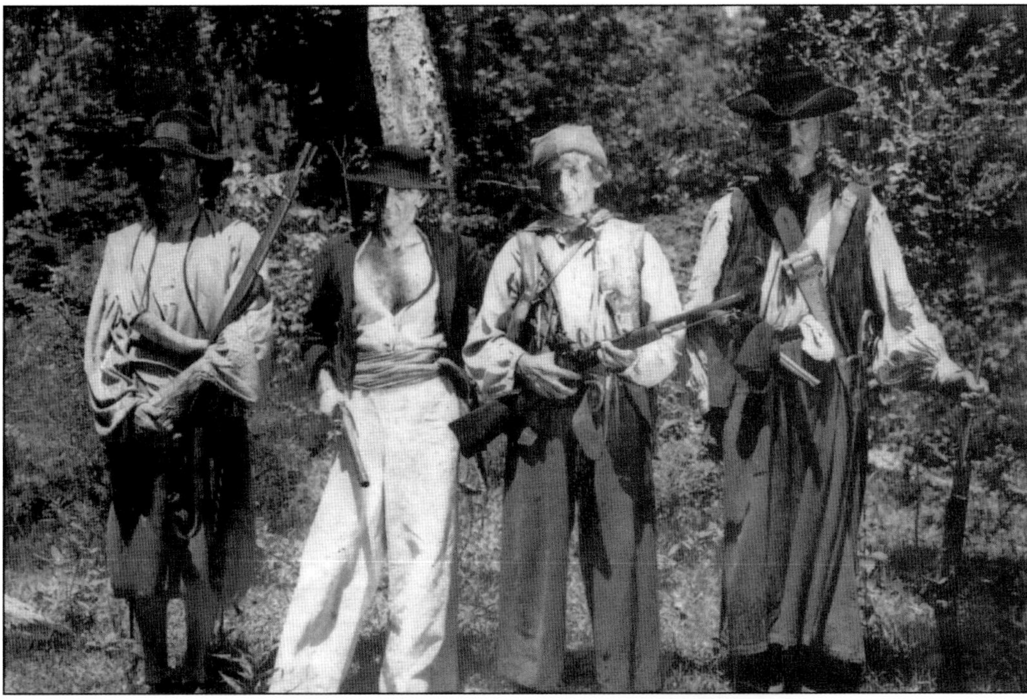

In the mid-1900s, attending dirt-track quarter horse races was a favorite Sunday afternoon pastime. The distance for the dirt track was seven *arpents* (193 feet), or approximately a quarter of a mile. Going to movies on Sunday afternoons was another popular form of entertainment. This July 1937 photograph shows the making of Paramount Studio's film *Buccaneer.* Pictured from left to right are Gaston Courville, Alfred "Buddy" Talley, Alonzo Latiolais, and Gill Verret, all residents of Catahoula.

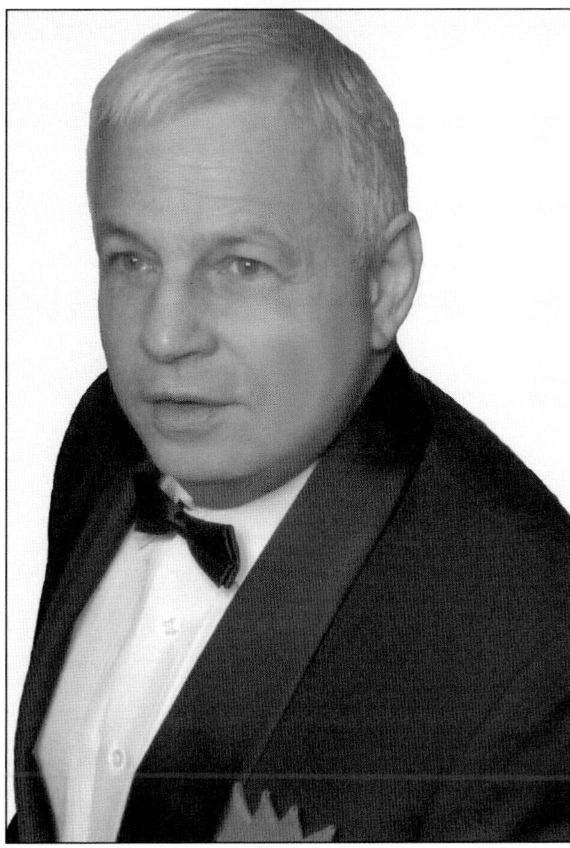

As a youth in New Iberia, Paul Muffoletto was drawn to the performing arts. He originated three local rock bands: the Lil Bits, the Gravel Road, and the Sheetrock Music Company. He attended USL as a voice major and was on the 1968 National Collegiate Championship Weightlifting Team. The singer has had an outstanding career in the gospel music ministry. In 1995, he began performing a musical tribute to Frank Sinatra, and now owns PM Music Studio.

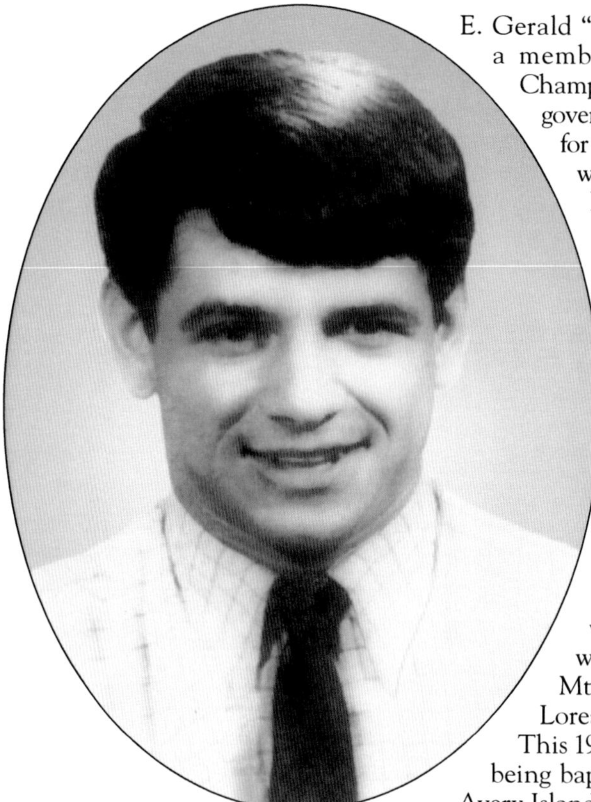

E. Gerald "T-Boy" Hebert, of Jeanerette, was also a member of the 1968 National Collegiate Championship Weightlifting team. Hebert is the governor's appointee to the Board of Supervisors for the Louisiana System of Higher Education, which oversees nine Louisiana universities. Hebert is serving his second six-year term. He is married to Martha C. Hebert and has one son, Gerald Paul "Jerry" Hebert, a ULL graduate in finance.

The citizenry of Iberia Parish was predominately Catholic. The sacred and the secular often intertwined, and the Church's rituals frequently were the center of daily life. Even public schools allowed students to receive religious instruction during the school day. In 1869, the Star Pilgrim Baptist Church was the first church for blacks, and next was the Boynton Chapel for Methodists, which opened in Hubertville. In 2010, Mt. Zion Baptist Church Number One in Loreauville celebrated its 100th anniversary. This 1920 photograph shows African Americans being baptized on Avery Island. (Courtesy of the Avery Island, Inc. Archives.)

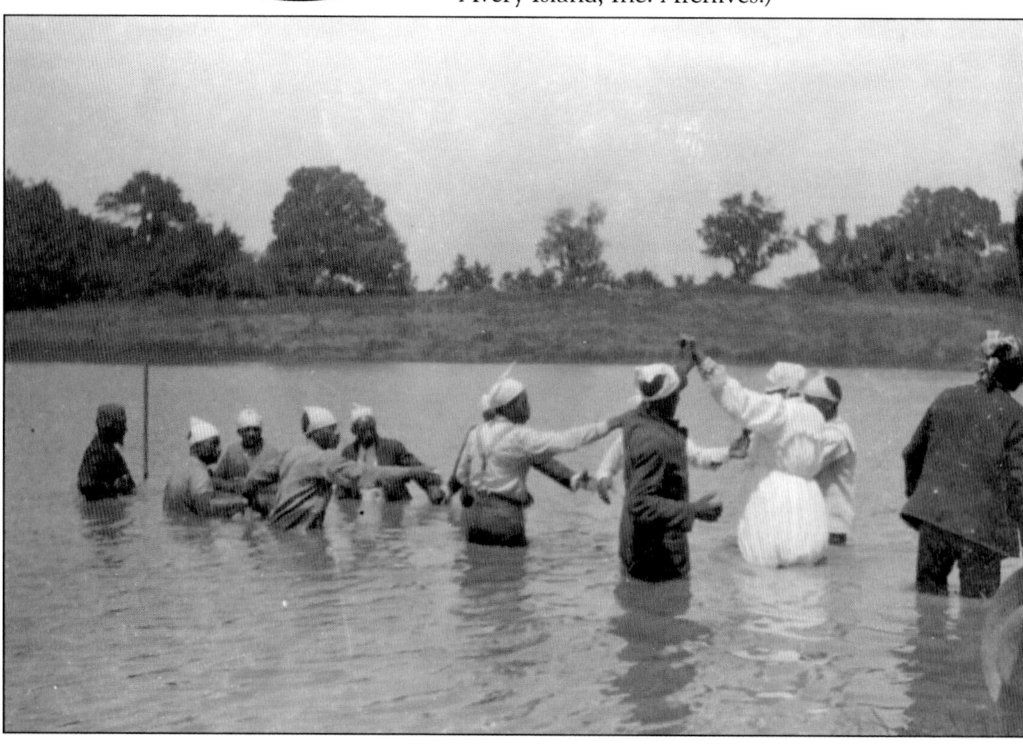

Epilogue

This is neither the complete story of Iberia Parish, nor is it the end. This is also not a complete listing of the many diverse peoples who played roles in the development and growth of the area. Clearly, Iberia Parish is a gumbo of cultures.

New Iberia continues to grow and prosper. As it was once a stopping place along the Old Spanish Trail and Highway 90, so it will continue to be when Interstate 49 is completed, making New Orleans less than a two-hour drive away. The building of a convention center, the expansion of the SugArena, the Port of Iberia, and the Acadiana Regional Airport Industrial Park should lead to continued economic growth. Promoting New Iberia as a retirement community with a focus on the arts offers promising future expansion opportunities.

Jeanerette has seen the closing of several industries, including sugar mills and the Fruit of the Loom Mill. Despite this, with the opening of the Hewes House as a meeting facility, the renovation of the Main Street area, the conservation of the beautiful stately homes, and the innovative promotion of economic growth utilizing the Jeanerette Mills building, there is renewed hope for the future.

Loreauville retains its small town feeling and remains a special place to raise a family. The community continues to come together for celebrations and tragedies because of its strong sense of civic commitment. The economy has been transformed from an agricultural focus to one that is more modern, based upon boatbuilding and house-moving businesses.

Delcambre is made up of hearty people who have survived the Lake Peigneur disaster, the BP oil spill, and several disastrous hurricanes and floods. High water may come again, but today, many homes have been elevated and there are plans underway to completely rebuild the community around the port area based upon cultural tourism.

Iberia Parish is an area with a rich history of strong-willed people who have come together over many years to live life to the fullest while also retaining a strong family unity. Businesses and the arts are growing, neighborhoods are expanding, and an air of excitement abounds. In October 2011, the Delta Regional Authority announced that $8.4 million would be granted toward expansion of the Port of Iberia's industrial complex by extending barge channel access to 108 acres of new development. The history of our people shows that they are hardworking and fun loving, but also serious and determined when there is a need to accomplish common goals.

In French, we say, "*Laissez les bons temps rouler*;" in Spanish, "*Alegria*;" and in English, "Let the Good Times Roll." Fate has been good to us, and our wish for future generations is much happiness, success, and prosperity.

Museum Mission Statements

The following are the mission statements of the three museums to which the profits from the sale of this book will be donated:

Acadian Museum
203 South Broadway, Erath, Louisiana, 70533
(337) 937-5468; 233-5832; www.acadianmuseum.com
The mission of the Acadian Museum is to commemorate and honor the Acadian heritage and Cajun people of Louisiana and to serve as a repository for records, artifacts, and memorabilia pertaining to the Acadian culture which has endured for over 400 years.

Bayou Teche Museum
131 E. Main Street, New Iberia, Louisiana, 70560
(337) 606-5977; www.bayoutechemuseum.org
The mission of Bayou Teche Museum is to educate the public about the Bayou Teche and its environs, to preserve the history and culture of New Iberia, and to emphasize the industries that have shaped the region.

Jeanerette Bicentennial Park and Museum
500 East Main Street, Jeanerette, Louisiana, 70544
(337) 276-4408; www.jeanerettemuseum.com
The mission is to foster, protect, and promote the best interests of the historical background of the City of Jeanerette and surrounding areas and to secure and protect artifacts and exhibits pertaining to the historical background of the City of Jeanerette and surrounding areas.

BIBLIOGRAPHY

Ancelet, Barry, Jay Edward, and Glen Pitre. *Cajun Country*. Jackson, Mississippi: University Press of Mississippi, 1991.

Ancelet, Barry, and Elemore Morgan Jr. *The Makers of Cajun Music*. Austin, Texas: University of Texas Press, 1984.

Bergerie, Maurine. *They Tasted Bayou Water*. Ann Arbor, Michigan: Edwards Brothers, 1962.

Bernard, Shane K. *The Cajuns: Americanization of a People*. Jackson, Mississippi: University Press of Mississippi, 2003.

——— *Cajuns and Their Acadian Ancestors: A Young Reader's History*. Jackson, Mississippi: University Press of Mississippi, 2008.

Brasseaux, Carl A. *Acadian to Cajun: Transformation of a People, 1803–1877*. Jackson, Mississippi: University Press of Mississippi, 1992.

——— *The Founding of New Acadia: The Beginnings of Acadian Life In Louisiana, 1765–1803*. Baton Rouge, Louisiana: Louisiana State University Press, 1987.

Comeaux, Malcolm L. *Atchafalaya Swamp Life: Settlement and Folk Occupations*. Baton Rouge, Louisiana: Louisiana State University Press, 1972.

Conrad, Glenn R., ed. *New Iberia*. Lafayette, Louisiana: Center for Louisiana Studies, University of Southwestern Louisiana, 1979.

Henry, Jacques. "From Acadien to Cajun to Cadien: Ethnic Labelization and Construction of Identity." *Journal of American Ethnic History*. Summer 1998: Vol. 17 No. 4.

Jobb, Dean. *The Cajuns*. Hoboken, New Jersey: John Wiley and Sons Canada, Ltd., 2005.

Kniffen, Fred B., Hiram F. Gregory, George A. Stokes. *The Historic Indian Tribes of Louisiana: From 1542 to the Present*. Baton Rouge, Louisiana: Louisiana State University Press, 1987.

LeBlanc, Dudley J. *The Acadian Miracle*. Lafayette, Louisiana: Evangeline Publishing Company, 1966.

Perrin, Warren A. *Acadian Redemption: From Beausoleil Broussard to the Queen's Royal Proclamation*. Opelousas, Louisiana: Andrepont Publishing, 2005.

Rushton, William F., *The Cajuns*. New York, 1979.

Wade, Michael G. *Sugar Dynasty, M.A. Patout & Son, Ltd.: 1791–1993*. Lafayette, Louisiana: Center for Louisiana Studies, University of Southwestern Louisiana, 1995.

West, Robert C. *An Atlas of Louisiana Surnames of French and Spanish Origin*. Baton Rouge, Louisiana: Louisiana State University, Geoscience Publications, 1986.